To Honor
and Comfort

D1199671

Native Quilters' Gathering Quilt, 1996–97

Made by Native Quilters' Gathering Participants in East Lansing, Michigan. 72.5 x 87 inches.

Collection of Michigan State University Museum

To Honor
and Comfort

NATIVE QUILTING
TRADITIONS

Edited by Marsha L. MacDowell
and C. Kurt Dewhurst

MUSEUM OF NEW MEXICO PRESS
in association with
MICHIGAN STATE UNIVERSITY MUSEUM

This book is dedicated to our daughter, Marit Dewhurst, who began accompanying us on field-work trips when only a few weeks old and was with us on nearly all visits with Native quilters. We thank her for the many hours of her patience, her ever-present willingness to learn new things, and her wonderful laugh.

—MARSHA L. MACDOWELL AND C. KURT DEWHURST

Manufactured in Hong Kong
10 9 8 7 6 5 4 3 2 1

Editorial Director: Mary Wachs
Art Direction and Design: David Skolkin
Project Editors: Mary Luders, Jenifer Blakemore, and Denice Anderson

Set in Novarese Book and Italic
with Belwe display

This book is a companion to the exhibition "To Honor and Comfort: Native Quilting Traditions," organized by Michigan State University Museum and the National Museum of the American Indian, Smithsonian Institution, and traveled nationally by Smithsonian Institution Traveling Exhibition Service.

A smaller version of this exhibition will be traveled by Michigan State University Museum.

Museum of New Mexico Press
Post Office Box 2087
Santa Fe, New Mexico 87504

Library of Congress
Cataloging-in-Publication Data

To honor and comfort : native quilting traditions/edited by
  Marsha L. MacDowell and C. Kurt Dewhurst.
      p.   cm.
    "In association with Michigan State University Museum."
    Includes bibliographical references and index.
    ISBN 0-89013-316-6 (hc). —ISBN 0-89013-317-4 (pb)
    1. Indian textile fabrics—North America—History.
2. Quilting—North America—History 3. Textile fabrics,
Hawaiian—History. 4. Quilting—Hawaii—History. I.
MacDowell, Marsha. II. Dewhurst, C. Kurt. III. Michigan State
University Museum.
E98.T35T6 1997
746.46'089'97—dc21   97-27063
                                                      CIP

Contents

Preface

Charlotte Heth (Cherokee)

Assistant Director for Public Programs,
National Museum of the American Indian,
Smithsonian Institution

G randma's house in Sallisaw, Oklahoma, brings memories of rows of cousins sleeping on pallets; memories of bags and bundles of scraps from dresses and shirts we all wore, linings from much-washed sheets, stuffings made from feathers of backyard chickens or well-worn blankets—quilts, comforters, and featherbeds, all handmade, all warm and comforting.

None of my relatives ever sold a quilt. They were all made as a matter of course to give away to family members and friends who needed them. The patterns were recognizable but the fabrics all had special meaning. When you made all your own clothes, as we did up until the 1950s, every piece was connected to someone. Every block and cover were artfully put together from material at hand, and we called it material, not fabric or cloth.

My family is mixed Cherokee and Euro-American, frontier people. My grandfathers were born in Indian Territory (now Oklahoma), my grandmothers in Texas and Georgia. My maternal grandmother, Ethel McEver, moved from Georgia to Indian Territory when she was six, traveling in a covered wagon, terrified by the Mississippi River crossing. After that she never traveled away from home except to see her children. She married my Cherokee grandfather, James Seabolt, reared eight children, cultivated a large garden, raised chickens, and made quilts.

My mother, Eula Seabolt Wilson, remembers the quilt frame hanging from the ceiling of their log cabin on my grandfather's allotment in Sequoyah County, Oklahoma. Most nights after supper Grandma and all the girls worked on quilts by lamplight. After they moved to Sallisaw, the county seat,

OPPOSITE PAGE:

Gwe Tes (Ojibwa) and son Jim Hanks, Sr., with birchbark canoe in 1940 at the Mille Lacs Trading Post.

vii

they made a new garden, got more chickens, and the quilting continued.

Just before I was born, Mother started a few quilt tops and then stopped. Urban work, Los Angeles commuting, and taking care of a family ate up her quiet time. She didn't finish them until after she retired in the 1980s, after my sister and I were grown. Later, after moving back to Oklahoma, she became a nonstop quilter and gardener—quilting in the winter and gardening in the summer. She must have been waiting to resume her old life. She filled a walk-in closet with quilts in various stages of completion, quilt pieces and blocks, templates for patterns, batting, and material. She got all the scraps from me and my sister, including the ones we were saving for some unknown purpose. And she started buying material. We all got quilts—hand pieced and hand quilted, some appliquéd or embroidered.

The sad story of Grandma Seabolt is that she had glaucoma and could not see for the last fifteen years of her life. For the past five years, Mother has been disabled by the same disease. When she started losing her sight, Mother hurriedly made quilts for my nephews (then fourteen and eighteen years old) and even made quilts for her unborn great-grandchildren.

We all sleep under these quilts and remember where they came from—the A-line dresses and wide summer pants we wore in the 1960s, the Gypsy-look calico petticoats of the 1970s, the Cherokee "tear dresses" that no longer fit and the country-western shirts of the 1980s—our quilts are a mosaic of memory and a reflection of a vital family.

Introduction

C. Kurt Dewhurst
Director, Michigan State University Museum

Marsha L. MacDowell
Curator of Folk Arts, Michigan State University Museum

Most ethnographers working in Native communities in the late nineteenth century were interested primarily in those aspects of North American Indian life perceived as culturally intact, showing little or no evidence of contact with European culture. They tended to ignore the changes occurring within Native American societies and instead concentrated on a glorified and romanticized depiction of Indian people as pure and primitive subjects of nobility.

The art market and the tourism industry that developed with the opening of the West perpetuated such cultural stereotyping, an influence that continues, if abated, to this day. It is not surprising, then, that few scholars, connoisseurs, or tourists have paid attention to the phenomenon of quiltmaking in Native communities. Quilts most likely were deemed too European to have value as marketable commodities or as markers of a Native way of life. Yet despite their relatively recent introduction into the Native community, quilts are as quintessentially Native as any other object that supports a Native belief system, worldview, or sense of identity.

Michigan State University Museum's Native Quilting Research and Exhibition Project, begun in 1984 to explore quilting traditions in Native Hawaiian and North American Indian communities, was created to illuminate tribal traditions and aesthetics in the quiltmaking arena.

Objects do not speak, people do. Successful interpretation thus relies on the ability of the interpreter to reveal the meaningful associations between an object and the cultural context from which it comes. To identify such associations for the quilts featured in what follows, we relied on multiple sources documenting the manufacture and use of quilts. Natives and non-Natives—quilters and quilt collectors, writers and scholars—have found quilting to have a significant role in Native life. Their contributions expand the interpretation and enhance the understanding of the quiltmaking traditions as practiced in Native communities across North America and in the Hawaiian Islands.

It is now evident that quiltmaking has had a rich and varied existence in Native communities, but the story of Native quilting has only begun to be shared. *To Honor and Comfort: Native Quilting Traditions*, both the book and related exhibition, examines the history and rich diversity of quiltmaking techniques, motifs, and meanings within Native communities. It pays special attention to significant, community-based, artistic expressive cultural traditions that are little known to non-Native peoples.

This book and exhibition pay tribute to Native quilters everywhere. Their stories are here to be shared, and we have much to learn from them. Sheree Bonaparte, a Mohawk quilter attending the Gathering of Native Quilters in Michigan in November 1996, may have expressed it best when she said: "People can't look at us [as] if something in the past were here right now . . . that's what I like about this project. This is happening now. *These women are here now*. And they can tell you their story."

We must learn to listen carefully and then join in the conversation.

HISTORICAL NOTE: Where possible, we have added the tribal affiliations of the Native American and Hawaiian quilters profiled in *To Honor and Comfort*. However, due to the complexities of the tribal system and because of forced migrations, it is beyond the scope of this publication to offer a precise history of these tribal affiliations.

To avoid confusion, we have selected the preferred tribal names and used them consistently throughout. For example, the Odawa are not referred to also as the Ottawa and the Ojibwa are not referred to also as the Chippewa.

In those cases where two tribal affliations are cited, such as Navajo/Seminole or Assiniboine/ Sioux, we have followed the Native American matrilineal line by placing the mother's tribal affiliation first.

To Honor and Comfort

Part I
A Gathering of Cultural Expression

North American Indian and Native Hawaiian Quiltmaking

by Marsha L. MacDowell

Of the various art forms that American Indians acquired as a result of contact with other cultures, the least well known is quiltmaking. Possibly because this art form appeared only after contact with "outside" cultures and perhaps because it spread so extensively into everyday life, quilts, until recently and unlike other Native arts, were not collected as items of either ethnographic, aesthetic, or marketplace value. However, throughout the entire postcontact period, Native quilters in the Hawaiian Islands and on the North American continent have used colors and designs distinctly their own to make quilts that function both similarly to those of other cultural groups and in ways that possess specific tribal or pan-Indian meanings.

Most historical formal portraits of Indians show little evidence of non-Native material culture. Photographers attempted to create the most "traditional Indian" look and often removed any item not considered "Indian" enough. It is thus surprising that many images exist of Indians wearing or sitting on quilts. This Arapaho man, wrapped in a quilt, holds a photo of a person who may have been a family member.

In Native and other cultures, quilts have been used as bedcovers, featured at fund-raisers, given as gifts for special occasions, and sold as a means of providing or supplementing income. The Potawatomi have utilized quilts along with rope as the basic material to create swing hammock cradles for babies. Quilts have been used by the Hopi as bedrolls for rooftop sleeping, by the Assiniboine to pictorially depict their history, and by the Chippewa at tribal senior centers for fund-raising raffles.

Production techniques (patchwork, appliqué, quilting, tied work), material preparation (batting, recycling cloth), patchwork patterns, quilting designs, and quilt names are shared among Native and non-Native quiltmakers. Yet choices of patterns, construction techniques, materials, and names are often tied to Native or tribal identity. In addition, quilts have become more popular as a format and technique for contemporary textile artists to express individual creativity linked clearly to ethnic and racial identity.

Quilts also have taken on meanings and functions unique to members of Native communities. For instance, the Odawa give quilts as gifts in naming ceremonies; the Ojibwa use quilts as a ground covering to protect a drum from contact with the earth; and the Sioux drape *star* quilts over their sweat lodges. At contemporary powwows, quilts are carried flat within the dance circle so that spectators can toss money to pay the dancers' or drummers' expenses.

Though little is known about the actual origin of quiltmaking within Native American communities, it is generally accepted that this art form was primarily learned through contact with Euro-American culture. Some evidence indicates that contact with African-Americans and peoples of Hispanic background influenced particular patterns, construction techniques, and uses, but the overwhelming influence was Euro-American. Traders, missionaries, government agents, and non-Native settlers all played key roles in introducing the fabrics, techniques, and uses that Native quiltmakers appropriated for their own purposes. Eventually, Native peoples began to pass on knowledge within their own communities and to use quilts for purposes unique to their culture and as instruments to convey a sense of identity and express feelings and ideas. Today, quilts are found in nearly all Native communities in the United States.

Early Contacts,   *N*ative peoples in the
Native Precedents   Hawaiian Islands and
North America have long traditions of textile production and use. The requisite materials and skills of quiltmaking had many precedents in these communities. When manufactured cloth and needles became available to Native peoples, it was not surprising that artisans adept at other crafts quickly picked up quiltmaking. Cree, Inuit, Yupik, and Odawa patched furs together with sinew to make clothing; Mohawk, Wasco, Cherokee, Pomo, and Ojibwa were basketmakers; Odawa were mat weavers and beadworkers; Sioux were buffalo-skin tipi and clothing producers; and Hopi and Navajo were cloth weavers. In the Hawaiian Islands there were several textile forerunners to quilts, including the *kapa moe*, a blanket of multiple layers of *tapa* (bark cloth) sewn together, decorated with designs, and used for clothing, bedding, and ceremonial purposes. Native Hawaiian women quickly appropriated the techniques and materials to create a distinctive type of quilt that reflected designs previously used on their kapa moe.

While it is known that cloth, needles, and blankets were among the items traded to Native peoples by explorers and fur traders, it is not yet known whether this early contact also involved the distribution of quilts and information about quiltmaking. Given the extensive presence of quilts within domestic households beginning in the late eighteenth century, it is likely that wherever non-Native women settled in trading outposts or military forts, quilts probably were part of their household inventory. In those contexts, at least some Native peoples would have seen quilts in use or may have been taught the rudiments of quilting. However, the primary agent in the initial conveyance of quilting skills to Native peoples occurred in the nineteenth century with the establishment of mission schools and churches in Native communities.

Missions and   *N*umerous references in
Quiltmaking   missionary diaries and
letters, mission records and newsletters, and in oral histories point to the substantial influence that Christian denominational mission churches and schools had in introducing quiltmaking to Native peoples. Through both formal instruction and in the context of affiliated women's social groups, missions promoted Euro-American domestic arts, including quiltmaking and other forms of needlework. Whether Mennonite missions on Hopi land, Mormon missions in Utah and Nevada, Quaker mission schools in Pennsylvania, or Catholic missions in frontier outposts, these Christian evangelical and educational efforts were instrumental in introducing and sustaining these crafts.

Several groups were particularly vital in conveying quilting to Native peoples. Most active by far, the Dakota Presbytery set up an

CLOCKWISE FROM TOP LEFT:

Julia Nyholm (Ojibwa) *created her* **Rabbit Pelt Quilt** *(1991, 64 x 74 inches) based on similar sewn bed covers she remembered from her childhood in northern Michigan.*

A Kashunak elder wears a bird-skin parka in this 1928 photograph, displaying a Nelson Island tradition.

This pony blanket–sized **Patchwork Crazy Quilt** (c. 1880–1900, 41 x 64 inches), made of hides, sinew, and beadwork, blends traditional South Dakota Sioux techniques and materials with the quilt form popular in the Victorian era.

Mrs. John Franks, of the White Earth Reservation in Minnesota, holds up her rabbit robe. Rabbit pelts were commonly used by Woodland Indians to create robes and blankets, sometimes referred to as "quilts," employing a form of knotting and finger-weaving techniques.

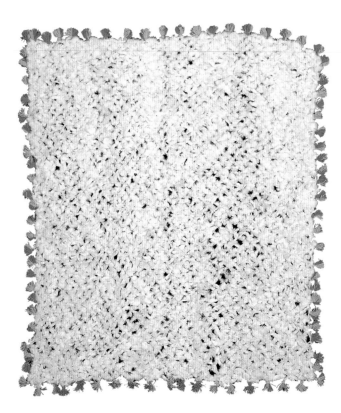

extensive system of missions and mission schools, sponsored the formation of Ladies' Aid Societies (where sewing skills were shared), and encouraged the making of quilts and the formation of quilting bees. Even today, annual gatherings of Dakota Presbytery women include the exhibition of quilts made by members.

The White Cross women, affiliated with the American Baptist church, have long been responsible for sending blankets, quilts, and precut quilt squares, known as White Cross squares, to quilters on reservations. At Oraibi, Arizona, Hopi quilters continue to receive bundles of these postcard-sized fabric pieces. In Michigan, many missions established by the United Methodist church have long served to revitalize older crafts as well as to introduce new ones, including quilting.

One of the earliest cultural contacts between Native Hawaiians and missionaries occurred when the brig *Thaddeus* brought the first missionary party to Oahu. Female members of the *ali'i*, or chiefly family, joined the missionary wives on board for a sewing party, as documented by Lucy Thurston in her journal on April 4, 1820: "Kalakua brought a web of white cambric to have a dress made for herself in the fashion of our ladies. . . . The four Native women of rank were furnished with calico patchwork to sew—a new employment for them."[1] Missionary wives established a number of sewing classes on the islands, and quilting was usually part of the curriculum. According to a visitor to a school in Wailuku on Maui in 1841, "[Miss Ogden] teaches them to make their own clothes, make straw bonnets, piece bed quilts and quilt them, to make samplers, and knit stockings."[2] Similarly, Mary O'Brien writes of the quilting activities of her Cherokee forebears who

This photo, taken on the Rosebud or Pine Ridge Reservation in South Dakota, c. 1930, shows Sioux women with quilts done in a variety of block patterns.

attended school at the Candy's Creek Mission in Tennessee, established in 1820.[3]

On the Rosebud Reservation in South Dakota, nuns from the St. Francis Indian Mission introduced Native American women to quiltmaking along with other forms of needlework. Missionary John P. Williamson's memoirs recall that women met every week to pray and quilt at the Yankton Agency School, established in the early 1870s on the Yankton Sioux Reservation: "One and sometimes two quilts were quilted nearly every week in the year [and] the women take turns bringing and serving a noon lunch." Just before he died, Williamson himself received an elaborate quilt made for him by the women of the reservation's Mayasan church.[4]

Two early-twentieth-century and nearly identical *star* quilts (see p. 32) were made by Odawa women living in the small Leelenau Peninsula in the northeastern part of Michigan's Lower Peninsula, most likely at one of the several mission churches. One, made about 1920, is attributed to either Margaret David or her mother, Anna, of Peshawbestown. The other, made in 1912, is attributed to a Mrs. Ogahmahgegedo (possibly also known as Catherine or Jenny Steele) from nearby Ahgosatown.[5]

A *hearts and gizzards* quilt was made about 1917 by Abelone Nielsen Larsen along with residents of the Oaks Indian Mission in Oklahoma. Larsen, a native of Denmark who worked at the mission for several years, later recalled:

> *Wednesday was normally quilting day. . . . The girls, staff, and neighbor women quilted two hours in the morning, broke for dinner, then resumed for several hours in the afternoon. The cotton batting was homegrown; the seeds were removed by hand and then it was hand carded. The quilts, always of the same pattern and always maroon and white, were sold for $3 each to raise money for the mission. The pattern was probably chosen by Mrs. Gertrude Nielsen, the wife of the founder of the mission, and supervisor of the work.[6]*

A quilt is spread out on the ground in front of this log house on the Devil's Lake Sioux Reservation, Jackson, North Dakota, in 1924.

In the Akwesasne communities of upstate New York, twentieth-century quilting bees were simply an outgrowth of mutual aid societies—societies of women and men bound together by clan, family, and community ties for the purpose of working on the tasks that needed to be done within the community. Here, too, the women shared in the work while enjoying the camaraderie and storytelling:

> *My mother [Sarah Lazore] used to invite all the neighbors in. Her mother and her aunt would come over and sew. And my father would end up doing the cooking while the women sewed. They used to do that in the wintertime, trading off stories. . . . You get to listen to them and you don't even realize how fast you are sewing.[7]*

Boxes of fabric as well as whole quilts were regularly sent to mission posts by home churches. A 1902 record book from the Devil's Lake Sioux Reservation in North Dakota lists donations of quilts (*owinja,* literally "to spread upon the ground") as well as dresses.[8] Many stories are told by Indians of receiving barrels and crates of fabric, clothing, and quilts on the reservations— especially at Christmas.

A study of quiltmaking on the Six Nation and New Credit Reserves in Ontario, Canada, notes that "by 1920, the various Christian religions were well integrated into . . . reserves, and quilting bees began to flourish as a related social and fund-raising activity."[9] Today, missions remain important spiritual, social, educational, and sometimes economic centers of Native community life, and quilting continues to support those functions.

Native Quilts in Mid-Nineteenth- to Early-Twentieth-Century Life Though missions were undoubtedly influential in bringing quiltmaking to Native communities,

**Hearts and Gizzards Quilt,
c. 1915**

*Made by Abelone Nielsen Larsen
and other unknown makers,
Oaks, Oklahoma. 77 x 65 inches.
Collection of Philip and
Florence Larsen*

knowledge of quiltmaking also spread whenever there was interaction between Native peoples and traders and other settlers whose family members already made or used quilts. In the course of research for *To Honor and Comfort*, Native quiltmakers were asked about their memories of family quilting activities. Time and again they recalled their mothers, grandmothers, and often great-grandmothers making quilts. Recent exhibits and studies on particular tribal quilting traditions also bear witness to quilts and quilting activities outside of missions.

In quiltmaker Mary O'Brien's Cherokee family, quilting goes back several generations. In her research, O'Brien found records indicating that "in 1842, many Cherokee families listed old and new quilts in their claims against the United States for possessions left behind during Removal [the forcible removal of Indians from their homelands in the eastern United States to tracts of land west of the Mississippi]. These quilts were generally valued at $5 to $6."[10]

A letter in the collections of the Cherokee Nation Museum illustrates another type of cross-cultural contact. In April 1864, Amanda Seal and Louisa Gibbs of Philadelphia wrote to John Ross, principal chief of the Cherokee Nation, requesting him to autograph and return an enclosed square of white silk. The block was to be used in a red, white, and blue *autograph* quilt they were making as a fundraiser for the Sanitary Fair in Philadelphia. (In Ross's reply it is difficult to discern if he actually sent a signed cloth back..[11])

In Mendocino County, California, through contact with local ranching and hop-farming families, Pomo Indians were commonly making quilts by the 1870s: "It was also established by this time that a good basketweaver made a good quiltmaker."[12]

Early quilts now in public and private collections provide further evidence of quilt-making's spread. A quilt made in 1868 by Sophia "Granny" (Chickasaw) in Oklahoma Indian Territory in honor of the birth of her son is now in the possession of one of her descendants in Bartlesville, Oklahoma.[13] An appliquéd *tulip* pattern quilt made about 1865 and owned by the Oklahoma Historical Society has stitched along the bottom the inscription: "the rina Bloom-maid in the Cherokee Nation—maid by Lydia A. Spangler—honor the pattern of the husbandry. Remember me and this you see will ceep huming." A *friendship* quilt in the same collection was made for a Mrs. Athenus Folsum Colbert by the women of Choctaw, Chickasaw, and Cherokee descent in 1869.[14] And in an 1894 *Scribner's* article, author Fanny Bergen reports that "Rev. J. Dorsey, of the Bureau of Ethnology, has kindly sent me three designs which were drawn for him by a Biloxi Indian from quilts pieced by his Indian wife."[15]

One of the earliest-known extant Native quilts in Canada, dated 1915, is attributed to an unidentified Ojibwa woman from the Saint Theodosie area of Quebec. Now in the collection of the Royal Ontario Museum, the *medallion*-style quilt (see p. 12) displays a large rondel and four leaf motifs appliquéd in blue on a white background. A quilt made about 1900 by Maggie Lowery Locklear, a descendant of Lumbee Indian Henry Berry Lowie, is on permanent display at the Pembroke Cultural Center, Pembroke State University, North Carolina.[16] Another quilt, made in the 1920s and 1930s by girls at the Chippewa Catholic Mission school in Bayfield, Wisconsin, is now owned by a woman who received it from her mother, who worked as a cook in the lumber camps around Bayfield.[17]

Two similar *pictorial* block quilts were made by Rebecca Blackwater around 1915 either in Santee, Nebraska, or Rosebud, South

Tulip Quilt, c. 1865

Made by Lydia Ann Spangler (Cherokee), Oklahoma. 82 x 71 inches. Collection of the Oklahoma Historical Society

Friendship Quilt, 1869

Makers unknown (Choctaw, Chickasaw, and Cherokee), Oklahoma. 81 x 68 inches. Collection of the Oklahoma Historical Society

Medallion Quilt, 1915

Maker unknown (Ojibwa),
Saint Theodosie area, Quebec,
Canada. 65 x 80 inches.
Collection of The Royal Ontario
Museum, Canada

Dakota. Blackwater was one of six Sioux women hired to help run the residence used by reservation superintendent Charles Eberle Burton and his wife, Ella. In the mornings the women did housework and cooking. In the afternoons, Mrs. Burton taught them to sew and quilt. Blackwater's quilt, made as a Christmas present to Ella, portrays the story of conflict between Indians and white men. According to Charles Burton Thomsen, a grandson and current owner of one of the quilts, "Grandmother asked Rebecca why she had the squaw riding and the brave walking when the Indians usually had it working the other way. Rebecca replied, 'That is one of the few customs of white men that I like so I decided to show it that way.'" Blackwater also commented on the evils of money by showing arrows pointed at an American shield, the shield representing the eagle found on most American currency.[18]

There also exist numerous quilts which, though unclear if made by Native quilters, were known to have been used in Native contexts. One such item is a *flower garden* quilt reportedly used in an Oklahoma Cherokee home during the Civil War.[19] One of the first non-Native nurses on the Navajo Reservation in New Mexico received a quilt from one of her Native American patients or friends. The quilt, in an appliquéd floral design, was probably not made by a Native American; in the early years of reservation

Pictorial Quilt, c. 1915

Made by Rebecca Blackwater
(Sioux), Santee, Nebraska.
70 x 78 inches. Private
collection

*The symbols and figures on this
quilt are believed to tell the story
of the conflict between Native
peoples and white men; in addition, they show representations
of everyday activities. A tomahawk above the peace pipe in the
upper left and vice versa in the
lower right are symbols, respectively, of war and peace.*

quilting only simpler economical patchwork quilts were common. More likely it had been given to the patient, either through a friend or a mission box, and she in turn gave it to the nurse as either payment for services, a token of appreciation, or as a way of honoring the nurse's work.[20] Countless historical photographs also document the use of quilts in everyday life in Native communities, though little or nothing is known about the quiltmakers or sources of the quilts.

Quilting Bees and Parties *Wh*ether quilting was done by an individual or a group depended on traditions specific to each tribe or community. Among the Sioux, for example, except for the mission- or church-related groups, most piecing and quilting was done by a person working alone.

Even today, Sioux quiltmakers tend to work alone unless there is an urgent need for making quilts quickly, such as for funerals.

Quilting bees and parties have long existed in some communities. A study of the Clifton Choctaw in Louisiana reveals that "quiltings were all-day affairs, held at someone's home, at which coffee and lunch were served."[21] Adolph L. Dial, a Lumbee historian, notes the process in his community:

> Quilts were made at quilting parties. Months in advance, a party's hostess began cutting squares of fabric from old clothes and empty flour sacks in her free time. Her children helped out by picking the seeds out of cotton from the family's fields. This cotton would be used as padding inside the quilt. Some evenings, children would be told they could not go to bed until they had filled their shoes with seeds.[22]

While the frequency of such quilting parties is not known, the following account by a former slave implies quilting promoted interracial and interethnic mingling:

While all were busily engaged quilting, a young brave, Martin Whistler, appeared upon the scene bearing a number of squirrels which he had killed and presented them to Betsy [a comely young Indian maid] for preparation for the noon meal. He took a chair near the object of his affections and would occasionally reach out and tap her on the shoulder. She would smilingly insist that he quit and in a coy manner pretend to draw away from his reach. To show that the attention paid her by the admiring youth was not unwelcome, she would soon have her chair scooted over to within reaching distance so that the gentle tapping would be repeated. This continued until late evening when the quilting was finished and the party, which was composed of both colored and Indian women, departed for their several homes. Of course, the young man found it to be convenient to go in the same direction, and at the same time, as the charmer of his life and, "lawsee de next mawnin we heead dey was mahied up."[23]

In Odawa and Ojibwa communities in northern Michigan, quilting bees were held in both mission churches and private homes. Ojibwa quilter Alice Fox remembers her family's quilting bees as times when she and her siblings would play, sometimes at their own peril:

When I was a child I used to watch my parents, my mother and my half-sister. . . . Anyway, she [my half sister] did all the work. Whatever my mother did, she was always the helper. And she made all our clothes. That was good, we were so poor. . . . They would have a quilting bee. . . . And then we would go under the table and under this quilt and pop our

*O*dawa elder Veronica Medicine of Harbor Springs, Michigan, recalled the importance of quilting bees to the passing on of knowledge in her community:

You learn a great deal because there are three generations of women there. We learn a great deal from each other. You listen to what the older ladies have to say and then the second generation and then quite often the third generation says very little because we're listening and learning. And to me it was a very valuable way of disseminating information from one generation to the other. Especially that type of information that is woman talk. . . . It's so very important especially in a culture that valued its women so highly, as the Odawa culture did. And it was the responsibility of the woman to teach the child or the children the history of the people. So, in this respect, the gathering to make quilts was very important. We did a lot of gossiping and a lot of small talk, too. But in the process we did learn.[24]

head under there you know. And they warned us, keep away from under there or else you're gonna get hurt. Somebody didn't listen. Came under the back, the blanket went up like this and a needle picked right on the head.[25]

The popularity of quilting parties and bees has fluctuated, even in communities where they historically occurred, but the growth of national and international activity in quilting and the concurrent rise of interest among Native quilters have caused an increase in quilting bees in the latter part of the twentieth century.

Learning Quilting within Family Contexts While missions and government programs were initially the most instrumental in spreading the skills of quiltmaking, the primary context for learning quickly became the family. Most Native quiltmakers of the twentieth century learned by watching and then working side by side with grandmothers, mothers, sisters, aunts, and other female members of their family and community. Many quilters still vividly recall these beginning experiences and the details of those lessons.

Eva Gagnon (Turtle Mountain Chippewa) of Dunseith, North Dakota, started quilting more than thirty-five years ago. When she was small her grandmother would turn a gallon pail over for her to sit on and then would give her scraps to sew. If Eva's stitches were too big or too far apart, her grandmother would make her take them out and do them again. Gagnon also remembers her grandmother telling her that as a child her family did not have irons to iron their quilting material. Instead, they made do by heating up metal spoons to smooth the fabric.[26]

Mary Woodward, a Cherokee quilter from Oklahoma known for her *wedding ring* quilts, remembers making her first quilt—a *nine patch*—at age four. Her mother taught her a variety of techniques and patterns using material from white meal sacks and twenty-five-pound feed sacks.[27] When Shirley Grady wanted to make a quilt, her mother insisted on her first learning to sew:

I wanted a baby quilt and my mother sat me down and said, "Sew!" I had to sit all day. Through this experience, I learned how to make mostly blouses, my own clothes, and Western shirts. . . . I told my mother I would start making quilts when I became a grandmother. In 1982, I became a grandmother and I started making my quilts big.[28]

Nellie Star Boy Menard of Rosebud, South Dakota, was taught during her four-day *Hunka* ceremony (the girls' coming-of-age ceremony) several crafts by her grandmother, Helen Leads the Horse.[29] She learned quilting, including the *star* pattern, from her mother, Grace Runs Clothes.

Pearl Spotted Tail, born in Rosebud in 1934, learned to make quilts when she was eleven years old from her grandmother, who, in turn, had learned from her mother and grandmother. Pearl remembers helping her grandmother for a few minutes every day after school by ironing and cutting fabric and sorting colors, sometimes working by lantern light in the tent in which her grandmother lived.[30]

Rae Jean Walking Eagle (Assiniboine/Sioux) of Brockton, Montana, is a very active quiltmaker who also serves as assistant to the Fort Peck Reservation tribal chairperson. Her stories about learning to quilt reveal how standards of excellence were part of the knowledge handed from one generation to the next:

My mother never told me to do this [quilt], it was just passed on. I wanted to do it [the star quilt] because I saw my mother make them. When I was little, I saw my mother take my quilt apart and redo it, because my hands were dirty, the thread was black, or the quality of the sewing was not good. This incident left a lasting impression in my mind. From then on, I was determined to do well. . . . There are the little challenges [in quilting]. A Smithsonian magazine article talked about good quilts having twenty-five stitches per inch. A friend from Denver sent it to me. The family jokes about having only twenty-five stitches per inch. We created our own competition as a result.[31]

For some, the memories of learning to quilt are connected to absorbing other aspects of culture. Sheilah Wahnetah remembers that while teaching her grandchildren to quilt, her grandmother would "tell us stories . . . you know the coyote and different stories . . . that's what was so nice about it."[32] For Hawaiian quilter Sharon Balai, her grandmother's spirit continues to help her quilting: "If I get stuck in an area, I'll just think about her and I'll go, 'Gram, can you give me some help here?' And I feel like she's around me and I can really hear her."[33]

Many contemporary quiltmakers who learned the skill from their mothers at an early age did not actively quilt until after they raised their families and/or retired from their jobs. With more time and resources, they make up for the years they did not quilt and are passing their skills and knowledge on to the next generation.

Native Quilters and Their Materials *U*ntil recently, nearly all North American Indian quilters used scraps of old fabrics or pieces torn from old clothing for their quilts. In Hawaii, Native quilters used scraps only for their patchwork-style work. Stories abound about the sources of and memories associated with these old fabrics. Pomo quilters tore up the men's old woolen suits or outdated ladies' dresses given to them by wealthy white families to make quilts. According to one Pomo elder, women competed for who had the lovelier quilts.

Another woman recalled how, after hop-picking time, quilts would be washed and put up on the line for all to admire and to imitate.[34]

One quilter from Warm Springs, Oregon, recalls recycling fabrics for quilts in the 1950s: "Remember poodle skirts and all? Yea, I ripped those things apart to make do because I had to have blankets for my kids. It was just out of necessity, and that's how I got involved making quilts."[35] Emil Her Many Horses' grandmother made a quilt with scraps of material left over from the dance shirts she had made for all the dancers in her family. Another quilt, given as a wedding gift by one of her best friends, was created from material left over from making satin dancing dresses.[36]

Feed, flour, sugar, and tobacco sacks were commonly used by many quilters for piecing quilts. Mary Woodward, a Cherokee quilter, recalls learning to sew on the sackcloth pieces her mother used:

> *. . . they used white meal sacks and flour sacks of twenty-five pounds and she'd turn down a hem . . . well I guess it would be an inch . . . and she would baste it down. Then I would do what we'd call the whipping . . . they call it a blind stitch now but it ain't very blind. So that's the way I learned to sew with Momma working at sewing and quilting.*[37]

Brother Simon in Pine Ridge, South Dakota, recalls seeing a photograph of a *star* quilt made of Bull Durham tobacco bags and recalls contemporary Sioux quilt-maker–artist Arthur Amiotte telling Simon of his grandmothers making quilts with tobacco bags.[38] Georgia Rae Easter, a home extension agent on the Pine Ridge Reservation in the 1930s, reported on Mary Scout's preparation and use of tobacco bags in Wounded Knee, South Dakota:

Crazy Quilt, 1996

Made by Melinda J. Doxtator
(Oneida), Oneida, Wisconsin.
62 x 87.5 inches. Collection of
Melinda J. Doxtator

Because portions of the quilt
were made at different times
over a twenty-year period, this
crazy quilt has an unusual
color design. Doxtator used
scraps of fabric left over from
other sewing projects, creating
a unique memory quilt of the
aprons, ribbon shirts, and
dresses she had made in the
past.

The ingenuity of this sixty-two-year-old Indian woman offers a splendid example of economy, patience, and splendid handiwork.

Men "roll" their own in the Sioux country, cowboy fashion, a custom which causes local traders to stock large quantities of sacked tobacco upon their shelves.

Mary saves every tobacco bag which her husband, Jasper, empties and hides away until she has a quantity sufficient to start work. The yellow draw strings are then carefully untied, pulled out, and laid in strands. The bags are turned wrong side out and the thread raveled from the lockstitched seams. Not one inch of thread is wasted, for practice enables Mary to rip a seam without breaking a thread.

Next comes preparation for wash day. Mary carries the water from the Creek, seventy-five paces from below the house, and allows it to stand overnight until all silt settles to the bottom. The water is heated with wood which she cuts herself—for the Indian country women often cut the wood. With homemade soap she washes the yellow draw strings, the thread taken from the ripped seams, and the muslin. When nicely ironed, the origin of the lovely white pieces of muslin could never be guessed.

In her original pattern, pieces of dress prints of the same size as the tobacco bag oblongs are combined . . . using thread that was salvaged from the seams and washed. But her most outstanding piece of work is made wholly from tobacco bag material which she dyed to carry out her color scheme for an eight-pointed star design. When the comfort tops are completed they are "tied" with the yellow cord which was once the draw string of a five cent tobacco bag. Mary's husband smokes about 430 bags of tobacco a year. She says that from 300 to 500 sacks are needed to piece one top. Since making her first quilt she has solicited sacks from relatives and friends and has now completed seven quilt tops.[39]

Ojibwa quilter Barbara Tazelaar, a resident of Michigan's Upper Peninsula, recalls the innovative use her mother made of materials from her father's occupation:

My mother made quilts . . . but I wouldn't exactly call them quilts. My dad was an upholsterer and they would always send samples up from Grand Rapids. They were oblong, probably a foot by a foot and a half. Some were velvets, which was nice. But mostly they were rough stuff [and a] lot of them were sprayed on the back with a rubber cement type stuff. . . . She sewed those together because we lived in a house in the country that the snow came through the walls. Those [quilts] kept the snow off you especially because of the rubber backing.[40]

Because so many materials in quilts were from relatives' clothing and were related to family members' occupations, the fabric pieces often prompt memories of people and experiences. Mohawk quilter Doris Benedict observes:

I remember as a child lying on the bed and sitting there looking at the big squares that my mom made out of my dad's coat or my grandfather's coat . . . it got to be a challenge to say, "That was Grandpa's and this was Mom's and that was Dad's," just from going through the patchwork as you lay there in the evening remembering who wore what and then what it looked like on them . . . it gave you a sense of warmth and closeness to other members of your family.[41]

When the memories are particularly strong, it may make it difficult to part with a quilt. As Mohawk quilter Elizabeth Perkins says, "All the pieces that I put together, all the dresses, the ribbon dresses I make, I know where each one of those pieces went to. So it's hard to sell them after that."[42]

In 1996, Eraina Palmer (Wasco Warm Springs Hoopa) made this quilt (64 x 86 inchs) in memory of her grandmother, Ruby Coone. Traditional Wasco believe that each person has an Indian spirit animal (Ta Wan Mus) for his or her medicine. When you are young you are sent on a journey up a mountain. On this trip, you will converse with a special animal and that animal will become your medicine power for all of your life. In the center of each log cabin block is fabric printed with an eagle, Coone's spirit animal. Collection of Michigan State University Museum

Wasco quilter Kate Jackson stands in front of her **Arrowhead Quilt**, a variation on the log cabin pattern.

A weaver and a quilter, Caroline Wilson (Navajo) of Mexican Springs, New Mexico, makes quilts in the same patterns as her Navajo rugs. This **Chief Blanket, Phase III Quilt** (1992, 61.25 x 53.75 inches) was intended as a baby quilt or a wall hanging. Collection of Michigan State University Museum

Navajo artist Mary Ann Henio creates quilts based on traditional Navajo woven rug designs. This quilt (c. 1990, 66 x 87 inches) utilizes only pieced triangles to replicate a rug pattern. Henio, of Thoreau, New Mexico, finds that quilting these patterns brings her closer to nature. Collection of Michigan State University Museum

Old quilts are recycled, usually as batting. Navajo quilter Alberta Lewis tells of local older women who cover two or three old quilts or blankets with new tops made of scraps pieced in no particular design. Tacked together with yarn, these quilts are very heavy and used only during winter.[43] Some contemporary Sioux quilters even recycle new quilts. In order to improve the workmanship or color scheme of a quilt they have received as a gift in a giveaway, they may completely disassemble and reconstruct it so that in turn they might feel good about giving the quilt to someone else.[44]

Native quiltmakers have been just as economical in their use of materials for batting as for quilt tops and backing. Depending on where they lived, quilters gleaned batting from natural or cultivated resources. In Hawaii, quilters first used the fluffy tops of a native fern for their quilts; later, when sheep were introduced to the island, they used wool.[45] In cotton-growing areas, batting was gathered from the fields, as recalled by Mary Woodward:

> We'd go after they'd turn it loose from pickin' . . . and take the scrap cotton, and then we'd lay it down where it would be warm in front of the stove and warm it and you can just push that seed out of there and then we'd use cotton cards [to take the seeds out] . . . we'd put up a quilt every morning and all three of us could lay them batts out and so we'd get the quilt out that day.[46]

Quilting through old blankets or quilts was difficult, as Veronica Medicine of Harbor Springs, Michigan, reminisced: "[For the batting] we used to use a light-weight blanket we put in between the shally back and then the light-weight blanket and the quilt top. And then quilt it. That's hard to do. It's hard on the fingers. Little tiny white stitches."[47]

While quilters today still use scraps of fabrics from other sewing projects or old clothing for tops and old quilts as batting, many now regularly incorporate polyester batting and new cloth, even when the selection is limited. New cloth, once readily available in trading posts or in now-defunct rural mercantile shops, is now mainly found in urban centers. In Sioux country, stores keep a stock of the solid-colored satins and cottons favored by Sioux quilters. The *Lakota Times*, one of the major newspapers serving Native peoples, regularly advertises sales of these fabrics, and stores sometimes have sales in conjunction with powwows.

Still, quilters will travel great distances to obtain the materials they need. Sioux quiltmaker Lula Red Cloud lives near Rapid City, South Dakota, yet gets all her fabric in Denver, Colorado, a seven-hour drive from her home. When she finds colors she likes, she buys the whole bolt.[48] Rae Jean Walking Eagle reports that news of fabric sales quickly prompts group excursions: "When quilters living on the reservation hear of a sale at one of the local stores, one of the women will pick up another four to five interested women and everyone will go to see what they can find at a good price."[49] The recent rise in mail-order catalogues specializing in fabrics for quilts has increased the options for quilters living in remote areas.

A North American Indian Quilt Aesthetic: Quilt Patterns, Colors, Fabrics, and Designs

Until the latter part of the twentieth century, most patterns and quilt techniques were shared in the context of mission-based activities, cooperatives, or families. Most native quilters, because they lived in remote or rural areas, did not have access to the full array of quilt patterns circulated regularly through newspaper columns or issued by pattern companies. Early Native quiltmakers generally followed simple patterns and made use of scrap rather than purchased cloth. Quilt patterns of great popularity across America invariably found their way into Native communities. Cherokee quilt-maker and quilt researcher Mary O'Brien notes that "in the early 1900s, many Cherokee women were collecting patterns from the *Kansas City Star* newspaper" and that although her grandmother's favorite pattern was a *star*, she frequently made *double wedding ring* and *Sunbonnet Sue* quilts.[50]

Some Euro-American patterns have been refigured and renamed. Wasco quilter Kate Jackson, for example, worked a traditional *log cabin* pattern into an *arrowhead* design. Odawa quilter Agnes Shawanessi renamed an *umbrella* pattern *turtle has an umbrella.* (see p. 24) O'Brien recently published two designs, *chief's daughter in diamond* and *double chief's daughter,* her interpretations of early quilt patterns influenced by Cherokee basket patterns.[51] Patchwork patterns named by Euro-Americans to refer directly to American Indian culture or to the natural world are also popular among many Native quiltmakers. Such patterns are *arrowhead*, *Indian head*, *Indian hatchet*, and *Indian trail* or *star*, *bear's paw*, *thunderbird*, and *maple leaf.*

A pattern similar to the *Sunbonnet Sue* and *Overall Andy* patterns, extremely popular in other circles, is the *Indian man and woman* quilt pattern. Originally designed by a VISTA volunteer in the mid-seventies, it appeared in an early *Lady's Circle Needlework* magazine and was reprinted and renamed *going to the fair* or *watching the sunset* in a September/ October 1989 issue of *Lady's Circle Patchwork Quilts* magazine.[52] Variations of this pattern show in each block either a single female and/or male viewed from the rear. Each

figure is "dressed" slightly differently by varying the fabrics for the clothes or adding fringe to dance shawls and braided black yarn to represent hair. Different variations reflect local clothing traditions, depending on the region of the country where the pattern is used. In Alaska, a version called *Kuspuk Kate* or *Parka Pete* is made; *kuspuk* is the Yupik word for a cloth parka worn by Eskimo girls and women.[53]

Though the making of quilts is infrequent within the Florida Seminole and Miccosukee tribal communities, a style of patchwork has, in the twentieth century, become one of the primary cultural features distinguishing these tribes from other Native American groups. Seminole patchwork generally refers to sewing solid pieces of cloth together to form designs in strips. The strips are joined to other similar or solid cloth strips to form bands of decorative cloth, which are then used to form or decorate skirts, blouses, jackets, and other garments. While its exact origins in these communities are not known, Seminole patchwork began some-time after the introduction of hand-cranked sewing machines into the camps of Miccosukee-speaking women in 1910 and, sometime later, by Muskogee-speaking women in Florida.

Seminole and Miccosukee patterns did not originally have names, but in the 1930s and 1940s Harriet M. Bedell, an Episcopal deaconess affiliated with the Glade Cross Mission in Florida, urged women to name their designs in order to help their sales in a fast-growing patchwork market. Designs and their names reflected the Florida landscape, weather, animals, and features of Indian life: *fire, lightning, storm, waves, arrowheads, alligator,* and *diamondback rattlesnake* are examples.[54]

Ribbonwork, another North American Indian textile tradition, involves creating decorative bands by appliquéing strips of

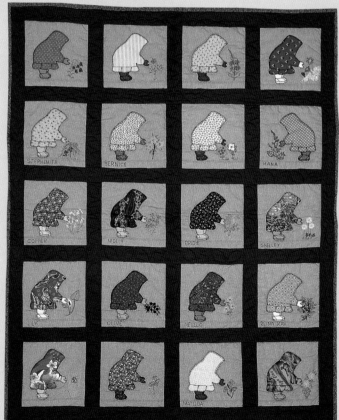

fabrics, cut in designs, onto other fabric strips of contrasting colors. These bands adorn clothing. While the process involves techniques used in creating patchwork and appliquéd quilts, few artists skilled in ribbonwork make quilts. Mary Big Horse, a well-known Osage regaliamaker in the ribbonwork style, is one of the few in her Oklahoma community to make quilts incorporating ribbonwork patterns.

Friendship quilts, sometimes also referred to as *autograph* or *signature* quilts, do not seem to have been popular among Native peoples, most likely because most Native quilters did not usually work in groups. One interesting early-twentieth-century exception is the *Hopland Friendship Quilt* (see p. 28), made in 1928 by Pomo Indians who lived in Hopland, California. Now owned by the Mendocino County Museum, the quilt was a project instigated by teachers at the Hopland Rancheria School for Indian children. Blocks preprinted with stenciled designs depicting colonial themes, such as "Standish Answers Indians" and "Pocahantas-Smith," or Eastern Plains Indians scenes were sent home with students to embroider and sign. (One square was done by the famous Pomo basketweaver Elsie Allen.[55])

Other examples include a *friendship* quilt made in 1954 by Olivia Black Elk Pourier (see p. 29) with her friends in Allen, South Dakota. A more contemporary *friendship* quilt was made by seniors at the Saginaw Chippewa Reservation senior center in Mount Pleasant, Michigan, in 1981. In this example, each block is embroidered with birds and flowers and the name of each quilter. The quilt now hangs in the casino located on the reservation.[56]

Sampler quilts also are rare in Native communities. Cherokee quilter Mary Woodward made several as reminders of quilt patterns that she was given but used them for everyday use. The Ka Hui Kapa Apana O Waimea quilt group on the Big Island of Hawaii has created several *sampler* quilts, each block made in a different pattern by a different member of the group. For the *sampler* quilt made in November 1996 by the twenty quilters who attended the Native Quilters' Gathering at Michigan State University Museum, each quilter contributed a block, mostly of original design, to a top that was then quilted by Paula White. A description of each block, written on muslin squares, was sewn to the back of the quilt.

For the quilting patterns used to stitch together the three layers of cloth—top, batting, and backing—many contemporary North American Indian textile artists favor stars, tipis, thunderbirds, pipes, warbonnets, and arrowheads, in addition to the clamshells, fans, or outline quilting used by non-Native quilters. The medicine wheel, an ancient religious symbol, also is often used. The wheel, broken into four quarters, variously represents the four stages of life, the four directions, the elements, or the four seasons. The associated four colors—red, yellow, white, and black—also represent the four human races. Alice Olsen Williams, an Anishnabe quilter from Ontario, always incorporates a small *pimaatisiwin* ("medicine wheel") in her quilt designs, making sure that the white quarter of the wheel is never dominant or on top, thus communicating her strong feelings about the history of Natives and non-Natives. Because the number four has such deep symbolism for Native peoples, quilts often contain images or designs in sets or multiples of four. Margaret Wood (Navajo/Seminole), a quilt artist from Phoenix, Arizona, usually produces new quilt designs in limited series of four.

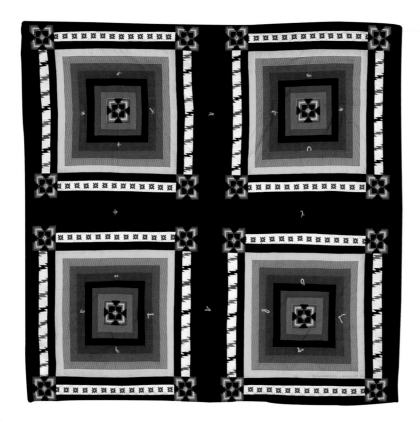

Well known for her finely crafted, colorful patchwork shirts, Virginia Osceola has turned in recent years to the making of pieced pillows and quilts, such as is shown above (c. 1994, 80 x 80 inches, Fort Lauderdale, Florida). Collection of Michigan State University Museum

Seminole woman with hand-cranked sewing machine, 1927.

Certain missions became centers of individualized quilt design traditions. For example, the missions established in the Odawa communities on Michigan's Leelenau Peninsula generated a style of quilt mixing Anglo-American and Woodland Indian designs. Quilts produced in this area incorporated a *star* pattern—thought to be based on a widely disseminated Euro-American quilt pattern—with floral motifs commonly used in Woodland appliqué and beadwork.

Commonly used quilt patterns tend to reflect designs or symbols important to a given community. Arapaho quilter Sara Angela Walker observes that "Arapaho designs are geometric. The Shoshone are known as the 'Flower People,' and their design is the traditional Shoshone rose."[57] One of Mary Big Horse's favorite quilts was done in the *spider* design, a sacred Osage design pertaining to the Spider clan. She remembers her grandmother telling her that "in the late 1800s the Spider clan had tattoos on their left hand. And they always wore a spider pattern in their clothing and in their ribbon work."[58]

Seminole and Miccosukee patchwork pattern designs called *crawdad*, *turtle*, and *lightning* are reminders of great myths or stories in those cultures.[59] Paula White uses symbols of the Native American church in her quilts, especially eagle feathers and arrows. At least two existing quilts carry the seal of the Cherokee Nation (see p. 33).

Clan symbols are frequently used by Native quilters. Alberta Lewis incorporates linear outlines representing buildings to reflect her Navajo clan, the House clan. Shirley Grady stitches a wolf, for she is of the Wolf clan, into her quilting pattern. Akwesasne quilter Beverly Cook Jackson has made several kinds of quilts and incorporates Mohawk symbols into her work:

Mary Big Horse (Osage) of Pawhuska, Oklahoma, is recognized in her community as an accomplished regalia-maker. She created this quilt (c. 1996, 58 x 87 inches) to resemble a traditional Osage tribal trade blanket.

Hopland Friendship Quilt, 1928

Blocks embroidered and autographed by Pomo Indians. Pieced and quilted by Geraldine Youd, Hopland, California. Double-bed size. Collection of the Mendocino County Museum

Students at the Hopland Rancheria school for Indian children were sent home with stenciled blocks to sign with their names, embroider, and return to the school for quilting. Block designs included depictions of eastern Indians as well as of colonial themes.

Olivia Black Elk Pourier (Sioux) remembers working on this **Friendship Crazy Quilt** (70.5 x 90 inches) with her friends in Allen, South Dakota, in 1954. Signed by the makers, this quilt was given to Ben Reifel; he later gave it to his daughter, Loyce Reifel Anderson.

I quilted the three clans, the Tree of Peace, Hiawatha, corn beans and squash, strawberries, drums and rattles. It was beautiful. One of the other parents at the Freedom School bought it because they couldn't stand for it to go anywhere out of the community. . . . I've been trying to do sky domes and symbols that depict what our culture and spirituality is about.[60]

Navajo quilter Mary Ives, of Chaparral, New Mexico, fashions quilts that contain appliquéd figures of Kachinas and Zuni hoop dancers.[61]

Within the Mohawk community in St. Regis, New York, quilts often possess symbols of the Turtle clan. A Tonawanda Seneca clan quilt made by Bessie Carpenter (Seneca) and Edna Parker (Cayuga) was part of a traveling exhibit circulated in 1976.[62] A block quilt made about 1994 by an anonymous Cherokee quilter carries embroidered renderings of the seven Cherokee clans as well as, in the Cherokee language, the clan names (see p. 35).

In Odawa and Ojibwa cultures, the strawberry is one of the first fruits to be gathered in the spring and figures prominently in harvest celebrations, feasts, burial rituals, dances, and legends. It is no surprise that Woodland Indian quiltmakers choose to make quilts with a *strawberry* design:

About the strawberry quilt. . . . My sister, Rita, made one like that. And then we went to Cross Village [an Odawa community with a Catholic mission in northern Michigan] and she donated her quilt to them. And it was navy blue background and strawberries with green leaves.[63]

Woodland quilters also make frequent use of the *thunderbird* image, either in a block pattern, a large *medallion* image, or incorporated into a *star* pattern. The Thunderbird (Animike) and the Underwater Panther (Jibshi) are two of the most important beings in Odawa cosmology.

Because most quilting was not shared intertribally, different tribes developed distinctive traditions. The Clifton Choctaw, for example, favored quilting done in the *fan* pattern with tops pieced in *crazy*-style, *double-bitted axe*, *star*, and *log cabin* patterns.[64]

Often Native quilters, irrespective of their own tribal background, will select printed fabrics that incorporate Southwest or pan-Indian imagery, such as eagles, running horses, or Navajo textile designs. Alice and Floyd Fox, Ojibwa living in the Upper Peninsula of Michigan, chose fabric printed with scenes of Inuit life for a backing of one of their quilts. Seniors at the Oneida United Methodist Church used handkerchiefs with Native American designs or scenes of Native American life to make a block quilt (see p. 34) as a gift for their pastor.[65] Eraina Palmer (Wasco) cuts out eagles from printed fabric to use as the center of her *log cabin* blocks.

Color choices often reflect the Native quilter's close spiritual ties to the natural world. Blue, the color of the sky, is often the background of an *eagle star* quilt design. Yellow, red, and orange—colors associated with the sun or fire—are frequently used in *star* variations. *Morning star* quilts are usually done in shades of blue—the color of the sky on cold winter mornings. When Sioux quilter Ollie Napesni of Rosebud, South Dakota, makes quilts for ceremonial purposes, she always uses "the six colors for [the four] directions and the sky and Mother Earth, that's blue and green."[66] Mary Ann Henio, a Navajo quilter from New Mexico, describes the colors in one of her quilts as representing "the four stages of life: black is the dark world, the mother's womb; turquoise is youth; red is adulthood; and white is for old age."[67]

Some quilters never use black as a background or dominant color, considering it unlucky. Others choose black as a symbol of grief or a troubling time. Paula White of Leech Lake Reservation in Minnesota typically uses a rainbow of colors set against a black background in her *star* quilts. For her, the color black is deeply symbolic of a sad period of her life: "I got into black about five years ago because I was going through healing, like grief. . . . [I was] in mourning because I had lost both my grandparents."[68] In 1990, as a social worker with a domestic violence women's support group, Toni Marie House urged the women to make a quilt as part of their therapy. Though normally she felt quilts should not have black backgrounds, she acquiesced when the women insisted on that color. The resulting quilt (see p. 38) was raffled to raise funds for the Oneida Social Services.[69]

In 1996, Native and non-Native members of the Calico Country Quilt Guild, Belcourt, North Dakota, joined together in creating this textile record, the **Turtle Mountain Chippewa Heritage Quilt** *(79 x 99 inches). The quilt includes important historical events, contemporary activities, buildings, and symbols related to tribal history. The central panel is an appliquéd and beaded floral design traditional to Woodland Indian culture.*

Members of the guild who contributed to this quilt include: Dolores Gourneau, Theresa Brien, Lori Weidemann, Maria Weidemann, Shirley Marion, Cecile Lemieux, Jenny Schindler, Verna Jeanotte, Nancy Fry, Josephine Jeanotte, Maureen Williams, and Ernestine Jeanotte. Collection of Michigan State University Museum

Lone Star Variation
Quilt, c. 1920

Made by Margaret [Anna]
David (Odawa), Peshawbestown,
Michigan. 76 x 91 inches.
Collection of Michigan State
University Museum

Quilt Patterns and Other Design Traditions Native artists have adapted the beadwork, rug weaving, and basket weaving patterns of their cultural heritage or of their own experience into their quilts. The quilts of Bernyce K. Courtney (Wasco/Tlingit) reflect the design patterns she uses in her woven fiber bags; Mary Big Horse (Osage), also a talented dancer, makes quilts with the designs of the regalia and blankets she makes for members of her tribe; Charlie and Julia Grinnell (Sioux) make quilts in patterns similar to their beadwork; in her New Mexico hogan, Caroline Wilson (Navajo) makes quilts and woven rugs in traditional weaving Navajo patterns; and Carole Stewart (Muscogee/j36Creek) produces *bandolier bag* quilts with patterns and motifs drawn from both the Delaware and Creek.

In southern Alabama, the Creek Indian Nation east of the Mississippi hosts a number of contemporary quilters who remember the scrap quilts made by their mothers and grandmothers. Today, most Creek women use traditional quilting patterns, but some are beginning to incorporate traditional motifs found in ancient Southeast Indian pottery.[70]

The Star Pattern Among the Sioux and other Plains Indians, the *star* and its variations have been by far the most popular quilt patterns used in the mid- to late twentieth century and have become an integral part of many native community-based traditions. As they witnessed the importance of the *star* pattern in Plains Indian life, the pattern increased in popularity among quilters of other tribes as well. Although well known among quilters of other cultural backgrounds, the image of the star has special meaning for Native peoples, and

As tribal communities have taken steps to strengthen their sovereign status, many have designed seals for use on tribal documents. The seal of the Cherokee Nation in the center of this quilt also carries words in the Cherokee language.

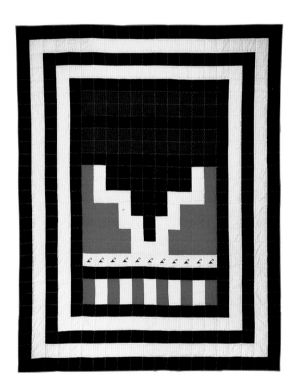

Pueblo Design Quilt, c. 1993

Made by Alberta Lewis (Navajo), Leupp, Arizona. 70.75 x 89.5 inches. Collection of Michigan State University Museum

Lewis embroidered a traditional Pueblo storm pattern above the pieced, stylized Pueblo architectural design. Her clan name translates to "building."

numerous stories are told of its origin and popularity.

George Horse Capture (Gros Ventre) sees a clear link between buffalo hides and the popularity of *star* quilts in Plains Indian cultures. Raised by his grandmother on the

Handkerchief Quilt, 1995

Made by the Oneida Seniors Sewing Group, Oneida, Wisconsin. 86 x 85 inches. Loaned by White Crow

The Oneida Seniors Sewing Group (Melinda Doxtator, Bertha Skenandore, Vera Perkins, Laretta Webster, and Margaret Summers) at the Oneida United Methodist Church used handkerchiefs with native imagery to make a quilt they gave to White Crow.

cultures. Raised by his grandmother on the Fort Belknap Reservation in north-central Montana, Horse Capture recalls sleeping under heavy quilts done in the *star* pattern. Years later, as a curator at the Plains Indian Museum of the Buffalo Bill Historical Center, he began to notice similar *star* designs in the center of painted buffalo hides in the museum's collection. When he had an opportunity to examine Native American painted buffalo-hide robes in the collections of the Musée de l'Homme in Paris, he recognized that the *star* quilt design was almost identical to a warbonnet painted on one of the robes.[71]

Brother C. M. Simon, S.J., who has spent a lifetime of service at the Red Cloud Indian School on the Pine Ridge Reservation in

South Dakota, has long taken an avid interest in documenting quiltmaking among the Sioux. He knows scores of quilters and has built a collection containing many examples of *star* quilts:

> *The oldest photo that I know of with a star quilt is a picture of Chief Red Cloud's cabin taken about the turn of the century. . . . When you look at photos of the 1920s, 1930s, they were all typical patchwork quilts, the log cabin quilt, the wedding ring quilt . . . the star quilt just faded out during the 1920s and 1930s, and it was the early '60s that the star quilt came back. And in the '60s it was almost a fad.[72]*

In an article tracing the origin of the *star* quilt, Karen McMurchie cites photographic and oral history as evidence of their popularity in turn-of-the-century Sioux life:

> *Marie Starboy, a Lakota quilter from Okreek, South Dakota, has a photo taken in 1908 on the occasion of her grandmother's fiftieth birthday. In it, several women are holding a star quilt, which was a gift to her. Marie says that both her mother and her grandmother made star quilts.[73]*

Ollie Napesni (Rosebud Sioux) was born in 1917 and has made more than four hundred quilts, many of them in the *star* pattern. She remembers seeing her first *star* quilt at a fair parade when she was only six or seven years old:

> *They had this big fair . . . in August. . . . We camped, and so I was in a tent looking out you know, sitting on a wagon seat there looking out and the parade was going by and here toward the last a covered wagon went by and here it had this quilt on there. That was the first time I saw a star quilt . . . it had diamonds that were really small and I never did forget that.[74]*

In some communities the transition from other patchwork patterns to the *star* pattern

Seven Clans Quilt, c. 1990s

Attributed to Minnie Clinton (Cherokee), Tahlequah, Oklahoma. 85 x 73 inches. Collection of Michigan State University Museum

The seven clans of the Cherokee Nation are embroidered in the blocks on this tied quilt. Clan names are given in both Cherokee and English.

Strawberries and Flowers, 1991

Made by Alice Olsen Williams (Anishnabe), Peterborough, Ontario, Canada. 60 x 60 inches. Collection of the artist

In Anishnabe culture, the strawberry is one of the first fruits to be gathered in the spring; thus, the fruit figures prominently in harvest celebrations, burial rituals, dances, and legends. It is no surprise that it is also used in quilts.

Paula White (Ojibwa), of Bena,
Minnesota, created this **Bright Star Quilt**
(1996, 82 x 58 inches) where two bands
of rainbow-colored fabrics at top and bottom frame a star of matching colors.
Unlike many quilters who shy away from
using black, White often employs this
color as a symbol of grieving and healing.
Collection of Michigan State University
Museum

**Tehashetase
(Rights of Passage), 1990**

*Made by Toni Marie House
(Oneida) and members of a
women's domestic violence
support group, Oneida,
Wisconsin. Double-bed size.
Collection of Vicki Cornelius*

*Social worker House urged
women of the support group to
create a quilt as part of their
therapy.*

Indian Cloud School, Pine Ridge, South Dakota, include many variations. A *star* quilt by Wilma Thin Elk features a rendering of James Earle Fraser's sculpture, E*nd of the Trail*. The original bronze became a wildly popular symbol of the American West after exhibition at the Pan-Pacific Exposition in 1915 and has been reproduced in a variety of media. Portions of the *star* pattern also are worked into dance shawls, shirts, and other elements of contemporary dance regalia.

Town, North Dakota, states: "My great-grandmothers, all our great-grandmothers and grandmothers made patchwork quilts. It was only in the 1950s that some people brought home some *star* quilts from the Sioux ladies . . . and then, all the ones that were sewing in my reservation picked up that *star* quilt."[75]

The basic eight- or six-pointed *star* pattern is most often produced, but artists also use a variety of *broken star* and *block star* pattern variations and incorporate·Indian heads, buffalo, pipes, tipis, warbonnets, and eagles into the central star design. Quilts in the collection of the Heritage Center at the Red

**Hawaiian
Quilt Patterns**
*H*awaii is famous for its distinctive quilt tradition in which a large design or pattern is appliquéd onto a base fabric of contrasting color to form the quilt top. One popular story of the origin of the Hawaiian quilt design relates how a Hawaiian woman laid out a large piece of cloth to dry in the shade of a tree on a sunny afternoon. The shadow the leaves and fruit of the tree (probably an *'ulu*, or breadfruit) cast on the cloth was so beautiful she decided to appliqué the design onto another cloth. Even today, quilters believe that in order to become good quilters the first quilt they make should be in the *'ulu* design.

The *lau*, or basic design pattern, is the personal creation of the quilt designer. The quilter makes the pattern by folding a large, usually quilt-sized, piece of paper in eighths of triangular shape and then cutting a design, in much the same way that paper snowflake designs are made. The design generally radiates from the center, or *piko* (navel), of the quilt. Should the quilter decide to give away or sell the quilt the ownership of its design is transferred to the recipient. When a quilter wants to use another's quilt pattern, she must have the permission of the owner. Even when quilt

Daybreak/Dawn Quilt, 1995

Made by Charlie Grinnell [designer and piecer] and Julia Grinnell [quilter] (Hidatsa), Parshall, North Dakota. 81 x 89 inches. Collection of Michigan State University Museum

In 1996, Carole Stewart, a Muscogee/Creek quiltmaker from Washington, Oklahoma, drew on both Creek and Delaware designs to create this large quilt (88.25 x 82.5 inches), an interpretation of a bandolier bag featuring strong, deep colors for a dramatic visual effect. Collection of Michigan State University Museum

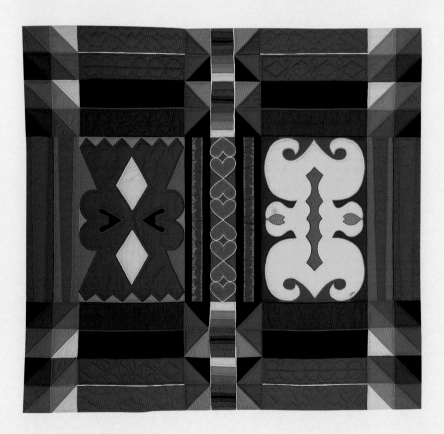

permission of the owner. Even when quilt pattern designs are in the public domain, most quilters alter them in some way to make them their own. Just changing the color of fabric is not enough; the design itself must be changed. Contemporary quilter Sharon Balai comments on the shifting practices pertaining to ownership of family patterns:

> In the past, Hawaiian quilts and their patterns were passed on only within families. Once in a while they shared with close friends, but certain patterns were not given to anyone. It was just passed within the family so that's how you can trace your family back, you know. It's like . . . a family crest, almost. And recently the women have started to share their patterns but still the ones that are basically family they won't let out.[76]

Many of the quilt patterns have both the Native Hawaiian name and its translation written on them. Quilters generally refer to the pattern by its Hawaiian name; thus, the language is perpetuated. Some pattern-makers give their designs names that carry a double meaning or symbolism known only to the maker.

Early Hawaiian *kuiki* (quilting) designs were derived from those found in *tapa* cloth and made by the *i'e kuku* (wooden mallet); *kuiki maka moena* translates literally as "quilting in *mat weave* design" and *kuiki papa pelena* as "quilting in *reef cracker* designs."[77] Today, most Hawaiian quilts use the traditional *kuiki lau* (echo or contour quilting) design that consists of repetitive lines of tiny stitches following the appliquéd design and done in rows out from the quilt's center.

Most Hawaiian quilters look to nature for inspiration, and many designs reflect the floral landscape indigenous to each island. Every island has a color and a particular blossom associated with it, and quilts made

One of the earliest photographs showing the use of a **star quilt** in Sioux life is this 1891 portrait of Chief Red Cloud at his home in Pine Ridge, South Dakota.

in those colors and floral designs are identified respectively. Creating a design is often a highly personal matter involving a spiritual process.

Sharon Balai, a quilter from Waimea, describes how she tries to capture the spirit of a natural form in her work:

> I'll take pieces of paper and do a sketch of the plant. . . . I try to sit close to the plant and talk to it in your mind, to connect with it. To get the plant to talk to you is easier than it is to translate it into a quilt pattern.[78]

For her first full-size quilt, Balai chose a *magnolia blossom* pattern as a tribute to her grandmother, a quilter who liked magnolias. Though considered by many to be a contemporary quilter, Balai adheres closely to certain fundamental traditions. Her designs are based on Hawaiian nature, are created on an eightfold or fourfold in two colors, and are quilted in echo quilting.

Harriet Soong grew up in the Waimea region of the Big Island of Hawaii. She

CLOCKWISE FROM TOP LEFT:

The Sioux have created countless variations on the star quilt pattern, many incorporating native images. An **Eagle Headdress Star Quilt** by an unknown Sioux maker (c. 1993, 76 x 85 inches) features a feather headdress set within a star, with small stars used in each of the eight points of the larger star.

Though no longer a source of food and clothing, the buffalo still retains a sacred place in the lives of Sioux people. This **Buffalo Head Star Quilt** (c. 1993, 83.5 x 85 inches), attributed to Philomena Frogg (Sioux), features a dramatic buffalo head as part of the pieced star design. Quilts are now acknowledged as the replacement for buffalo robes in many Sioux ceremonies.

This star quilt (c. 1960, 97.25 x 105.25 inches) is unusual in that the star is set with corners of white cloth with colorful embroidered floral and grid designs. The previous owner acquired it from a New Mexican woman of Hispanic and Pueblo Indian background, known only as "Bobo," who died in 1965 at the age of ninety-two.

This **Star Baby Quilt** (1996, 37.5 x 37.5 inches) was made by Ella Louise Weaver (Southern Ute) of Ignacio, Colorado.

All from the Collection of Michigan State University Museum

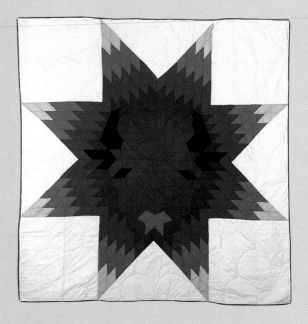

found that the area's year-round rain, suggested itself as an appropriate name for the quilt she recently made her granddaughter, Sarah Kamuela:

> This is Waimea's Rain . . . ; Kamuela is up there [mountain]. . . , the rain, it was called Ka Ua Kipu'upu'u Waimea after the Kamehameha warriors. [Like the warriors] the rain comes at you with a force. In [my quilt] there are the four spears. . . . I wanted it in green and white because that's how Waimea is. It rains all the time. We were always wet . . . and so it was always green.[79]

Many people consider completed quilts to be instilled with the *mana*, or spirit, of the quilter and therefore the quilts are highly regarded as family treasures. Junedale Lauwaeomakana Quinories recalls that, as a child, "when there was a tidal alert, my mother grabbed up her Hawaiian quilts and wrapped them in a bundle . . . and go off to higher and safer ground until the alert was over."[80]

Quilts and Everyday Use within Native Communities The overwhelming majority of quilts are made as bedcovers for the simple everyday function of providing warmth. A quilt also may be used in almost any situation demanding a blanket or blanket-sized cloth. Depending on the climate or community tradition, quilts may be used to help insulate dwellings, to cover the ground for sitting or sleeping, or to provide shade.

Paula Chaco Montoya (Hopi) remembers her family rolling up quilts when they slept on the roofs of their adobe homes on warm summer nights.[81] Another type of bedroll common in the ranching country of the West

One of the younger generation of Native Hawaiian quilters in the Ka Hui Kapa Apana O Waimea Club, Sharon Balai of Waimea, Hawaii, is known for her ability to create innovative and complex patterns. She is also a strong advocate for protecting the cultural rights of ownership of traditional Hawaiian quilt patterns. She explains how this quilt, "Kaumoha Koli'i" (1996–97, 96 x 101 inches), represents and speaks of marriage and was designed specifically to symbolize the union of Hawaii's cultural past with the introduced materials, ideas, and influence from other cultures. Nothing on or of this quilt is native to Hawaii but for the Hawaiian cultural system that brought in the traditions and the unique expansive concept of the eightfold process. The pattern of open hearts has a message to all who see it, saying, "Na pua o Hawaii aloha" (from the flowers [children] of Hawaii, greetings of love). As is customary in Hawaii, the name also has a second meaning: Kaumoha is a heaviness or burden due to a troubling situation, such as sadness or grief; Koli'i is a disappearing or diminishing, such as water evaporating or a ship sailing off into the horizon. This quilt's other name, "diminishing burden," refers to the quilter's sustained thoughts and feelings while this quilt was in progress.

and used by both Native and non-Native families are thick quilts, sometimes called *soogans*. Soogans often are made of patched denims or other sturdy material that can withstand hard use.

Quilts have also been worn, much like shawls, as thick outerwear to keep a body warm or to swaddle a baby. Papooses—textile bags constructed to carry a baby and keep it warm—have been patched, appliquéd, and quilted. Swing cradles, constructed of a piece of cloth folded over two pieces of suspended rope and used by many Native peoples, have been made of both blankets and quilts.

Numerous historical and contemporary photographs document quilts used as coverings over doorways and windows to keep shelters warm, be they wigwams, tipis, tents, cabins, framed houses, or mobile trailers. On the Warm Springs Reservation in Warm Springs, Oregon, the inside ground perimeter of sweat lodges is sealed with square-shaped, denim patchwork quilts. One of the most unusual uses of quilts as shelter is documented in a 1948 photograph (see p. 46) of Martin Kegg (Ojibwa), who used a quilt to make his tentlike ice-fishing shanty at Lake Mille Lacs, Minnesota.

When quilts were not in use they were generally stored between mattresses or in trunks. Hopi quilter Marlene Sekaquaptewa recalls keeping quilts and other textiles folded and stored up on the ridge poles.[82] Barbara Tazelaar remembers her aunt storing her quilts out of reach in black-ash baskets up in the rafters.[83]

While quilts are inherently functional, their symbolic value as expressions of honor is sometimes of greater importance. Quiltmakers often do not own examples of their own work as their quilts are primarily made to be given away. When asked if she uses any of the many *star* quilts she has made in her lifetime, Marietta Four Bear responds:

> I *tease my grandchildren [by telling them] the only time I get to use a star quilt is when I come to visit you. They will all bring out their star quilts when I come to visit. They wrap themselves up in their quilts and occasionally wrap me up in one, too.*[84]

Sara Angela Walker, an Arapaho quilter from Ethete, Wyoming, jokes when she is asked the same question: "I'm like a carpenter, you don't get to live in your own home [the one you build], and I don't have my own quilt."[85]

Some quiltmakers recall that certain quilts, considered special, were brought out only when guests visited. Barbara Tazelaar notes:

> I *remember my grandmother . . . back in the 1940s when I was born. Upstairs there was a great big wood [cedar] closet . . . [where] the good quilts were kept. Grandma almost died. The doctor came quite often. Whenever the doctor came she always had the tied quilt ripped off her bed and some nice quilts put on . . . ; they were kept for company.*[86]

Whether used for everyday wear or reserved for special occasions, quilts are worn and recycled, with few extant examples surviving from one generation to the next.

Quilts in Rituals and Ceremonies Throughout time, quilts have been used in Native communities in practices related to traditional as well as Christian religious rituals and ceremonies. In Hopi culture, quilts are a fundamental ingredient in baby-naming ceremonies, one of the most important events in Hopi society. Along with the gift of names for a newborn, members of a clan give the

Harriet Soong (Native Hawaiian) of Kailua-Kona, Hawaii, received the pattern for this quilt from her mother Hattie, (née Kahohina) Kauwe of Kauai. Entitled "Ke Kahi O Ka'iulani" (The Comb of Ka'iulani), it incorporates symbols of Hawaiian royalty, including crowns, leis, and the combs (or kahi) worn in the hair of Princess Kaiulani (1875–99). Kaiulani was the daughter of Oahu Governor Archibald Cleghorn and Princess Miriam Likelike and was niece to the last two reigning monarchs of Hawaii—King Kalahaua and Queen Lili'uokalani.

A member of the Ka Hui Kapa Apana O Waimea quilting group on the Big Island, Soong is considered by many to be a master of the old-style traditional Hawaiian quilting. In this quilt (1996–97, 98 x 99.5 inches), she uses many of the traditional quilting designs (piko) derived from those used on tapa cloth: parallel lines, diagonal lines, diamond squares, leaves, papa pelena (soda cracker), maka muena (lauhua mat), i'e kuku (carved wooden mallets used to create watermarks on tapa), maka upena (eye of the net), pupu (shell), and kua honu (back of the turtle). The stars represent the eight main islands of Hawaii. Collection of Michigan State University Museum

This c. 1925 photo shows quilts, along with other clothes, hanging at a campsite.

To provide protection and warmth, Martin Kegg (Ojibwa) used a quilt in the construction of his ice-fishing shanty at Lake Mille Lacs, Minnesota, in April 1948.

child a quilt. This practice of using a quilt has replaced the historical tradition of having the child's father or grandfather weave a special blanket for the child, although the use of a handmade cloth remains important. In Oklahoma, quilts are also used in ceremonies for babies as a key feature of Osage cradleboard ceremonies. As quiltmaker Mary Big Horse explains, the quilt is presented to the person who gives a newborn their cradleboard:

> *[When someone tells a parent], "I'm bringing something for your baby," the parent has food ready for them and a quilt. After the visitor dresses the baby and ties the child to the board, they hand the baby in the cradleboard to the mother and father. Then the parents usually give the visitor money and wrap the quilt around them.*[87]

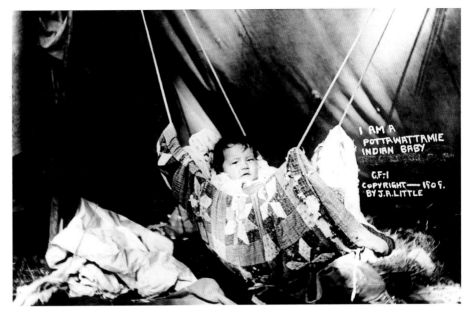

CLOCKWISE FROM TOP LEFT:

In this c. 1925 photograph, Tom and Mary Wind, with their baby in a quilt baby carrier, visit Miller's Tea Room Store on Wigwam Bay at the Mille Lacs Reservation in Minnesota.

This 1909 photo from Michigan shows a Potawatomi baby in a sling hammock made by folding a quilt over suspended ropes. (The photographer incorrectly spelled Potawatomi.)

Quilts were used as window coverings to keep out drafts and light, as shown in this 1924 photograph of an Indian home.

Temporary or semipermanent camps were set up in the woods during maple syrup and sugar-making season. In this 1908 photograph, a quilt is shown being used as an entrance covering to a tent at a "sugar camp" at the White Earth Reservation in Minnesota.

Among the Nelson Island Eskimos, quilts are part of the ceremonies marking the annual cyclical events in the community. Strips of cloth are distributed at parties marking the first bearded seals taken that season. Later in the year, during the Winter dance, the strips reappear, this time assembled into quilts and bedspreads, which are again distributed by parents, in the name of their children, to elders or honored guests.[88]

A turn-of-the-century photograph (see p. 50) shows a Midewin practitioner in a medicine lodge at Lac Court Oreilles, Wisconsin, wrapped in one quilt; another quilt hangs from the entrance of the lodge. In another photograph, a patchwork quilt is one of the valuable goods displayed among ceremonial objects of a deceased high-ranking Tlingit leader lying in state (see p. 50). Quilts are sometimes hung behind the casket at Winnebago funerals, then given as a gift to the person responsible for conducting the ceremony.[89]

At Sioux funeral services, a folded *star* quilt often is placed on the coffin of the deceased, and *star* quilts are presented to each of the pallbearers as well as to the person who conducts the funeral ceremony. Because death is often unexpected, the demand for quilts can be sudden, causing women to work through the nights preceding the funeral in order to have the quilts completed in time. The Sioux in Montana, North Dakota, and South Dakota commonly wrap additional *star* quilts and matching pillows around tombstones until their unveiling.[90]

The Seminole and Creek in Oklahoma traditionally enfold their deceased in a quilt prior to burial, and the coffin may have a quilt placed upon it before interment. Carole Stewart (Muscogee/Creek) says that in her tribe "the quilt is an important part of the burial tradition. One of the last gestures the family is able to perform for the deceased is to drape a handmade quilt over the coffin before it is buried."[91] According to Creek elder Jackson Narcomey, whose mother and grandmother quilted, everyone keeps a quilt on hand for this purpose. But he admitted that the younger generation is not keeping up as well with this tradition.[92] In some Native communities, when a person died all of his personal belongings, such as clothing and quilts, were burned so spirits did not come back to haunt those still living.

Among the Sioux, a *star* quilt is used as an outer wrapping to warm individuals on a vision quest. *Star* quilts also play a critical role in the Lakota *yuwipi*, a nighttime curing ceremony in which a medicine man is wrapped and the spirits are summoned to aid in healing. The ritual follows strict traditions, including the choice of wrap and the process of wrapping. Formerly buffalo robes were used; now the *star* quilt is. The quilt used in the ceremony or quilts made from other cloth in the ceremonies are then utilized as medicinal coverings to help heal someone suffering from respiratory illness.[93]

In Sioux country, *star* quilts often are draped over altars and hung on the walls of Catholic and Episcopal churches. Brother Simon reports how "several years ago, when Charles Chapu, a Roman Catholic priest of Native American decent, was consecrated bishop of Rapid City, South Dakota, four giant-sized *star* quilts decorated the walls of the cathedral."[94] The quilts usually are made for churches as expressions of the quilters' faith or to honor people. When Osage quilter and regaliamaker Mary Big Horse was commissioned by her Catholic church to make an altar cloth, she refused payment: "I feel like God gave me this gift, and I don't think I should charge you."[95]

A *star* quilt may be selected as a symbol of Indian identity and belief systems. In Oklahoma, a Comanche group holds its church ceremonies outdoors, centered around a drum placed upon a *star* quilt. A Winnebago drum is protected from touching the earth by quilts spread under it. Other textiles are likely available, but quilts are the materials of choice because, as handmade objects, they represent an investment of time, thought, and self.

In two c. 1940 photographs (above), Sioux twins sit on a bear claw pattern quilt, and Garfield and Eunice Quick Bear (Sioux) of St. Francis on the Rosebud Reservation in South Dakota hold their baby, who is wrapped in a patchwork quilt.

Historically, quilts have been used to wrap and carry babies. Coth pieced in the star pattern (above) has been used to make a Sioux papoose carrier (maker unknown, c. 1993, 13 x 29.25 inches, Rapid City, South Dakota). Collection of Michigan State University Museum

Quilts and the Tradition of Honoring

*G*iving quilts in recognition of special achievements, occasions, or activities is a common practice in Native circles, just as it is in many other cultures. Quilts are given at births, graduations, weddings, and anniversaries. In Hopi culture, the gift of quilts is an integral part of the traditional baby-naming ceremony. Among the Sioux, few things measure up to the meaning inherent in the gift of a *star* quilt. Lydia Whirlwind Soldier of Mission, South Dakota, eloquently describes that

by making quilts and giving them away—it's like almost giving away part of yourself

because you're putting a lot of your own energy into it and your own creative thoughts come in. I think it really fits into our whole culture. . . . You can't compare it to going to the store and buying a gift and giving it to somebody else. The quilts that you work on sometimes might take you two or three years of your time, and time that you really don't have, but you make that time because you love that person and you want to make something special for him. You know, it's just really easy to go to the store and buy something and give it away. I think that star quilts are just really special. Sometimes, when you go into Indian homes, you see the children's beds all covered

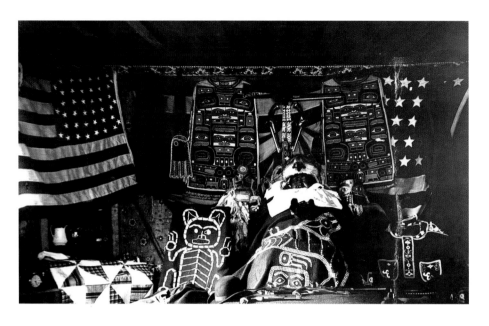

Traditional Northwest Indian burial ceremonies involve a give-away. In this photograph (n.d.) entitled **"Takou Chief Lying in State, Alaska,"** a high-ranking Tlingit leader is surrounded by prized possessions, including a patchwork quilt.

RIGHT: In this c.1899 ceremony in a medicine lodge at Lac Court Oreilles, Wisconsin, some of the participants, including the midé priest in the center, wear quilts draped over their shoulders. A quilt also was hung at the entrance to the lodge.

with star quilts. I sometimes wonder if the children really realize the honor that was given to them when that star quilt was given to them.[96]

At Pine Ridge, a star quilt is often presented to baseball teams that have won tournaments or championship games; the quilt sometimes incorporates a baseball in the center of the star. In Warm Springs, Kate Jackson made a quilt in honor of the members of the winning high school girls' track team. Each block of the quilt incorporated colors, symbols, and images associated with each individual member of the team.[97]

In Sioux country, quilts are often given to members of the military service when they return home from duty and to veterans on Memorial Day or Veterans Day. These quilts, referred to as veterans quilts, are usually red, white, and blue and often contain eagles and stars and stripes. Quilts also have been presented by various tribal groups to individuals who have played prominent roles in

furthering American Indian causes. Many state and national representatives, religious leaders, and private citizens have been the recipients of star quilts.

Dispersing quilts in ceremonies, called giveaways, has very significant meaning within Native culture. Generally conducted under the supervision of a female member of a clan or family, giveaways represent sharing material wealth with others in honor of a loved family member. Giveaways, particularly in the Plains region, are often held by families for baby-naming ceremonies, weddings, graduation parties, and memorial feasts for the dead. The latter, held approximately a year after a loved one's death, may, when the sponsor can afford it, involve as many as three hundred guests and the giving away of up to a hundred quilts.

Large giveaways involving many quilts—sometimes purchased from quilters from other tribes—are becoming increasingly

common at contemporary powwows in several parts of the country. Sponsored by the host committee, powwow giveaways are intended to thank the elders, head dancers, drummers, arena directors, veterans, and other dignitaries for participating in the event. Sometimes a gift is given to all involved in the event. Though tobacco, blankets, trunks, food staples, fruit, clothing, and beadwork are typical gifts, quilts are becoming increasingly popular as a giveaway item. The 1993 Pequot Schemitzun PowWow in Hartford, Connecticut, included more than fifty quilts, most made by Sioux quilters.[98]

Occasionally a whole community participates in a giveaway. In Rosebud, quilts and cakes are presented to men at the powwow held closest to Father's Day in June. In this same community, it has become customary to honor high school and college graduates with a *star* quilt at graduation commence-

ments and parties. When graduates of St. Francis Indian School on the Rosebud Reservation enter the gymnasium for high school commencement exercises, they find each chair covered with a brand-new *star* quilt purchased by the school from several community quilters. At the end of the ceremonies, graduates exit the room either carrying the quilt folded over their arms or wearing it around their shoulders. Sometimes, as they go through a congratulatory receiving line, the graduates are given additional quilts by relatives and friends.[99]

For some thirty years the basketball tournament *star* quilt ceremony has been a critical component of the eastern Montana regional high school boys' and girls' basketball tournaments. Quilts made by team parents and community members of high schools on the Fort Peck Reservation are presented during a tournament game to

Baseball Star Quilt, 1996

*Made by Nora Brings Him
Back (Sioux), Oglala, South
Dakota. 80.75 x 93 inches.
Collection of Michigan State
University Museum*

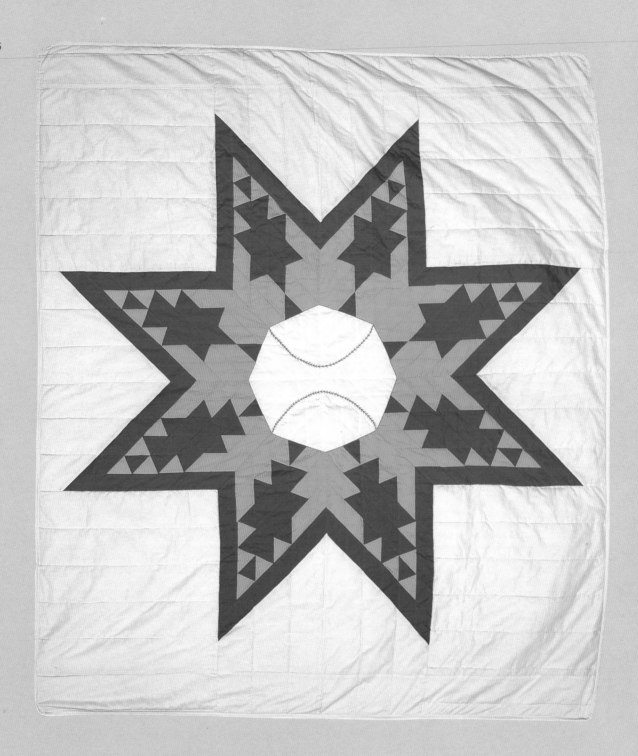

Ollie Napesni (Rosebud Sioux), of St. Francis, South Dakota, created this **Veterans Quilt** (1996, 78 x 84 inches) as one of the many honors accorded by Native communities to military veterans when they return from the service. In Sioux communities, veterans quilts are usually made of red, white, and blue cloth and often incorporate eagles and the stars and stripes of the American flag. Collection of Michigan State University Museum

honor opposing team members who have displayed exceptional qualities of good sportsmanship throughout the basketball season. Often these *star* quilts incorporate appliquéd basketball representations in the center of the star or in the four corners.[100]

The giving and receiving of quilts is a measure of a family's material wealth. In a giveaway ceremony, the family will give as many quilts as it can financially afford in order to honor someone. However, the exchange of quilts is also a measure of a family's spiritual and emotional wealth, as acknowledged by Lula Red Cloud:

> My mother used to say that a person who does not get star quilts or who does not own bead-work is a poor person. . . . They're like an orphan because if you have relatives who loved you and really cared about you they'd make you beadwork and they'd give you star quilts.[101]

Quilts and Traditional Myths and Legends
In May 1994 a group of women from the Warm Springs Reservation in Oregon gathered to talk about their quilt-making experiences. Several recalled the storytelling—including Coyote stories—that went on while their grandmothers and mothers quilted.[102] Pat Courtney Gold (Wasco), basketmaker and quiltmaker, believes most Native Americans grew up listening to stories of the Coyote trickster and specializes in wall hangings (see p. 56) depicting his legends.

On Manitoulin Island, Ontario, in the community of Wikwemikong, quilter Rita Corbiere (Ojibwa) often uses the thunderbird image as well as the colors red, black, white, and yellow in her original quilt designs. She collaborated with her sister Alice Fox and nephew Floyd Fox on a

thunderbird block quilt (see p. 60), which Alice Fox relates to this story:

> Nanabush and his grandma, they lived together, and they were very happy. The grandmother took care of her grandson and taught him about life—everything that she knew. And one day the grandmother said, "The Thunderbirds are coming to visit us. They're on their way east and they're stopping here." So Nanabush, just a teenager, he was so happy to think they were going to have visitors. So when the Thunderbirds arrived, they heard a rumble like the thunder. And they arrived with all their feathers. And they had drums.
>
> Nanabush said, "You're going east? I'd like to go with you. Take me."
>
> The older Thunderbird said, "Oh, I don't think you can follow the rules. I don't think that would be a good idea." So finally some other Thunderbird said, "Oh, yes, I think he'll listen. I think he's a good boy. He'll listen." Then finally the leader said, "OK. You follow the rules. If you don't, you're going to come tumbling out of the sky."
>
> And Nanabush was frightened. "I'll follow the rules carefully."
>
> And the Thunderbird ahead of you—where he steps, that's where you step."
>
> And they also gave him the drum. And they said, "When you hear drumming, and the ones around you are drumming, you go easy on your drum because if you go too loud, you'll scare the people down below on the earth."
>
> And they left, and he hugged his grandma bye-bye. And she said, "Be good. Listen. Do what you're told." And away they went—the big Thunderbird, the older ones first, and then the second group, and then he was in the third group—the younger ones. And later he heard

The Underwater Panther and the Thunderbird are important figures in Woodland Indian cosmology. For this quilt
(c. 1991, 63 x 72 inches), Ojibwa quilter Rita Corbiere
of Wikwemikong, Canada, incorporated a thunderbird in
the star as well as in the four corners of the quilting
pattern. Corbiere also used the traditional Native colors of
red, yellow, black, and white, representing the four races of
man and the directions of north, south, east, and west.
Collection of Michigan State University Museum

$\mathcal{P}$at Courtney Gold (Wasco) relates this parable to accompany her quilt, **Coyote Helps to Create the Night Sky** (1995, 46 x 39 inches) *Collection of Michigan State University Museum*

Coyote wanted to help the Great Spirit put stars in the night sky. Coyote was told that there were many, many stars and that he would be very busy for a long, long time.

Coyote assured the Great Spirit that he could do it, no problem. But after Coyote worked for a few years, he decided it was too boring to place each star up in the night sky. "I think I'll make designs," thought Coyote, but he could not think of any.

Bear came along and said, "Coyote, put me up in the sky. Put me right near the center of the sky where everyone can see me and I can guide them." Coyote agreed. We call the Bear star design the Big Dipper.

Then Rabbit hopped up, saw Bear in the night sky, and said, "Coyote, since you put Bear in the sky, you must put me there with my whole family. Everyone likes rabbits." Mouse overheard Rabbit and squeaked, "Coyote, you need little creatures in the night sky. You must put me in along with all my family." Owl was out hunting, and flying overhead, he listened to Mouse and Rabbit. Owl hooted, "Don't forget all us birds, Coyote, you must put all of us in the night sky, too."

Coyote said, "There is too much arguing and too much noise. I can't put everyone in the sky. Putting the stars in the night sky is too much work."

So Coyote grabbed all the remaining stars and threw them up into the sky. This is how Coyote made the Milky Way.[103]

the first group, the older ones, they were drumming. And then the second group were drumming, and then the younger ones. And he followed the rules. Finally, again they were drumming again. Same thing. Finally the third time, the older ones were going louder, and the middle ones—they too were going louder, and the younger ones were going louder, and they were just having a grand time. And he was. He didn't care. He forgot that he is not supposed to drum loud. They had told him, "Drum easy, don't scare the people down below." And he was drumming and drumming away with all his might and the people down below were so frightened, oh, they were scared.

And all of a sudden, looking up at the sky, they saw something coming out of the sky. It was coming down. The thing fell into the marsh. So they all gathered. "Let's go see what that thing was that fell into the marsh." They went over there and out of the mud came Nanabush. His eyes were blinking, and he was just full of mud, his eyes were just full of mud. And the people said, "Oh, we might have known. We should have known it was Nanabush. We know the way he is." I guess when he was out with friends, he was really terrible.[104]

A 1983 exhibit of quilts from the Six Nations and New Credit Reserves in Ontario included an original cotton, white-on-white quilt titled *The Legend Quilt*. Made in the 1970s by Mrs. Marion Martin, the piece incorporated floral and geometric quilting designs and referred to a legend of her Anishnabe heritage. The exhibit also included a block quilt titled *Floral Motifs* made in the early 1980s by the Wikwemikong Homemakers, a group of Odawa, Ojibwa, and Métis women living on Manitoulin Island, Ontario. Each block carried a variation of a basic Woodland Indian floral design.[105]

Quilts as Pictorial Stories

*O*ccasionally, quilts convey, in pictorial images or symbols, information about people, places, or events. The earliest-known extant pictorial quilts are a similar pair attributed to Rebecca Blackwater (see p. 13), a Sioux woman living in either South Dakota or Nebraska, and completed about 1915. Appliquéd riders on horses, tipis, and figures engaged in hunting, cooking, singing, and dancing on a black background mirror similar depictions found in buffalo-hide painting dating from the seventeenth century.

Important events in Assiniboine history are relayed in a series of pictorial images in two block-style quilts (see p. 58) made at Wolf Point, Montana, on the Fort Peck Reservation in 1939–40. James Garfield, an Assiniboine tribal member, drew the designs, and his wife, Nora (Assiniboine/Sioux), did the embroidery. Thirty squares depict images of men, women, and children involved in hunting, cooking, healing, burial, and other activities.[106]

The *Grand Entry Lone Star* quilt (see p. 59) made in 1995 by Shirley Grady includes embroidered renderings of the primary male and female dance categories included in powwows in her community. In a written statement accompanying the quilt, she explains the images:

> *The Grand Entry was made to represent the dances of the Three Affiliated Tribes, Fort Berthold Reservation, New Town, North Dakota. They are Mandan, Hidatsa, and Arickara Tribes, which had lived along the banks of the Missouri River by what is now Bismarck and Mandan area. . . . The dances are Men's Traditional and Straight Grass Dance for the men; Ladies Traditional and Shawl Dance for women. Long ago the women did not dance mixed with the men like they do today. Before, each woman belonged to their different society dances. Men also belonged to societies too. . . . I took the traditional star quilt and added my own designs, drew the pictures and hand quilted it. The big face pictures were made by my son; I traced them as I do not draw faces good. I have won first prize on all the quilts I made, no two quilts the same in detail.[107]*

In 1987, Della Oliver, a member of the Greensky Hill Indian Church near Charlevoix, Michigan (originally established as the Methodist Pine River Mission in 1859), celebrated the sesquicentennial of Michigan's statehood by making a pictorial quilt. Around a central block picturing a peace dove and the United Methodist cross-and-flame symbol she placed blocks depicting each of the Indian churches in Michigan today as well as Indian symbols and a picture of the original Greensky church.[108]

A quilt made by members of the Calico Country Quilt Guild tells of both historical and contemporary activities in the Fort Berthold Reservation. Surrounding a central rectangle containing a floral design embellished with beadwork, the eighteen blocks include images of the first schoolhouse, a mission church, a log cabin, a tipi encampment, a Métis fiddler and jig dancer, and a group of dancers in powwow regalia. To represent the activities of the guild, one block shows a seated woman quilting in front of quilts displayed on a clothesline.

In Hawaiian quilt patterns, the allusions to events, places, and people are more abstract in design. Symbols of Hawaiian royalty (*ali'i*) appearing in many quilts include crowns (*kalaunu*), royal standards (*kahili*), the queens' fans and combs, the Hawaiian Kingdom's Coat of Arms, and special features of the royal residences, such as a chandelier, vase, and gaslights. *Manu Lawe*

**Assiniboine History
Quilt, 1939–40**

*Made by Nora
(Assiniboine/Sioux) and
James Garfield (Assiniboine),
Fort Peck Reservation,
Montana. Double-bed size.
Collection of the Denver
Museum of Natural History*

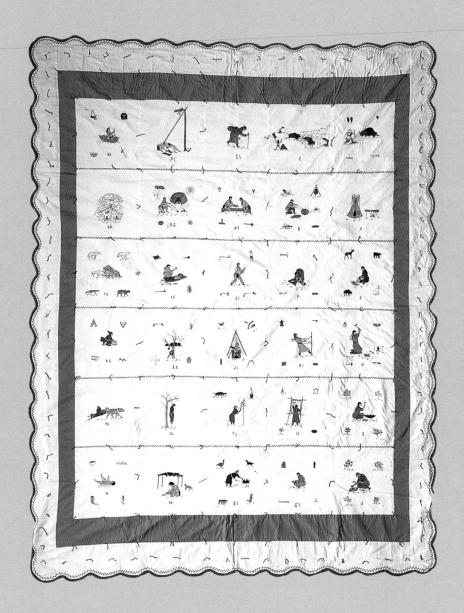

Shirley Grady (Hidatsa), of New Town, North Dakota, created this innovative version of the star quilt, incorporating appliquéd feathers in the corners and a border of pieced star tips. For this **Grand Entry Lone Star Quilt** (1995, 80 x 93 inches), the quilting includes an elaborate rendition of a pow wow "grand entry" as well as feathers and many other figures. Grady has won numerous awards for her work. Collection of Michigan State University Museum

Thunderbird Block Quilt, c. 1985

Made by Alice Fox, Rita Corbiere, and Floyd Fox (Ojibwa), Manitoulin Island, Ontario, Canada, and Sault Sainte. Marie, Michigan. 74 x 87 inches. Collection of Michigan State University Museum

This pattern features thunderbirds set in squares. Sisters Alice Fox and Rita Corbiere are well-known porcupine quillwork artists who use the thunderbird symbol on their quilts and quill boxes.

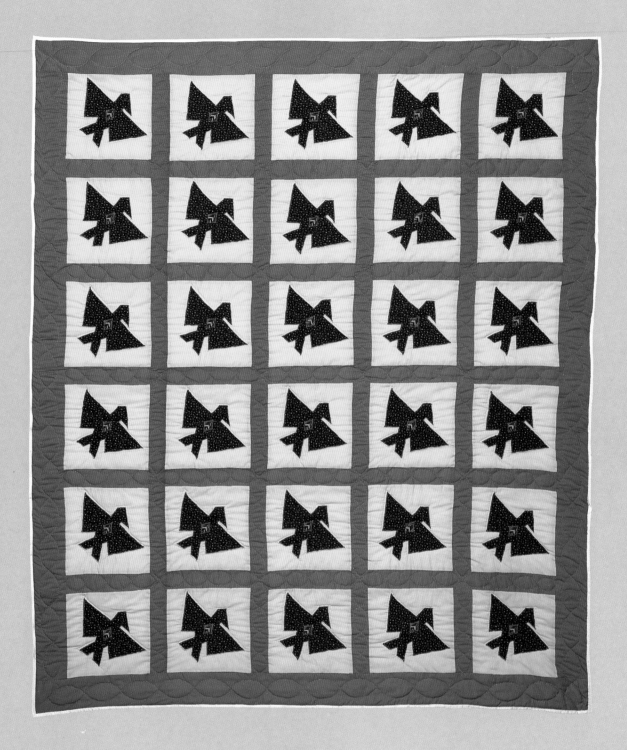

Leka (Carrier Pigeon) was said to record the beginning of regular mail service to the island of Kauai; Nani O Niumalu (Niumalu Beauty) celebrated the new harbor at Nawiliwili on Kauai; Ka Hoku Hele O Ka Pakipika (The Traveling Star of the Pacific) recorded the appearance of Halley's Comet in 1910; 'Ehu Kai O Niakala (Mist of Niagara Falls) memorialized a visit to those falls. Quilts also have been made to commemorate the annual Merrie Monarch Festival, an annual hula competition in Hilo, and the inaugural issue of the Garden Island, the first weekly newspaper on Kauai.[109]

Government Programs and Quiltmaking   Federal programs, such as the Bureau of Indian Affairs, issued quiltmaking instruction books early in this century and have continued to sponsor exhibition catalogues on quiltmaking in a variety of Native communities. Documentation exists of women home extension agents and wives of U.S. Indian Service agents teaching quiltmaking in the areas where they lived. Alice Janet Reifel, wife of Sioux farm agent and later South Dakota state representative Ben Reifel, studied home economics in college and was asked to teach and set up a quiltmaking factory in Pine Ridge, South Dakota, as part of a 1930s Works Progress Administration (WPA) project.[110] Eraina Palmer, a Wasco home extension agent and now curator at the Museum at Warm Springs, taught quiltmaking to scores of women in the Warm Springs, Oregon, area in the 1970s and 1980s.[111]

During the 1930s, several issues of Indians at Work, a news sheet published for Indians by the Office of Indian Affairs in Washington, D.C., included articles on reservation-based educational and arts activities. Mylie Lawyer (Sioux/Nez Perce), a home economics gradu-ate of Willamette University in Salem, Oregon, reported in the October 15, 1933, issue on her work with women in Two Medicine Camp on the Blackfeet Reservation:

> Four of the full-blood women have started embroidery work, using the old Blackfeet designs on table runners and luncheon cloths. These have been completed and the women have started some embroidery of their own, using their own original designs. Three quilts have been completed, the women using their own materials and designs. One industrious woman has carded and combed wool by hand, and quilted the design by hand. Mr. Hagarty, the Camp Manager, donated the lumber for a quilt frame, and it is being used by these women.[112]

A November 1933 issue carried a letter to Mae Frazier from Myron Sippi (Apache) detailing her work among women in family camps on the San Carlos Reservation in Arizona:

> The women are getting [on] nicely with their sewing. They had made one quilt and [are] still sewing pieces to make another quilt. The Asst. stay in the camp all the time to see everything to keep in order each day. We have the women to do the work at home in morning, cleaning their home such as any washing to be done. In afternoon about 2 o'clock we have our sewing class, all the young women, some are cutting quilt pieces. . . . All these women are anxious to make quilts more than anything. I wish you and friend see them at work. The way we do to give out these quilts when finish, who ever takes quilt gives me a dollar. So I take this dollar and buy some more goods with it, in that we can carry on work. All I asked for was cotton at Office. All these women seem to think it fair. So in this way they all have quilt by next Spring.[113]

Gussie Bento (Native Hawaiian), of Kaneohe, Hawaii, was inspired to begin quilting when, in her twenties, she saw examples of her grandmother's work. Bento continues to sew a few hours every day, making quilts and pillows in traditional as well as new designs. She is also a leader in the Hawaiian Quilt Research Project. In 1989 she made this quilt, **Na Koehili Ame Na Kalaunu** (The Kahili(s) and Crowns of King Kamehameha IV), as a variation of an 1880s traditional pattern that is now in the public domain (100 x 106 inches).

Cooperatives were established in some parts of the country to help support the production and marketing of quilts produced by Indian women. In 1934, Norman Ewing, the business manager for the Sioux Indian Women's Arts and Crafts Club of Wagner, South Dakota, wrote to John Collier, commissioner of Indian Affairs in Washington, D.C., about copyright protection for the women:

> I wish to request your advice concerning the security of Trade protection and copyright for an exclusive product which these women are making and which I am seeking a market for this [in] the east. I refer especially to the Sioux star quilt. This is a very beautiful hand pieced quilt containing an ancient Sioux eight-pointed star design and I believe if we do not protect this product on the market and reserve for these workers the right to manufacture and sell this product exclusively, plenty of manufacturers and cheap dealers will soon exploit it and make it be machine and undersell the Indians and force them to cease making it. . . . I am giving a great deal of my time towards the promotion of this club and have encouraged similar organizations among many other Indian tribes and communities.[114]

Concerns about the appropriation of Native designs by other quilters continue to be an issue today as mass-produced quilt pattern books increasingly include Indian designs, sometimes uncredited. Issues of artistic ownership and design copyright have inflamed controversy in Hawaii, where unscrupulous individuals are importing from China and the Philippines cheaply made and poorly constructed copies of Hawaiian quilters' designs. Hawaiian quilters and their supporters are now seeking means of obstructing the importation and sale of these textiles, falsely marketed as "authentic Hawaiian quilts."

Quiltmaking and Economics in Native Life

Quiltmaking has enabled many Natives, particularly women, to participate in economic activities that garner tangible or symbolic wealth. The exchange of quilts, as in Sioux giveaway ceremonies, is one of symbolic reciprocity. The number of quilts given at these occasions represents not only the wealth of a clan or family but the extent to which it wishes to honor the recipient.

In a similar way, Native women in Ontario historically brought honor to their community by participating in the donation of quilts to the Canadian Red Cross Society, which between 1939 and 1945 sent many quilts to war zones in Britain and Europe.[115] On local levels, quilters in many communities donate quilts to those without sufficient blankets, especially when families lose their belongings to fires or other calamities.

On an individual basis, quilts have been used to barter or trade for other goods or services. An early-twentieth-century Odawa quilt now in the collection at Michigan State University Museum was originally acquired as a trade for farm goods.[116] Ojibwa quilter Barbara Tazelaar remembers "a really good quiltmaker who lived around Sterling [Michigan, who sold] . . . her quilts to buy fuel oil," fetching $100 for a king-sized, hand-sewn quilt.[117]

Quilts also have helped individuals earn or augment a living. Award-winning author Sherman Alexie's mother supported her family by working at the Wellpinit Trading Post and selling quilts on the Spokane Reservation northwest of the city of Spokane, Washington.[118] Bernice Blakney, a cultural arts instructor at Nebraska Indian Community College in Santee, Nebraska, and a quilter for more than twenty-five years, makes about thirty to forty quilts a

This photo of an Oklahoma quilting bee was included in the 1938 publication Indians at Work, issued by the U.S. Department of Interior Office of Indian Affairs.

year that sell for $400 to $600 each.[119] Several Sioux quilters tell of earning enough money from selling quilts to send their children to college or to pay their own way through school.

The majority of contemporary quilters acknowledge, however, that it is difficult to earn a living making quilts; market prices are so low that they must sell in volume. Sharon Balai started a cottage industry in her home making Hawaiian quilt pillowcases. Although she was working constantly and her sewing projects took over the house, Balai soon found she could not make enough money to support even one person, let alone a family.[120] Thus, most quilters rely on quilting as only an occasional or supplemental source of income. But a few have attempted to market their own quilts as well as others' through establishing craft shops or mail-order businesses, such as Leedom Indian Crafts on the Winnebago Reservation in Nebraska. Run by Florence Leedom, a

Santee Sioux, and her son, it is one of the few sources of quilts for the tribes in eastern Nebraska.[121] In 1937 Nellie Star Boy Menard established an arts and crafts shop on the Rosebud Reservation in South Dakota that still sells locally made quilts.

Many church-affiliated groups make quilts for activities related to church needs, either for local or for worldwide relief or mission efforts. Quilts also are created for fundraisers for a wide variety of other local and national Native causes, organizations, and activities.

On a more direct level, quilts are sometimes given to individuals or groups to symbolically honor and financially support their activities; in such cases, the recipients sell the quilts. Brother Simon describes how quilts are used at Pine Ridge to support members of local baseball teams and drum groups:

> As I understand it, during a tournament, the team will be given a quilt. And what can nine, twelve, thirteen players do with a quilt? They sell it and then they split the money. The same things happens at a powwow. Someone will give the drum group the quilt. How can they divide one quilt amongst six, seven singers? So they sell the quilt.[122]

A communitywide fund-raising initiative occurs every year in St. Regis, New York, on the Akwesasne Mohawk Reservation. In 1980, Sheree Bonaparte, one of the founders of the Akwesasne Freedom School, was looking for donations to support the school. It was suggested that quilts be auctioned off. At first just a few parents and community members provided the quilts, but soon all parents with children enrolled in the school had to participate in the auction, either by making a quilt or by buying one. Now in its seventeenth year, the auction is a weekend event filled with other activities, attracting donations and buyers from great distances. Sometimes as much as $25,000 to $30,000 is made in one weekend.

Quilting Instruction Today 	 Today, the majority of Native peoples learn to quilt in church groups and in parks and recreation programs, at senior citizen centers, and by association with family members. Nationally broadcast televised quilting shows and quilting how-to video-tapes have increased the availability of the technical aspects of quiltmaking. In addition, Native quiltmakers now teach their craft in formally organized classes at several tribal colleges.

Helen Hoskins, director of the Southern Ute Tribal Museum in Ignacio, Colorado, shares her quilting skills with others both informally and under the auspices of the Colorado Arts Council Traditional Arts Apprenticeship Program.[123]

Some contemporary quilters, such as Mary Henio, learned their skills at such places as the Navajo cooperative in Thoreau, New Mexico. There, Henio learned from other women and guest instructors and has now become an avid quiltmaker.[124]

In Hawaii, many museums, large resort hotels, and shopping centers host quilting demonstrations and classes. "Auntie" Deborah Kepola Kakalia demonstrates and teaches twice a week at the Mauna Loa Shopping Mall and once a week at the Bishop Museum, where she and her students also have an annual show of their work. Harriet Soong demonstrates at the Kona Village Inn resort on the Big Island.

At Hopi, quilters attend quilt workshops taught by non-Indian volunteers, many of them members of the Arizona Quilt Guild.

Delaware quilters at work on a moon, sun, and stars quilt at the Delaware Senior Citizens Center in Moraviantown, Ontario, in 1989.

Members of the Tsali Manor Senior Sewing Club of Cherokee, North Carolina, work on blocks with Cherokee Indian figures in 1995.

Navajo/Seminole quilter Margaret Wood taught at one of the Hopi workshops and has taught workshops in other Native communities.[125]

Quilting Groups Today 	 Today, Native quilt groups meet in senior centers and community halls across the country. At the Ojibwa Senior Center in Baraga, in the Upper Peninsula of Michigan, women gather to make ribbon shirts, beadwork, baskets, and quilts.[126] At the Tsali Manor Senior Citizens Center in Cherokee, North Carolina, one room is dedicated to the activities of the center's quilt group, which meets every Wednesday morning to piece and quilt a variety of patterns. Proceeds from the sale of quilts, patchwork

Ella Louise Weaver (Southern Ute) works with master quiltmaker Helen Hoskins under a Colorado Folk Arts Master/Apprenticeship Grant Program in the 1940s. Weaver began quilting as part of a workshop at the Southern Ute Reservation Museum and cultural center, where Hoskins serves as director.

Quilts made by Tohono O' Odham seniors are displayed in the back of a pickup truck at the 1980 Elderly Parade at San Xavier, Arizona.

aprons, pot holders, and quilting tops fund other social and educational activities. The group enjoys the social time and the chance to converse in Cherokee and share common experiences.[127]

Under the guidance of elder Lou Scott, a dozen seniors at the Grand Traverse Band Health Building in Peshawbestown, Michigan, have completed several quilts, including ones with fifty blocks embroidered with pan-Indian designs (see p. 73), which they raffle off to raise funds for other senior programs.[128] At the Mazakute Memorial Church in St. Paul, Minnesota, a group of Winnebago and Dakota Sioux women met in the late 1970s to do fan quilting and some decorative quilting.[129]

In 1988, members of the New Mexico Quilters Association began teaching quilting to women at Cañoncito, a Navajo Reservation, and at Isleta Pueblo, south of Albuquerque. Although most speak only their Native languages, quilt association members and the Native women easily share materials, patterns, and techniques.[130]

The Calico Country Quilt Guild at the Turtle Mountain Chippewa Reservation in North Dakota includes both Native and non-Native members. Started by Theresa Brien and Dolores Gourneau about 1988, the group meets twice a month and hosts many special activities, including birthday clubs, a Christmas potluck, and an annual all-night quilting and camping trip at a church-based Anishnabe center. Members regularly demonstrate quilting during Turtle Mountain Days at the Turtle Mountain Heritage Center, where they also hold an annual quilt show.[131]

Among the many quilt groups active in the Hawaiian Islands, several have sizable numbers of Native Hawaiians. One such group, the Ka Hui Kapa Apana O Waimea, meets monthly in the town of Waimea on the Big Island. The group maintains a large collection of traditional patterns and mounts a biannual exhibit of members' works. According to information in their self-published 1995 book *Hawaiian Quilting*, the group was formed in 1972 as a nonprofit organization with two essential objectives: to gather members of mutual interest in friendly fellowship; and to preserve, perpetuate, and encourage the art and culture of Hawaii in the field of Hawaiian quilting. Through generous cooperation, members contribute Hawaiian quilt patterns to a collection that the organization maintains and makes accessible to all members. Added to over the years, the large pattern library now forms the foundation for an ongoing resource.[132]

Hawaiian names for patterns and quilting techniques are employed, thus helping to maintain the Native language. In addition to sharing patterns, quilting techniques, and a potluck meal every month, the group also collaborates on quilts it donates to local health, educational, and social institutions. Permanently displayed in these community-based sites, the quilts are enjoyed by local residents.

Contemporary Quilt Cooperatives   Quilt cooperatives, most located in the Plains and Southwest regions, remain a vital source of economic activity in some communities. One contemporary cooperative, the Gathering Place, was established by Angela Bianca, a nun from New York who came to the Navajo Reservation in Thoreau, New Mexico, as a volunteer. Bianca saw the potential of a sewing co-op as a place for women to learn new skills while augmenting their incomes through sales of their handwork and enjoying social time together. For the most part, the quilters worked with patterns not specific to the reservation, but some experimented with traditional Navajo designs, particularly those used in woven rugs.[133]

Through the Sioux quilt cooperatives, several types of quilts can be purchased: *prince baby* and *princess baby* quilts (block patterns depicting children dressed in Native attire and seen from the backside); quilt wall hangings; gift sets of receiving blanket–sized *star* quilts with beaded infant booties in matching colors (choice of blue or pink); and quilted tote and diaper bags. Some cooperatives, such as Missouri Breaks, specialize in producing patterns for *star* quilts; others feature clothing with patched and appliquéd stars.

In 1992, the Lands' End company commissioned a limited number of *American eagle star* quilts (see p. 70) made by the joint efforts of the Bear Soldier Quilters Co-op in Bismarck, South Dakota; the African-American Freedom Quilting Bee in Alberta, Alabama; and the Euro-American Cabin Creek Quilters of Malden, West Virginia. Sold through the company's mail-order catalogue, the quilts were an immediate success, quickly selling out and prompting orders for other quilts from all three cooperatives.[134]

Quilts as Commentary on Contemporary Issues   Some quilts serve as a visual forum for expressing ideas or feelings about issues important in North American Indian and Native Hawaiian life. Some such quilts are meant to be shared widely; others, much like diaries, are personal statements to be shared only privately, if at all.

In a quilt she calls *Indian Woman* (see p. 74), Margaret Wood comments on the chal-

Hawaiian Flag Quilt, 1997

Made by Harriet Soong (quilter) and Sharon Balai (designer) (Native Hawaiian), Waimea and Kailua-Kona, Hawaii. 56 x 54 inches. Collection of Michigan State University Museum

This Hawaiian flag quilt features the Hawaiian Coat of Arms, adopted in 1845, and the royan crown flanked by two warrior chiefs wearing feather cloaks and helmets.

Ka Ua Kipu'upu'u O Waimea (The Kipu'upu'u Rain of Waimea), c. 1975

Made by Harriet Soong (Native Hawaiian), Honolulu, Hawaii. Collection of the artist.

Thunderbird Quilt, c. 1996

Made by Ruth and Vera Tyler (Choctaw), Clifton, Louisiana. 49 x 58 inches. Collection of Michigan State University Museum

The thunderbird holds special meaning for many Native people and is a popular design motif for quilts and other art forms. This quilt was made by Ruth Tyler and her daughter Vera, who sell their quilts at an American Indian Arts and Crafts Co-op owned by members of the Clifton Choctaw in Louisiana.

American Eagle Star Quilt, 1992

Made by the Bear Soldier Quilters Co-op, Bismarck, South Dakota, Cabin Creek Quilters, Malden, West Virginia, and African-American Freedom Quilting Bee, Alberta, Alabama. 90.5 x 100 inches. Collection of Michigan State University Museum

Cooperatives have been involved in the making of quilts for sale on some reservations. In 1992, the Lands' End company commissioned this American Eagle star quilt design by three cooperatives. The limited-edition quilts quickly sold out.

lenge of being a woman in two cultural worlds. The quilt depicts a life-sized, appliquéd woman viewed from the back, one half dressed in traditional Navajo attire, the other in a business suit. Says Wood: "I know all women juggle things but I think Indian women juggle them a little bit more because not only do we juggle family, job, and marriage, but we are stepping back and forth between two cultures."[135]

In Hawaii, quilters express their allegiance to Hawaiian sovereignty by making quilts containing all or part of the Hawaiian flag along with symbols of Hawaiian royalty and the Hawaiian coat of arms. The eight stripes of the flag represent the eight islands, and the Union Jack represents the islands' close ties to Great Britain. Quilts named *Ku'u Hae Aloha* (My Beloved Flag), depicting the flag of the Hawaiian Kingdom, probably appeared as early as 1843. A resurgence of interest in *flag* quilts accompanied the two times in history when the flag came down. Today, the *Hawaiian flag* quilt continues to have meaning for many Native Hawaiians.

Akwesasne quilter Sheree Bonaparte creates *tree of peace* quilts in response to violence in her community. The first was a top made in 1991 for the annual Freedom School Quilt Auction. Underneath the traditional tree of peace symbol she stitched two crossed war clubs: "Around the top are fifty figures, patched in solid purple fabric with white quilted stitching, holding hands; the figures represent the fifty chiefs of the Iroquois Confederacy who will hold strong if there is ever any danger to the peace within their nations."[136] A second quilt incorporates the three sisters (corn, squash, and beans) at the base of the tree as a symbol of life and hope. Underneath the tree, the artist

A *group of Odawa women sells baskets and patchwork pillows alongside the road at Omena, Michigan, c. 1910. In this northern Michigan resort area, many Native craftspeople have made a living or supplemented their income through the sale of their work.*

added AK-47s to the war clubs to symbolize that the weapons should be buried. The two quilts, powerful statements about community disruption and peacemaking efforts, strongly resonate with the Akwesasne people who see it. Bonaparte comments: "If it is something that happened in your time, it has to affect you. I think that's why that quilt affects people, because that happened in our time and it's important."[137]

Alice Olsen Williams of Curved Lake Reserve, Ontario, quilted *The Tree of Peace Saves the Earth* to commemorate the 1990 Mohawk incident in New York. Atop an evergreen, whose roots embrace the back of a turtle, sits an eagle, the sacred bird who helps look after all beings. A sun around the eagle represents the life-giving force. Underneath the turtle, which represents Turtle Island (the American continent), are a crossed club and tomahawk representing the tools of oppression, which should be buried in the earth. In another version, Williams included the shattered buildings of the

Sheree "Peachy" Bonaparte (Mohawk), made this **Tree of Peace Quilt** (1991–92, 85 x 62.5 inches) for the annual Mohawk Freedom School Quilt Auction as a call to stop the violence on the Akwesasne Mohawk Reservation. In the purple border band, quilted figures holding hands represent the Chiefs of the Iroquois Confederacy, who, united, will maintain the strength of their nations. Bonaparte explained: "In the beginning of the Haudenosaunee Confederacy, the tree of peace was uprooted and the weapons and words of war were thrown into the hole and buried so that people could live in peace. During the time I was working on the quilt, automatic weapons were heard so frequently on the river that people no longer reacted to the horrible noise. And the words that were being used so often had lost the respect and love our people had for each other. So, when I started sewing the weapons of war beneath the tree, I stitched in the war club, but that didn't seem quite enough. The war club was too distant to the reality we were living. So I decided to sew an AK-47. I was real nervous about doing it. It was almost sacrilegious to mess with a traditional symbol. My heart raced while I stitched. To calm down, I stitched in the Three Sisters, the corn, beans, and squash, at the base of the tree. They are the sustainers of the life of our people."

In many tribal communities, senior centers are frequently where elders gather to quilt. This quilt (92.5 x 80 inches), made in Suttons Bay, Michigan, 1993 by the Grand Traverse Band of Odawa and Ojibwa Indian elders, features blocks with embroidered images of symbolic importance as well as images of everyday Native life. Collection of Grand Traverse Band of Odawa and Ojibwa

Another quilt, made by Assiniboine quilter Almira Buffalo Bone Jackson, is called the *Red Bottom Tepee*, or *The Story of the Assiniboine Quilt*, (see p. 78) incorporating colors, motifs, and an arrangement of design elements that symbolically reflect the history of the quilter's people. As she writes:

The four red, petal-like corners represent the four cardinal winds and directions. When we pray we do everything four times. The tepees in a circle means there is strength and unity, and the four in the corners means there are other clans of Assiniboine scattered to the four winds, but we still remember them and they us. . . . The darker blue in the center is the river waters—they used to cross the Missouri. . . . The octagonal center represents the shield the braves had to carry to protect themselves.[139]

Sometimes a quilter can use just a single patched or appliquéd block to convey a strong message. One such block in the Calico Country Quilt Guild's *Turtle Mountain History* quilt contains a map and a written tribute to Louis Riel, a Métis who was hung for his efforts to preserve his nation. In an excerpt from the written statement accompanying her *bear paw* block contributed to the 1996 *Native Quilters' Gathering Quilt*, Alice Olsen Williams sums up her insight into the Native perspective of her work:

I chose to submit the bear paw block because it is a block that is familiar to people from the dominant culture as well as being an important theme in the lives of the First Nations People of this great and sacred Turtle Island. The way I did this block represents many values of First Nations People. I started out by wanting to do a perfect job, but then kept making mistakes—so much that I had to patch the patches! Then I realized that this is what is really important: that we do a good job and have good workmanship. In our teachings

In this quilt entitled **"Indian Woman"** (1991, 56 x 83.5 inches), Margaret Wood (Navajo/Seminole) of Phoenix, Arizona, expresses the challenge of being a woman in two cultural worlds—Native and non-Native.

Canadian Parliament. She explains:

I personally want to pay tribute to and honor the Mohawk people because, against great odds, they made known to the world and brought up-to-date the fact that we aboriginal peoples all over the world are still trying to regain our rights to our lands, our cultures, our relatives, our languages, our beliefs, and customs.[138]

we are taught to live life in a good way. . . .
Often our Peoples don't have the resources and
belief system that everything has to perfectly
match up. What is important to us is that we
love and enjoy what we're doing and that we
do all these things in a good way which will all
reveal itself in our creations and work. We're
not living up to someone else's judgment of
us. . . . In spite of all the rules I broke, my
block is still beautiful.[140]

Judy Toppings of the White Earth Reservation in Minnesota has been a long-time activist for Native rights. Her *News from Native Country* (see p. 80) was made to make people aware of the struggles of Native American people and to recognize some who have worked hard for the causes of Native peoples. In the quilt's center is a phototransfer of the poster "1993 Declared the Year of the Indigenous People." Portraits of key individuals imprisoned for their activities are included.

The Healing Power of Quilts and Quilting

$\mathcal{Q}$uiltmaking has been a source of solace and healing for many quilters. Whether reflecting on past injustices, current hardships, or the stresses of daily living, piecing and quilting have brought comfort to many. As Sheree Bonaparte expresses it: "When you just sit there and quilt, all of sudden things just start to calm down . . . to finally get down to the last stitches, you've become a better person for it . . . the act of quilting is healing."[141]

Sometimes Native quilters use their quilts and quilting activity to express past injustices directed toward their people. Lula Red Cloud finds inspiration for her work in a variety of sources, including the hardships and tragedies that her great-great-grandfather Chief Red Cloud endured.[142] In one

block in her quilt, *Honor the First Nations* (see p. 79) , Pat Courtney Gold "wanted to show respect for the elders in the block. I chose the clothing style during transition from the traditional ways to the 'white man' ways. I felt this was a painful time in tribal history, and the strength of the generation was passed to us."[143]

Many quilters speak of piecing and quilting to work through hard times, dependencies, illnesses, and deaths. Quilter Nancy Naranjo, while caring for an ill family member, explained: "I hope that soon I can find some answers and help. My art is all that keeps me sane at times."[144] Mary Big Horse turned from making regalia to making quilts when her father was in the hospital:

My quilting started one fall [when] my father
had two strokes. He was in the hospital. I
started seeing him every day and I was just so
upset worrying over him. . . . I just needed to
be busy and I didn't want to do ribbonwork, so

This photo, taken in 1898, records the lowering of the Hawaiian flag at the Republic of Hawaii annexation ceremonies. Many Native Hawaiians made quilts with Hawaiian flag imagery as a statement of their strong feelings about the removal of the flag and their identification with a Hawaiian sovereignty.

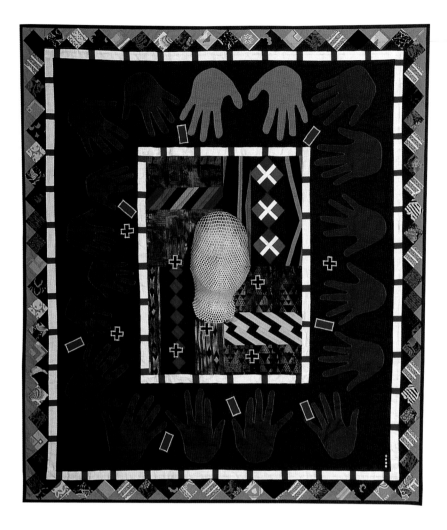

Charlie Wood's Stoma Quilt, 1996

Made by Margaret Wood (Navajo/Seminole),
Phoenix, Arizona. 44.75 x 50.75 inches.
Collection of the artist

I started doing piecework on cloth. So he got to
see my first quilt and he told me, "What
you've done is one of a kind and it's unique,
and don't ever stop because you've really captured something for our tribe." And to that
tribute I've maintained it. I lost my dad that
same year but I've carried on.[145]

Margaret Wood describes Charlie Wood's
Stoma, a quilt made after an extended
period when she was the primary caregiver
for her ailing father:

In the center is a white plastic mesh face, which
is the actual radiation mask my father used for
six weeks. The x's on the quilt represent the x's
marked by radiologists on my father's face and
chest to pinpoint where radiation treatment
was to be directed. I put in Seminole patchwork because my father is Seminole and blue
colors since his favorite color was blue. The red-
and-white borders represent the cigarettes that
caused the cancer, and the appliquéd hands
symbolize some of the people, especially family,
that helped him on his healing journey.[146]

When Ollie Napesni's son was murdered,
quilting helped his mother through this particularly hard period of her life, especially as
she made them for the memorial giveaway
in Rosebud:

I started to get ready for the memorial. I sat
down to sew in January of 1994. I took an
administrative leave and then every morning I
get up at 4:00 and I just cry and sew . . . so a
lot of the quilts I have there have teardrops on
them I'm sure.[147]

Pearl Spotted Tail, also from Rosebud,
tells of making *broken star* quilts to heal sadness: "When my mom died I made that for
her. . . . I put it on top of her casket because
I had a broken heart. [It was] all in deep pur-
ples."[148] Spotted Tail burns a small bit of
sage and says a prayer for peace and health

before she begins to piece her quilts. She thinks of her ancestors who died, and they give her inspiration to begin.

While grief and sadness are expressed, the Native way stresses the feelings of hope and love that go hand in hand with quilting. Lydia Whirlwind Soldier sees quilting time as an important time for reflection and for sharing with her family:

I guess what I really like about it is it's kind of a time to sit and think [to be] . . . creative with your hands. It's kind of therapy; . . . [and] if you're sitting and quilting with your daughters—that's a good quality time to think and be with them.[149]

When Mary Henio was asked why she quilts, she said quickly, "Oh, it's for my heart. I mean, I just love doing it. It's the caring that goes into it and you love doing it. It's just like raising your child, you know? . . . That's the way I think about my quilt."[150]

Anger has no place in quilting, and some quilts should not be made when the makers are sad, as Warm Springs, Oregon, quilter Eraina Palmer explains:

Well, I think there's something special in each quilt. They [the quilters I taught] never work on a quilt when they're feeling bad or sad because we do a lot of baby quilts and there's a lot of love and heart goes into it. That's what's special about it. You're putting yourself into it and thinking about the meaning of the quilt. . . . We're taught in the Indian way, you know, that you don't cook or sew in an angry way.[151]

One of the most emotionally charged ways that patched and appliquéd textiles are used today is in producing panels for the NAMES Project to honor the memory of someone who has died of AIDS. In Michigan, Orin Fallis and members of his family made a panel for his daughter Toni Simpson, a Saginaw Chippewa. Fallis made a beaded

An especially accomplished Sioux quilter, Pearl Spotted Tail of Parmelee, South Dakota, makes variations of star quilts for many giveaway occasions and for sale. She tells of making **Broken Star quilts** *such as this one (top; c. 1994, 82 x 86 inches), "when you are sad or when your heart is broken." Collection of Michigan State University Museum*

This turquoise blue panel (bottom), made in memory of James ("Chip") Hartfield, was added to the NAMES **Project Quilt** *in the fall of 1996 in Washington, D.C. Members of the Cheyenne River Reservation, South Dakota, participated in ceremonies and activities associated with the display.*

Red Bottom Tepee, or The Story of the Assiniboine Quilt, c. 1979–80

Made by Almira Buffalo Bone Jackson (Assiniboine), Fort Wolf Point, Montana. 72 x 87 inches. Florence Pulford Collection of Morning Star Quilts in the care of Annie Pulford Wilson

Jackson has incorporated colors, motifs and an arrangement of design elements that symbolically reflects the history of her people. She writes: "The four red, petal-like corners represent the four cardinal winds and directions. When we pray we do everything four times. The tepees in a circle means there is strength and unity, and the four in the corners means there are other clans of Assiniboine scattered to the four winds, but we still remember them and they us. . . . The darker blue in the center is the river waters they used to cross the Missouri. . . . The octagonal center represents the shield the braves had to carry to protect themselves."

WHENEVER STATESMEN ASSEMBLE, THEY SHALL OFFER THANKS TO THE EARTH WHERE MEN DWELL, TO THE STREAMS AND LAKES, TO THE MAIZE AND FRUITS.
GREAT LAW OF THE HODENSAUNEE (IROQUOIS)
PRE-1700

TREAT ALL MEN ALIKE. GIVE THEM ALL THE SAME LAW. GIVE THEM ALL AN EVEN CHANCE TO LIVE AND GROW. ALL MEN WERE MADE BY THE SAME GREAT SPIRIT.
CHIEF JOSEPH, NEZ PERCE
1879

SELL A COUNTRY? WHY NOT SELL THE AIR, THE CLOUDS, THE SEA, AS WELL AS THE EARTH. DID NOT THE GREAT SPIRIT MAKE ALL FOR THE USE OF HIS CHILDREN?
TECUMSEH, SHAWNEE
1792

TRIBAL GOVERNMENTS ARE MUCH OLDER THAN EUROPEAN GOVERNMENTS. KNOW WHERE WE'VE BEEN TO SEE WHERE WE ARE GOING 10, 100, 500 YEARS FROM NOW.
CHIEF WILMA MANKILLER, CHEROKEE
1992

Honor the First Nations Quilt, 1996

Made by Pat Courtney Gold (Wasco), Scappoose, Oregon. 69 x 85 inches. Collection of Michigan State University Museum

Gold says of this quilt, "I wanted to do a quilt to represent various tribal entities throughout the United States. I could not include all nations, and it was hard picking the art forms on this quilt. Each block represents a different tribal art and/or region. I especially wanted to show respect for the elders in a block. I chose the clothing style during transition from the 'traditional ways' to the 'white man' ways. I felt this was a painful time in tribal history, and the strength of the generation was passed to us."

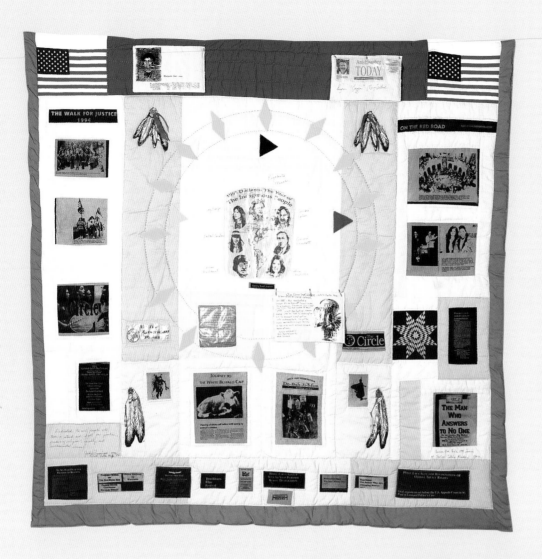

Ojibwa/Anishnabe quiltmaker Judy Toppings of the White Earth Reservation, Waubun, Minnesota, selected and transferred onto fabric articles from the Indian Country News for this pictorial history quilt, entitled "News from Native Country" (1996, 74 x 72 inches). She hopes the quilt will make people aware of the struggles and notable achievements of Native peoples. Collection of Michigan State University Museum

By combining painted and dyed fabric with appliquéd and embroidered detailed images, Eastern Cherokee quilter Nancy Naranjo of Frederick, Maryland, achieves a painterly effect in this quilt titled "A New Time" (1996, 82 x 58 inches). She has embroidered at the bottom: "In the early Spring morning, The People begin reuniting from small, wintering groups. Emissaries of Morning Star and White Buffalo Calf Woman come, carrying The Pipe. The time of healing, of coming back together to start a new time, is here." Collection of Michigan State University Museum

Navajo rugs serve as design inspirations for Navajo quilters such as Mary Ann Henio of Thoreau, New Mexico. This quilt was named **"Tony's Quilt"** (c. 1990, 82.5 x 102.5 inches) in honor of her husband, who died shortly after the quilt was finished. Henio explains that the colors represent "the four stages of life: black is the dark world, the mother's womb; turquoise is youth; red is adulthood; and white is for old age."

eagle staff to accompany the panel. On the front, a richly beaded border surrounds a portrait of Toni; on the reverse side are the outlines of the hands of those who worked on the panel.[152]

The Takini High School on the Cheyenne River Reservation in South Dakota was the first Native American school to pilot the NAMES Project High School Quilt Program. With help from community members, high school students designed and constructed two panels in honor of James ("Chip") Hartfield (see p. 77). Students, faculty, community members, and visiting artists and other speakers joined in "A Week to Remember," a week of HIV/AIDS prevention education activities. Ceremonies in honor of Heartfield included a group of men carrying the panel on horseback on the path to Wounded Knee. One panel was dedicated to the NAMES Project in San Francisco and was displayed as part of the National NAMES Project AIDS Memorial Quilt Display in October 1996 in Washington, D.C. The other panel will remain on display in the school.[153]

A History of Exhibiting and Judging Native Quilts

As early as the mid-nineteenth century, American Indians were known to have held exhibitions of quilts. In 1913 a Choctaw woman, Sarah Ann Harlan, reminisced about a quilting party she attended in 1857 shortly after moving to Skullyville, the Choctaw Indian Agency west of Fort Smith, Arkansas. Her memoirs, published in *The Chronicles of Oklahoma*, recalled:

> So, not long after this, there came a lot of Indian women to invite me to a quilting. Quilting was the order of the day then, and they always had a big powwow. The men furnished the meat and barbecued it, and wild

The Exhibit Hall of the 1912 Standing Rock Fair in Fort Yates, North Dakota (top), displays locally made Sioux quilts as part of the fair exhibition.

Mr. and Mrs. Joe Claymore (Sioux) exhibit a wide variety of Sioux crafts, including pieced and floral appliqué quilts, in this c. 1910–20 photograph (bottom).

A *collection of Hawaiian quilts is shown in this 1933 photograph* (top) *taken at the Mokihana Club, a Kauai women's literary, civic, and social club.*

At *the 1933 Mokihana Club exhibit on Kauai* (bottom), *a group of women gathered around a quilting frame as Kalei Montgomery* (far right) *quilted.*

game as well. Well, I went to the first one, and saw barbecued beeves, hogs, venison, and thought it enough to satisfy an army. I was always treated royally. The Indians kept coming until I verily believe there must have been six or seven hundred people at this quilting. They had arbors all over the ground, and the quilts were hung in them. They were beautifully pieced. Here I prided myself that my mother had taught me to quilt beautifully; knew my quilting would not be criticized. An old [Choctaw] lady by the name of [Susan] Hall who ran a hotel at Skullyville, and who, by the way, was my brother's mother-in-law, was one of the examiners of the quilting. When she got to me she said, "Well, you quilt fine." I remarked to her, "Mother taught me to quilt."

Now you see, this was bordering on civilization. Prizes were given to the best quilters. I received a strand of white-and-red beads. They were real pretty. I wish that I had had sense enough to preserve those beads. Even to this day I watch bead counters to see if I can duplicate those beads. I would enjoy myself at these big gatherings, but they failed to drive the tears away. You know Old Man Time does all those healing properties.[154]

Little visual evidence of these events has been found, but quilt shows continue to be held in association with powwows in North America. For example, every year or two a quilt show is held at the powwow on Walpole Island, Ontario, Canada.

Historical photographs also document the inclusion of quilts in agricultural expositions and county fairs early in the century. Some of these fairs were specifically for Native peoples; others included all residents of a region. Photographs taken from about 1910 through the early 1930s at the Midwinter Fair in Browning, Montana, and

**Navajo Basket Quilt,
c. 1992**

*Made by Caroline Wilson
(Navajo), Mexican Springs,
New Mexico. 78.5 x 78.75
inches. Collection of Michigan
State University Museum*

*Quiltmakers find inspiration for
designs, color schemes, and
patterns in other forms of material culture important to their
heritage, such as this Navajo
basket pattern, designed by
Sara Ann McLennand.*

Navajo Quilt, c. 1996

Made by Vera and Ruth Tyler (Choctaw), Clifton, Louisiana. 78.5 x 100 inches. Collection of Michigan State University Museum

As there are few design symbols or motifs commonly used in Choctaw material culture, the Tylers look to other tribal communities for their quilt designs, such as the Navajo rug design used for this king-size quilt.

the Standing Rock Fairs on the Fort Yates Reservation show exhibitions of a variety of block-style, *crazy*, and *star* quilt patterns.

In 1983, Tom Hill, director of the Woodland Indian Cultural Educational Centre in Brantford, Ontario, organized an exhibition of quilts from the Six Nations and New Credit Reserves. The catalogue accompanying the exhibit reports on the presence of quilting in agricultural fairs as early as 1872.[155] Quilts continue to be entered by Native textile artists in provincial and county fair competitions.

Less well documented is the inclusion of Native-made quilts in local, state, regional, or national quilt shows. A 1938 *Detroit News* article about the fifth annual *Detroit News* Quilt Show carried a photograph of judges admiring a "quilt made by an Indian squaw. Bright colors predominate and the combination of flowers and patches is interesting."[156]

Quilts are regularly included in textile or separate quilt categories at juried tribal art shows. Every year since 1989, at least one quiltmaker has been awarded one of the top prizes in the textile category at the United Tribes Indian Art Expo in Bismarck, North Dakota. Judy Toppings (White Earth Ojibwa) won Best of Show at the Ojibwa Art Expo 1992 with her satin quilt *Migizi*. The Northern Plains Indian Art Show in Sioux City, Iowa, and the Spring Art Exhibit at the Five Civilized Tribes Museum in Muskogee, Oklahoma, are examples of juried shows that include quilts as a separate category. Seminole and Miccosukee patchwork on apparel is showcased and judged in fashion shows and dress competitions at the Miccosukee Arts and Crafts Festival and the Seminole Tribal Fair. Featuring cash prizes offered by the tribe, work is judged in a variety of categories.

Quilts of a variety of patterns are on display in this c. 1915 Shawnee Indian Agency agricultural exhibit. The Indian profile is made of grains attached to a background board.

Three years ago there was a quilt show in New Town [North Dakota]. The first prize was $100 and second prize was $75. When I quilt, I don't move. I put a pink quilt together for the quilt show and quilted designs around the edge. Three girls and I did the quilting and finished it in three hours. By one o'clock in the afternoon, I got the quilt in the show. I took second place. That was a rush job! The quilt that won first place had little quilted animals within the design. [That quilter] may have been preparing her quilt for a year before the show.[157]

Hawaiian quiltmaking was brought to the attention of many through early exhibitions, including one held at the Lihue Parish Hall in March 1933 by the Mokihana Club, a Kauai women's literary, civic, and social club. The exhibition included 108 quilts, including many of the *Hawaiian flag* design.[158] Museums in all of the islands have sponsored shows; more recently, through the

Native Hawaiian quilters are pictured with a traditional Hawaiian floral quilt in this promotional photo (n.d.).

𝒥nterest by contemporary quilt designers in Native American arts has led to an increase in the number of published quilt patterns incorporating Native motifs, patterns, and images. Quilt cooperatives such as Missouri Breaks also have begun to market a variety of patterns as well as kits for *star* pattern quilts. Sara Ann McLennand designed *Duck Island basket*, a pattern based on a Southwest Indian coiled basket she found in her grandparents' cabin on Duck Island in Michigan. A ribbon winner at the Fourth Annual Show and Contest of the American Quilter's Society in 1988, the pattern was printed in Sandra L. O'Brien's *Great American Quilts* (1992). A copy made its way to the Gathering Place in Thoreau, New Mexico, where weaver and quiltmaker Caroline Wilson (Navajo) of Mexican Springs, New Mexico, saw and replicated it in what she refers to as the *Navajo basket* quilt (see p. 85).[160] Books are now available on appliqué patterns drawn from Native American beadwork designs, ribbonwork, woven blankets, pottery, and baskets.

efforts of the Hawaiian Quilt Research Project, quilt festivals are held in convention centers. In addition to exhibitions of quilts, the festivals feature demonstrations, lectures, and workshops on Hawaiian quilting.

Individual quilts made by North American Indian and Native Hawaiian textile artists have been included in late-twentieth-century exhibitions. A few quilters have had one-person shows; others regularly have their work exhibited in museum and gallery shows, where they often win awards. In addition, quilts drawn from specific tribal traditions also have been the subject of exhibitions.

Near Pine Ridge, South Dakota, exhibitions have been held of quilts exclusively made to honor veterans of military service. These quilts are usually done in predominantly red, white, and blue colors and feature the star, eagle, and flag.[157]

Today, all quiltmakers have far greater access to quilt patterns and techniques through the increasing number of available of books and mass-distributed periodicals. More importantly, through nationally syndicated quilting programs, quilting information is accessible to almost anyone who has a television. It is not surprising that women are expanding their repertoire of patterns, skills, and forms of quilts. Some patterns are drawn from other cultural traditions, including other Native cultures. For instance, one of Mohawk quilter Sarah Jacobs's treasured quilts is done in a Hawaiian-style pattern, and Louisiana Choctaw quilters Vera Tyler and her daughter Ruth make quilts in both *thunderbird* and Navajo patterns. Margaret Wood of Phoenix finds inspiration for her ideas, designs, color palette, and motifs in her own tribal heritage and in those of others. She has created quilts and quilted soft-sculpture pieces incorporating patchwork Seminole pieces of her father's heritage and the Navajo jewelry of her mother's family as well as work derived from a Sioux tipi, a Blackfeet Indian boy's shirt, Mimbres pottery, and even the textile traditions of the Ainu, the aboriginal peoples in Japan.

Using both published patterns and their own designs, non-Native quilters also are turning to Native American culture for inspiration. Some, such as Dawn Amos, who is married to a Sioux, are well acquainted with Native American symbols and traditions. Others, such as Joanne Adams Duncan, who makes quilts in the Navajo "eye dazzler" rug design, are trying to make sense of distant and sometimes nearly obscure connections with Native American ancestors.

Other non-Native quilters simply find Native patterns an inspiration or design source for their work. Marva E. Dalebout of St. George, Utah, has completed a series of pictorial quilts, titled *Indian Working Women*, that depicts various traditional activities of Native women from western tribes. A quilt by Helen Ocwig of Arizona, now in the collection of the Museum of Anthropology, University of British Columbia, represents a Kwakiutl ceremonial curtain from Kingcome Inlet. Celine McKenzie Vukson of Bradford, Ontario, specializes in *crazy* quilts made of tanned hide and embellished with beadwork. Winifrede Burry's work was first inspired by the paintings and drawings of Ontario Native artist Norval Morrisseau, and now most of her work is infused with references to Anishnabek art.

Rose Momsen, a quilter living in Hawaii, combines Euro-American techniques and patterns with a variety of Native Hawaiian quilt techniques, patterns, symbols, and legends into her highly personal work. One of the quilts in her self-portrait series, *Ulupalakua: Rest Stop on the Wheel of Fortune*, refers to the Haleakala crater in Ulupalakua. The quilt contains piecework and Hawaiian appliqué and is executed in a brown-gold color scheme.[161] In one unusual collaboration, Fran Soika, an Ohio artist, joined with Acoma potter Drew Lewis to create a quilt portraying motifs from his pottery. The finished quilt now hangs in Acoma while several of Lewis's pots are in Soika's home.[162]

Some quiltmakers who employ Native designs in their work are careful to not use sacred images and to give credit to their sources; others are not aware of either the source or the meaning of the images. Sioux quiltmaker Lula Red Cloud observes that there are all sorts of items—including jewelry, clothing, even dishes—in the marketplace with Indian designs on them. "Some of those designs are very precious to us but they don't give credit to the American Indian people. They don't give credit to the Sioux for a lot of our symbols. They call it Southwest designs . . . which is ridiculous." The theme of one of her recent quilts was a tribute to the invisible people who first used these symbols.[163]

Public Recognition to Native Quilting and Quilters Native Hawaiian and North American quilting has been featured in a variety of museum, festival, and park interpretive public programs. At the Bishop Museum in Honolulu, Native Hawaiian quilters are a fundamental part of the educational programming of the museum

Loon Quilt, 1996

Made by Diane O'Leary
(Comanche), Garibaldi,
Oregon. 90 x 116 inches.
Private collection

O'Leary, a painter by training,
uses a painterly approach in her
quilts. This one, made for her
son and as part of a series of
bird quilts, features a loon in an
impressionistic landscape.

and regularly conduct classes and demonstrations. Hidatsa Mandan quilters have participated in the Smithsonian Festival of American Folklife, Clifton Choctaw quilters in the Louisiana Folklife Festival, Seminole quilters in the Florida Folklife Festival, and Odawa and Ojibwa quilters at the Festival of Michigan Folklife. At the Miccosukee Museum, quilters demonstrate during the annual Miccosukee Fair.

Native quilters have participated as master artists in traditional arts apprenticeship programs run by several state arts programs, including Florida, Michigan, North Dakota, Minnesota, and Nebraska. Two Native quilters have been honored as recipients of National Heritage Fellowships awarded by the National Endowment for the Arts: Nellie Star Boy Menard (Rosebud Sioux) in September 1995 and Mealii Kalama (Native Hawaiian) in 1985.

Recently, there has been more general public attention directed toward these traditions than ever before. Increasingly, quilts are being used as decorative elements in graphic designs for such items as book covers. Part of a *star* quilt pattern serves as the basis for the design of the logo of the Indy Reds, the Indianapolis, Indiana, farm team of the Cincinnati Reds professional baseball team. Whole-cloth appliquéd quilts, along with the hula, ukulele music, and the luau, are among the chief symbols of indigenous culture in Hawaii.

Native Quilting into the Twenty-First Century

The latter part of the twentieth century has witnessed an explosion of interest in quilting—making quilts, building collections of quilts, exhibiting quilts, marketing quilts, and researching and publishing on a wide array of contemporary and historical quilt-related topics. This interest has expanded to the formation of international quilt exhibitions and conferences. As more knowledge about historical and contemporary Native quilting is shared with the worldwide community, this exchange between quilting in Native and other cultures will undoubtedly continue to affect the textile traditions of the respective communities.

On the local level, in Native communities across North America and in the Hawaiian Islands, women and men still meet in homes, churches, tribal centers, and other community places to teach, learn, and share their quilting skills and their knowledge with family members, neighbors, and new friends. Along the way, these quilters are leaving tangible and visual evidence of their Native heritage. Through the quilts and the stories and practices associated with making and using them, Native peoples are passing on an artistic and cultural legacy to be treasured.

Part II
Tradition and Identity

Learning the Threads: Sioux Quiltmaking in South Dakota

by Laurie N. Anderson (Sioux)

Although quilting is a fairly recent phenomenon in Sioux society, the tradition of sewing in Sioux culture predates non-Native migration and has been passed down from generation to generation. The presence of sewing skills is evidenced in the following account by D. C. Poole of everyday life in Spotted Tail's camp about 1869–70: "The women are working and gossiping, always at a distance from the men, and the girls too small to carry burdens were playing with the crude dolls or acquiring knowledge of the needle with dried sinews for thread."[1] The materials used by the girls were traditional, natural skins and sinew, even though cotton thread (as well as calicos) could be found in trading posts in the Dakota Territory at that time. In fact, Poole listed

This typical scene of an Indian boarding school sewing class was taken in Fort Yates, South Dakota, c. 1930.

cloth and needles among the items he first brought to the Indians during his time as Indian agent:

> The first issue of annuity goods made to the Indians, as has been shown, was entirely insufficient, the majority of them not receiving anything; consequently, I made an effort to procure more, stating the number of blankets, yards of Indian cloth, kettles, butcher knives, buckskin needles and quantity of tobacco, which would be required to satisfy in part their desires.[2]

From the mid-1700s until the end of the nineteenth century, the area now known as North Dakota, South Dakota, and Montana was primarily Sioux domain. Beginning in the early part of the nineteenth century, pioneers, missionaries, and military people relocating from the East began to settle this region. By the 1880s, the U.S. government provided the Sioux certain protection through the creation of reservations. However, the loss of their territory and

disappearance of their food supply were devastating to the Native population. Conflicts between the Sioux and settlers did not subside until Sitting Bull, one of the great Sioux leaders, was captured in 1881. Shortly thereafter, on November 2, 1889, the Dakota Territory became the states of North and South Dakota. Although since that time reservation land has been further reduced, most of the Sioux population now resides on reservations spread throughout the states of North and South Dakota and Montana.

In the nineteenth century, organized Christian denominations in the East, in an alliance with the federal government, worked to create institutionalized educational systems that would assimilate Indians into a Western European–based culture. To that end, missionary schools sprang up on territorial and, later, reservation lands. The curriculum of the schools was highly structured and, for young girls, focused on acquiring domestic skills, as the Episcopalian Minutes of the Fifty-Fifth Annual Convocation of the District of South Dakota in 1939 reveals:

> Education—Every student who comes to St. Mary's [located in Santee, Nebraska Territory] is important to the faculty. We try to help each girl find her particular place in the world and then to fit her for it. Along with the formal education, the girls acquire as many skills and interests as possible. Sewing, cooking, housework, crafts, music and organizations will help her to find her place in the home, church, and community.[3]

Mission schools and mission societies first introduced quiltmaking—as part of the set of requisite domestic skills—to Sioux women. Virginia Driving Hawk Sneve writes about how her great-grandmother, Hannah

Indian Head Star Quilt, c. 1994

Made by Evelyn Douville (Sioux), Parmelee, South Dakota. 78 x 82 inches. Collection of Michigan State University Museum

A display of needlework produced at the St. Francis Mission was part of the May 21, 1936, celebration of the mission's fiftieth anniversary on the Rosebud Reservation in South Dakota. This photo (top) records Sister Olnida's mission sewing class.

Lakota Sioux members of the St. Mary Society of the Holy Rosary Mission in Pine Ridge, South Dakota, display samples of their quilting in this 1938 photo (bottom).

Frasier, learned to make patchwork quilts from Mary Riggs, a missionary in Santee:

> Mary and her husband, Stephen R. Riggs, were the first Presbyterian missionaries in Santee. They [the Sioux women] learned how

to make crazy quilts and mostly flannel with probably old wool used as batting in between. Some of these quilts were tied and some were quilted. The Presbyterians were the first missionaries to bring out women to work with the Indian women.[4]

In addition to learning quilting at the mission schools, Sioux women also learned through quilting societies established by the wives of missionaries, evidenced by the many copious letters, diaries, and documents kept by the missionary families. In the Dakota Territory, the Presbyterian church and the Episcopal church established women's church groups called, respectively, the Ladies' Aid Society and the Women's Auxiliary, both of which usually held weekly quilting sessions. The activities of these gatherings helped raise funds for building chapels, supported schools and orphanages, and covered the expenses of their own congregation. Sometimes they even supported further missionary work in other countries. Virginia Driving Hawk Sneve, in *That They May Have Life*, states:

> The early women missionaries of Bishop Hare's time faced all of the hardships of pioneer women in a harsh land. Yet, many of them devoted the major part of their lives to the Indians and to South Dakota.
>
> One of the primary purposes of the missionary women was to work with the Indian women, teaching them sewing, cooking, and housekeeping, along with the word of God. Soon after the Church was established in new missions, there came into existence little bands of Indian women, aided by white women, to form guilds. They immediately set about saving pennies, or did beadwork, made quilts, and other craftwork, to sell and make money to build a chapel. They not only contributed to the expenses of their own congregations, but also to the native clergy fund, missions in

Japan, orphanages in China, the church schools in South Dakota, and innumerable other enterprises.[5]

Some churchgoing Natives decided to independently create their own women's groups. Sister Margaret Hawk gives this account at St. Elizabeth's Episcopal Church on the Standing Rock Reservation:

We had . . . a person in the women's group [who seemed like the owner of the church and the congregation] and I didn't dare go to Women's Group because she was always saying that the young ladies did not know how to sew. She would rip my sewing out and she never showed us how. She was always criticizing. She became sick but she was entirent [a tyrant] until her death and after she died we really evaluted [evaluated] her. She was telling us something in her own way, if you don't know how to sew, go somewhere and learn and come back. This way the young ones didn't come to church to the women's groups. We had a bright idea, we said let's form the Daughters of the King, so we did and we called ourselves the Martha and Mary Group. The elderly people called us the M&Ms.[6]

Leonard Bruguier, director of the Institute of American Indian Studies at the University of South Dakota, fondly recalls: "My mother used to take me with her to the Martha and Mary Group quilting session every Wednesday night every week. I can remember running under the quilt while they were working on it."[7]

Native women wanted to pursue the activities introduced to them by the missionary women, yet differences in teaching and learning styles sometimes made it difficult for the Sioux women to accept what they considered to be inappropriate behavior. For instance, criticizing and admonishing others in order to make the quilt "good" was simply

Missionaries and Native quilters, Howe Creek Episcopal Church at Santee, Nebraska, c. 1920.

not practiced among the Sioux; moreover, it was considered offensive. Rather than giving up altogether, Native women adhered to Sioux values by forming the alternative, independent Martha and Mary Group.

In the early twentieth century, Lucy Burning Breast, a Sioux quiltmaker from Parmelee, Rosebud Reservation, South Dakota, organized an Episcopalian Women's Society group to teach both quilting and the new techniques of sanitation she had learned from missionaries. Albert Reifel, the youngest of her five boys, remembers her raising a white flag to let the other women know the quilt group was being held. Reifel also recalls his mother inspecting the other women's hands to ensure they were clean before working on the quilt.[8] Nellie Menard gives a very similar portrayal of her aunt Lucy:

And then, when they would want to quilt . . . they would have Women's Society meeting, they all quilt. They make a block each and my aunt has to measure it to see. And they fix the centers and then they make the quilt top. And when they were going to quilt . . . my auntie will say, "There's a basin there and hot water there. There's a little tea kettle there." . . . She made each one wash their hands and dry them and then, they start quilting. So she

was really strict. And if somebody's new, and
then they're going to start quilting, she'd give
them a little rag and she'd test their stitches.
She'd give them a needle and thread and
they'd have to show her how they stitch it.[9]

In addition to missionaries and church
groups giving instruction in quiltmaking, the
Works Progress Administration (WPA) hired
women to teach quilting techniques to the
Native women during the Great Depression.
Alice Johnson Reifel, a first-generation
Norwegian-American, married Burning
Breast's son, Benjamin Reifel, and moved
with him to Oglala, South Dakota, on July 1,
1933. There she was hired by the WPA, an
experience she later wrote about:

We hadn't been settled many months before I
was asked to take a job in Pine Ridge. WPA
had set up a quilt-making factory to employ
the Indian women. They needed a Home
Economist to supervise. I was the only one in
the area so I began driving the fifteen miles
from Oglala to Pine Ridge each day while Ben
worked in the Oglala office.[10]

Her daughter, Loyce Anderson, reflects,
"Native women never made the same size
quilts, so Mom went out to the factory to
help to standardize sizes used for bed
quilts."[11]

Young Sioux girls often would take their
newly learned sewing and quilting skills
home. Madonna Swan recalls doing this as
a young girl in 1937:

It was snowing hard, and the wind howled and
shook the windows. The winter of 1937 was a
cold one. Dad had taken Shirley and I home
from school for Christmas. In those days we had
no television or radio. We did a lot of things like
quilt or crochet or sew.[12]

At home these young girls shared their
quilting and other new sewing techniques
with their elders. Aside from the group quilting done in schools, churches, and in other
Anglo domestic spheres, Native women more
often were content to quilt alone at home.

Quiltmaking quickly moved into more traditional Sioux contexts for instruction. For
instance, during the four-day Buffalo (Hunka)
Ceremony, young girls learned to make moccasins, do beadwork, or quill in order to
develop their skills in "womanly arts" and to
learn the virtues of industry, wisdom, and
cheerfulness. Quilting was one of the arts
learned during the ceremony by the young
women, such as Nellie Star Boy Menard of
Rosebud, South Dakota. Now in her mid-
eighties, she recalls:

Well, I didn't know how to quilt . . . I always
saw my mother making star quilts. And she'll
be quilting it and I'll be playing. But I never
bother about it because that was her art. And
then, you know, I went through that ceremony
[the Hunka ceremony] . . . and that is when [I
learned].[13]

Madonna Swan also gives this account of
her Buffalo ceremony held sometime in the
1940s:

Among the Lakota people, we have a way of
marking a ceremony for young women when
they have their first moon, or monthly cycle.
The day that I got my first moon, we were living outside Cherry Creek [South Dakota].
Mom and Grandma closed off a little space for
me to stay with ropes and blankets. I moved in
Grandma's little cabin, and that is where
Grandma said I must stay for the next four
days and four nights.

Grandma Julia instructed me not to look
out the windows. I was not to stand at the door
and peek out or let my thoughts go outside
that little enclosure. She said, "You are to stay
busy doing something all the time; if you are
not cooking, washing, or cleaning the house

you should be sewing or beading. Whatever you do, if you are sewing and you make a mistake, you should not rip it out. If you do, you will be that way the rest of your life. If you do rip it out, it will be your habit in all things during your life time. So just keep going and the next time do it better," she instructed.

I didn't have to try very hard, because Mom or Grandma were there to remind me and show me the right way to do things the whole time. I made a doll with a cloth Indian dress, beaded moccasins, and leggings. I had never done beadwork before. I sewed buttons on all my dad's and brother's shirts. I sewed all my mom's old dresses. I sewed up and patched up bib overalls. Then Grandma Julia cut some quilt blocks, and I made them up into two quilt tops. She taught me how to cook in the old ways that her mother had taught her.

About two days later they made a feast and invited everyone in Cherry Creek. They gave away what I had made and many things they had been making and put aside for this day. Grandma gave a talk about what had taken place, instructing other women to do the same with their daughters, so that they could have good lives. Then she prayed and fed all visitors and gave them a gift of a shawl, a quilt, or food.[14]

Contemporary Sioux quiltmakers share many stories that reflect on the process of informal learning that now occurs in their communities. According to Iris Red Elk Allrunner of Wolfpoint, Montana: "My mother, Josephine Red Elk, sewed, did beadwork, spoke Sioux, and recognized God-given talent in her own children." Red Elk Allrunner learned how to sew from her mother when she was in the sixth grade and began making her own clothes. She fondly recalls the day her mother asked her to come over to help with a quilt project. Her mother told her, "I've looked at colors so much I can't put them together:

So she gave me three bags of colors and said, "Put these together." Mom only quilts when she wants to. She made several star tops. I fretted over my mother's potential acceptance or nonacceptance of the color choices I would make. It took me a while to drum up the courage to show my mother the completed quilt tops. Eventually, I showed my mother the tops. My mother loved them![15]

To Red Elk Allrunner, her mother's approval also conveyed her general acknowledgment of Iris's quilting expertise: "I had learned well from my teacher [mother]. It is another thing to have your teacher [mother] learn from you. It is both a great feeling and an honor." Continuing in her mother's path, Red Elk Allrunner taught her daughter how to sew and quilt and is now in the process of teaching her grandchildren.

Sometimes young people seek out elders in their communities to teach them how to quilt. Others relied on extended family to teach them, as Pearl Four Bear remembers:

I used to watch my mother sew, but it was my aunt, Virginia Spotted Bird, who really showed me how to quilt. Nina First, my other aunt, taught me how to cut diamonds. My mother learned how to quilt from my father's cousins and from her sister-in-law. Three of my father's cousins sewed a lot. My mother is eighty-seven years old now and still sews.[16]

Tillie Walker, who lives in Mandaree, North Dakota, learned how to sew from her mother and also helped her mother put quilts together by tying them. Tillie recalls that her church received mission barrels:

These were often filled with beautiful fur coats, old shoes, and quilt pieces, which were taken to various communities and were to be used by people in need. A room for distribution was set up, much like a secondhand store, in my

Grandmother's Flower Garden Quilt, 1996

Made by Bernice Blakney (Santee Sioux), Niobrara, Nebraska. 90 x 96.5 inches. Collection of Michigan State University Museum

Blakney makes quilts for burials, memorial giveaways, to honor returning veterans, graduates, newborn babies, and when sundancers finish their four-year pledge period. She is known both for her star quilts and versions of the Grandmother's flower garden pattern.

church. Here, people could come and gather what they needed. I went to school in the mission. I was a mission kid. I was involved with my church. Quilts were generally made for our beds. We used quilts in the sleigh out of necessity. The quilts were used in the back of the pickup, or wagon. Many times, we would take quilts off our beds and use them for the sleigh. A quilt was an everyday type of article and was made to be used.[17]

Loyce Anderson, Lucy Burning Breast's granddaughter, remembers a star quilt Lucy had made of satin and velvet, where she incorporated fancy handwork consisting of quilting and embroidery stitches.

She probably got her materials from the mission boxes in the church. Eastern women used to send fancy velvet and satin dresses in them. Where could you go dressed in velvet and satin dresses on the reservation? Yet, the old crazy quilts were full of these materials, and few people living on the reservation could have afforded them.[18]

In the twentieth century, quilts—especially those in the *star* pattern—have become one of the definitive cultural symbols of the Sioux people. Though quiltmaking was introduced to the Sioux through contexts outside of Sioux tradition, quiltmaking has, over the years, become thoroughly embedded in Sioux life. Today, quiltmaking has extended well beyond the mission schools and societies, most likely learned in the home from a family elder. At the same time "the threads are learned," Sioux values and beliefs are imparted and perpetuated.

*O*riginally from New Mexico, a Pueblo woman, Ramoná Malnourie, married a man from the Fort Berthold Reservation in North Dakota. She became interested in the *star* quilt pattern when they lived in Colorado in the 1960s:

I give all my credit in sewing star quilts to a lady; she just passed away last year. That's where I learned my making quilts. Her name was Mercy Walker [Tillie Walker's mother]. She's originally from this reservation. We met when we used to live in Denver. I used to watch her. She came often to visit her daughter, who was employed in Denver. I had never ever seen star quilts until I had seen some of their work and it was so complicated, you know. In New Mexico, you don't see those star quilts down in the Southwest pueblos. So I've never seen one like that and I used to watch her and I was just kind of determined to make one. And, she used to tell me, "You can do it. You know, it is easy." It didn't look easy. So she got me started on making just a plain . . . they call it nine-patch to sewing squares together. That came out okay. We just put that on the floor, and she crawled all over it to really think it over and see if my stitching was right, you know. So then she got me going on these star quilts. From there, I caught on. It was hard, but with her constant help and at her side all the time, I worked with her and so I managed to put one out. Of course, I didn't start with a big one. I kind of made a small one just to get the feeling of the star quit. That's a tedious job [as well as] the cutting of the diamonds.[19]

The Craft of Identity:

Quilting Traditions of the

Waccamaw-Siouan Tribe

by Jill Hemming

It's not what you'd say, an Indian thing. You know, quilting's not. It's a thing for everyone, but quilting has been a way here, in this community and with this tribe—gosh, I'd never remember back when the first quilt was made. . . . But I know it has been passed down for over a hundred years, if not more.[1]

When I heard this statement from a Waccamaw-Siouan quilter during an interview, I thought I'd just heard a contradiction. How, I wondered, could she acknowledge quilting as a long-standing tradition of a historic Indian community yet not see it linked to her Native identity? Was it possible that quilts indeed were neutral, that they had no meaning or use that was specifically Waccamaw?

For two years I traveled the back roads of North Carolina, to the Indian community of Buckhead, to study quiltmaking in the Waccamaw-Siouan tribe. I systematically

recorded their quilts and quilt history through interviews, photographs, and written surveys and learned much about the tribe's historical background. This research engages the important discussion of identity, specifically as it relates to Native Americans. The tribe downplays local handicraft to outsiders unless it is an art associated with pan-Indian imagery, such as beadwork, pottery, or regalia. When the tribe ran a local craft cooperative in the early 1970s, it was these uncontested ethnic crafts that were displayed and sold. Local traditions such as quilting and cornhusk weaving were not included. Chief Priscilla Freeman Jacobs describes the past social life of the tribe, saying that while there were few activities outside church and school

the women would sit around the quilt. I would have to say quilting has been one of the most consistent things that has gone on in my lifetime here, as far as arts and crafts . . . but we

Bicentennial Quilt, c. 1985

Made by Juanita Jacobs (Waccamaw-Siouan), Buckhead or Bolton, North Carolina. 90 x 90 inches. Collection of the artist

Jacobs receives high praise in the community for her stylish quilting and impeccable workmanship.

considered it a necessity. . . . It's one of those things that is like, you just had to do . . . it was like cooking. This was something that the women had to do. You had to keep enough quilts to keep the people warm.[2]

The longevity of the craft into the present, when quilts are no longer a necessity to keep people warm, supports its status as a long-standing traditional feature of Waccamaw-Siouan life.

The Waccamaw-Sioux are not federally recognized as Native American. Along with the other remnants of small tribes that managed to stay and survive in the East following the Indian Removal Act of 1830, the Waccamaw seemingly disappeared as the United States concentrated its removal efforts on larger, more powerful groups of Indians.

With the relocation of such bodies as the Cherokee Nation to Oklahoma came the myth that all Indians now lived in the West. However, the smaller tribes were left behind physically and socially; their isolation increased because they tended to live in remote tracts of land. The Waccamaw tribe's journey has been one of adjustments and creativity as the tribe has seized the political, social, and cultural tools it needs to remain intact. Much of that path to the present has been the gradual emergence of the tribe from a private knowledge of its Indian ancestry to a self-conscious proclamation of its Indianness both for tribal members and outsiders.

Through consistent patterns of racial intermarriage and the passage of land through families, the Waccamaw carved out all-Indian settlements in the Waccamaw Lake region in North Carolina, including the Buckhead, St. James, and Columbus settlements. Sometime during the nineteenth century, English replaced their Native language, and tribal members adopted the clothing and household styles of their neighbors, primarily of Scotch, English, and African descent. As the tribe increased its economic and social interaction with its neighbors, members added their influence to the development of the region. Even as they adopted new customs, and despite having no federal and little local recognition as a tribe, the Waccamaw kept alive a consciousness of their Indian origins.

James E. Alexander, a California journalist, was one of the first to help the Waccamaw compile their history in order to pursue federal recognition status. On his way through North Carolina in the late 1940s he heard about the Waccamaw and decided to investigate in pursuit of a possible story. Instead, Alexander found himself personally drawn into the struggle of the tribe for day-to-day survival. Unschooled and living at a subsistence level, the Waccamaw asked Alexander to stay with them long enough to research their origins and to help them create a case for federal recognition. After repeated requests at county and state levels to receive basic funding for schools, drainage, and roads, the tribe felt that federal attention was the only way to move out of poverty and be given credibility on the local level. Alexander, deeply moved by their situation, eventually led a tribal delegation to Washington, D.C., in 1950.[3]

Though the tribe has yet to succeed in its bid for federal recognition, living conditions have slowly improved for the community and a variety of activities have contributed to their growing sense of Indian identity. The 1970s brought an era of spirited organizing within all of the tribes in North Carolina. A state organization was created and tribes established tribal grounds, community centers, and development strategies. For the Waccamaw, part of their efforts centered on their genealogy. In the early 1980s, Patricia Lerch, a local anthropologist, was hired to research for the tribe. Early census records systematically designated the predecessors of community family members as "all other free persons," a label that implies African-American origins, but into the nineteenth century, census records in North Carolina only had three categories: white, slave, and all other free persons.[4,5]

The community has survived generations with marginal resources, disputed origins, and few advocates. In the face of challenges to their group identity, their early history shows them presenting themselves in terms of racial difference. For instance, they fought for years to receive county funding for an all-Indian school. With the advent of civil rights, the emerging popularity of pan-Indianism, and the upheaval of desegregation, the tribesmen entered the public arena with more self-conscious attempts to represent themselves as Indian. Rather than arguing racial identity, they tapped into a broader cultural Indian identity.

The label pan-Indianism has wide definitions and refers to a decades-long movement among Native Americans toward common Indian interests and identity nationwide rather than at a tribal level. Here the term is

*F*olklorist Shalom Staub has looked at the dynamics of cultural layering in communities—how groups of people often present different "versions" of their own culture in different situations.[6] An ethnic restaurant might have one menu for outsiders and another for real Natives. A community might have a dance troupe that wears flamboyant traditional costumes and dances a certain repertoire at a festival while the dancing done within the community is distinctly different from the public presentation. In the same way, labeling certain crafts as "Indian" and "not an Indian thing" may represent cultural layering within the Waccamaw community. The powwows, dancing, and drumming that take place in public arenas bring recognition from outsiders and provide an easily accessible way to reinforce tribal and individual identity. However, quilting has not really been used as a way to identify tribal members to outsiders—it is more just the way things have always been.

Yet quilts play a significant role in the Waccamaw community, passing through families as treasured heirlooms. Older women labor long hours to ensure that every child and grandchild own one of their quilts. Newlyweds and babies inevitably receive at least one quilt, if not several more. For a few women, quilting offers a means of making money in a way that they enjoy. Quilting is also a communal activity for many of the elderly, who gather together and help one another finish quilt projects. Over the years, quilts have been a fundraising tool in the community—whether to raise money for new fire suits at the volunteer fire department or to raise funds for repairs to local buildings.

used for the cultural symbols commonly owned and adopted by tribes as uncontestably Indian: powwows, tipis, fry bread, beadwork, drumming, feather headdresses, and other dance regalia. These crafts, food, clothes, housing types, and social gatherings have become the shared property of tribes across the United States, whether indigenous to particular groups or not. The powwow, especially, has become a powerful means of forging a pan-Indian identity as well as a specific tribal one:

> Some of these men and women [who leave the reservations] will be lost in the general population but others will seek to retain or create an Indian identity. . . . It seems highly likely that people whose homeland was reservation or tribe will continue to call themselves Indians, though they may not be readily identifiable either in appearance or life style as such. The Pan-Indian base will probably encompass not only Indians fresh from the reservation but also many who have lived in the larger society for generations.[7]

The adoption of pan-Indian elements by the Waccamaw came largely through the efforts and interest of tribal women. They saw in this movement an exciting and living heritage with which to connect their children—something to set them apart from those outside the tribe.

The institution of the tribal powwow meshed with long-standing Waccamaw community gatherings. What was new was holding a gathering that incorporated features identifiable as Indian as a means to invite outsiders into the community. Priscilla Jacobs describes this time around the beginning of the powwow:

> [We were] trying to recapture our heritage. . . . Not that we had lost it or anything, but it was just that we didn't get together and share. I

mean, the quilting was going on ever since I can remember. These things have always been there, but it was like we didn't come together for a special occasion other than at church. And really, back in that time, I met at the church with the [Indian] dancers, we did crafts in the church, about everything we did we did in the church because we didn't have anyplace to meet.[8]

By incorporating dancing, drumming, beadwork, and regalia into the event, local female leaders hoped to engage the youth and redefine the tribe in terms irrefutably Indian. The powwow offered the potential to strengthen themselves both internally and externally. By not including some local cultural traditions less known as Indian, the choice of cultural performances expressed the struggle for nonreserved southeastern tribes to sustain themselves as distinct from their neighbors.

Another interesting example of this conscious act of self-definition is seen in the local high school's publication *Kin'lin'*.[9] Following the Foxfire method, high school students gathered oral histories and information about their community. Waccamaw students participated in several of the issues and interviewed members of their tribe. While the students reported on handiwork practiced by their community, such as sewing and chair-bottom weaving, aspects of culture that were just a part of ordinary, everyday practice for all who lived in the region were too familiar to be valued by Waccamaw as expressive of a cultural or ethnic identity. How could Waccamaw crafts and customs be seen as their own when there were so many similarities with their neighbors? As the Waccamaw continue their search for a usable identity, their efforts have centered on recovering aboriginal cul-

tural elements that anthropology and archaeology have uncovered and looking to uncontested reservated tribes for cultural borrowings, whether locally indigenous or not.

This study of quilts suggests that quilts are a viable feature of Waccamaw identity. Originally, I expected to find quilts that physically conveyed an Indianness through their use of particular colors, motifs, or symbols. Indian motifs did appear in some of the quilts surveyed in the Waccamaw community, and I could have limited my search to these quilts and come away with a confirmed belief that Native American quilts "look Indian." However, many more quilts surveyed defied stereotyping.

Waccamaw quilting has followed the changes in the community. Just as Buckhead's wood houses shifted to cinder block to brick to trailers, quilts evolved with the quilters' lives. Generally, older Waccamaw quilts, which date from 1920 to 1970, are mostly remnants and scraps made into single large blocks, pieced blocks with sashing, strips, or medallion tops. Either stitching or tacking holds the quilt together, and the stitching is invariably the *fan* or *windowpane* design. Fillings vary according to the maker, and quilt borders tend to look more like a use for leftover strips than a visual frame. The Waccamaw women do not shy from bright colors; their tops attest to colorful family clothing.

Quilts from the 1970s onward show the tribe's increased prosperity. Because life is not so hard as in the past, women have the luxury of shopping for new materials and buying cloth big enough to make piecing postage stamp–size scraps no longer necessary. The availability of whole cloth tops with a quilt pattern on the surface has encouraged younger quilters to abandon

Medallion Quilt, c. 1960

Made by Lee Jacobs, (Waccamaw-Siouan), Bolton, North Carolina. Double-bed size. Collection of the artist

This quilt is one of several medallion-style quilts made by Jacobs from old scraps and fabrics.

fan-shaped stitching for quilting that follows the printed design. This has carried over into quilts they piece themselves. In addition, patterns readily enter the community via magazines and books, resulting in such popular designs as the *Irish chain* and *Grandmother's flower garden*. The tendency to create certain forms has given way to a flurry of creative endeavor that leaves the older patterns behind, and wild color arrays have been subdued by preprinted tops and the effort to color coordinate.

Placing the older tradition in the general context of southern quilts is hard. Much variation exists due to personal taste, socioeconomic conditions, and region, but

general patterns would include use of scraps; asymmetrical designs; colors balanced by weight; unusual but successful combinations of colors and fabrics; unemphasized borders; and the commonly used medallion shape. Buckhead's stitches average around five stitches to the inch. The batting consists of everything from polyester to cotton, rags, tobacco sacks, and blankets.

In the Waccamaw tribe, quilting is a living tradition that goes beyond commonly accepted Indian motifs. Waccamaw quilts undermine the stereotypical expectations of what Indian craft, or Indianness, is. Though some Waccamaw quilts display distinct patterns and characteristics that represent a local aesthetic, they do not have to carry traditional representations to be of value. Rather, they are of value *because* of their persistence and importance within family and community and for their representation of a rich material history built from the intersection of cultures. What distinguishes the quilts is not their Indian icons but their craftsmanship and their role in building and maintaining community relationships.

Work by such scholars as Rayna Green raises the battle cry for more honest, contemporary representations of just who Native Americans are and have been—to allow them to remove the feathers and put on their jeans. Focusing on a thriving quilting tradition in a little-known tribe abates the romantic clichés and may give the Waccamaw the vision to more actively define their own local traditions as Indian rather than rely on the safe and publicly uncontested pan-Indian elements that dominate their public presentations. In a 1993 speech, "Repatriating Images: Indians and Photography," Green calls upon all Indians to actively engage themselves in the act of reinventing themselves *for themselves* using whatever images they choose.[10] Even if those images are created by the outside, Native peoples can seize control of what those images will mean to the inside.

Indian Head Quilt, c. 1980

Shirley Freeman (Waccamaw-Siouan) of Bolton, North Carolina, works on an Indian Head quilt, c. 1980, derived from the Waccamaw-Siouan Development Association's letterhead. Double-bed size. Collection of the artist.

Lakota Star Quilts:

Commodity, Ceremony, and

Economic Development

by Beatrice Medicine (Sioux)

During the nineteenth and early twentieth centuries, most Native peoples living in North America were subjected to great cultural disruption, displacement, and relocation by the U.S. government. As Native peoples resettled, they found new ways of maintaining traditional practices, as commented on by Ella Deloria in *Speaking of Indians*:

The people began to make ingenious adaptations of some elements of their old life to the new. For instance, at one period they transferred the art decorations of the tipi to the log house. Out of G.I. muslin they made very large wall coverings, a carry over from the dew-curtain of the tipi and called by the same term, ozan. *On these they painted beautiful designs and made lively black-and-white drawings of historical scenes or hunting or battle or peace-making between tribes, and courtship scenes, games, and suchlike activities of the past. People went visiting just to see one*

another's pictographs and to hear the stories they preserved.[1]

Quilts made to provide warmth have been part of Lakota Sioux households in North Dakota, South Dakota, and Montana since the beginning of the reservation period. Lakota Sioux women of the Northern Plains reservations began making patchwork quilts as utilitarian replacements for buffalo robes and other skin bed coverings. According to ethnohistorian Christian Feest, "Nowhere . . . did patchwork quilting become of importance as on the northern Plains, where quilts were used increasingly as substitutes for painted skins after large scale hunting had been abandoned."[2] The introduction of quilts into the western Sioux reservations was undoubtedly linked to the presence of missions on the early reservations.[3]

Everyday quilts made of tops with simple square or geometric patterns and scraps of wool, cotton, and other materials and filled

Lakota Sioux quiltmaker Lula Red Cloud from the Pine Ridge Reservation in South Dakota makes quilts in star patterns for ceremonial uses as well as quilts in other patterns for other uses. The vibrant colors she prefers carry meaning; in this **Morning Star Quilt** (1996, 78 x 79 inches), they refer to the colors of the morning sun, the earth, and the sky. Collection of Michigan State University Museum

with batting were commonly called *owanke* (to spread) or *owinza* (to cover). Called *sina ek cheka* (translated as ordinary shawls or blankets), they have long been a favored textile in Lakota Sioux households. Feest notes that "the predominant use of the *star* quilt or *sunburst* design may best be understood as a direct continuation of one of the earlier symbolic hide painting traditions."[4] Originally labeled *wichapi shina* (*star* robes), these quilts assumed distinctive values in Lakota life.

Female quilting groups formed and continued in the pattern of the older traditional porcupine quillwork societies; involvement in these societies fostered the recognition of women's contributions to the community. Women's groups also were fostered by missionaries to promote industriousness. Excelling in quiltmaking became a status symbol for many Lakota women as well as an important economic enterprise, and quilts began to function as both commodity and ceremonial object.[5] But the dispersal of these quilts seems less important than their economic and ritual roles in contemporary Lakota Sioux reservation life.

Seldom is a *star* quilt used as an ordinary bed covering in reservation homes; rather, *star* quilts are used in ways that distinguish their meaning and role within Lakota Sioux life. They are employed as door coverings for dwellings or shelters at ceremonial events and are worn by healers in the *yuwipi* (curing) ceremonies. More importantly, *star* quilts have long been a critical element in giveaways and, from birth to death, the life-cycle events of Sioux peoples.

Miniature *star* quilts often are made or obtained by members of a *tiospaye* (extended family, usually sister of the father) for a newborn child. As cradleboards and cradleboard coverings are nonfunctional in contemporary

times, a gift of a *star* quilt to a child is purely honorific, serving to recognize the child's entrance into the extended family. This practice, most often observed by "traditional" and/or full-blooded families, gives the item, called *alesza* (to urinate upon), added symbolic value. This gesture also validates the Lakota term for child: *wakan yesa* (a sacred being).

Interestingly, many paternal aunts (the father's sisters) give this gift whether the child is a result of a legal marriage or a consensual one; recognition of the child is the significant issue. Some children receive the gift of a *star* quilt later in childhood or at a naming ceremony, which may be in adolescence. At whatever age, the *star* quilt is a symbol of prestige, sentiment, and "belongingness." Some youths take their *star* quilts with them when they venture out of the community to search for work, recreation, or to attend college. This may represent an emotional tie to kin and community.

From the establishment of the reservations until very recently, every "proper" Lakota maiden was expected to have a hand-quilted *star* quilt in the household goods she took to her new home upon marriage. This custom may have declined due to the prevalence of consensual or "Indian" marriages and the waning of the "exchange" feature in contemporary marriages.

Today, *star* quilts are the most valued and prestigious items in the death customs of the Lakota. In prior times, the buffalo robe, painted with a *star* motif, was used to wrap the body of the deceased for scaffold burials. Now, a *star* quilt often is used to cover the coffin. Most families bury the quilt with the departed; some remove the quilt and give it, as recompense, to the religious practitioner who conducts the ceremony. Until recently, it was only given to a Christian

This remarkable photo records a
series of quilts draped over
horses in the July 4th, 1924,
parade in Fort Totten, North
Dakota.

minister; now it may also be given to the
individual conducting a traditional ceremony. Traditionally, the Lakota threw
beaded moccasins into the grave to assist
the departed on the Lakota steps to the
Milky Way—*Wanagi Omani*, or a Spirit
Road—and the entrance into the Land of
Deceased Relatives. For those who do not
have beaded moccasins, the *star* quilt now
serves this purpose. Some acculturated
Lakota have begun to substitute commercially made Pendleton blankets for the *star*
quilts, although quilts are preferred.

No matter how poor a Lakota family may
be, there is a concerted effort to obtain a
star quilt for funerary rites. Upon hearing of
a death in their family, many women of all
ages quickly gather to make the requisite
quilts. Working efficiently, they are able to
produce one in approximately four hours.
These may be hand quilted or simply "tied"
with yarn or thread. If the quilters are not
paid immediately in cash, they are compen

sated a year later during the memorial feast
by receiving gifts.

At the memorial feast *star* quilts reach
their apex in ceremony and prestige in many
of the Lakota Sioux and Dakota Sioux reservations. In this *Wanagi Yuhapi* ("keeping the
spirit" of the deceased), the *wasiglapi*
(affronted) keep a lock of hair of the deceased
for a year. During this time, the entire *tiospaye*
begins to make and collect items for the
release of the dead person's *nagi* (spirit) at
the memorial feast. This time of mourning is
also a time of industry for all. It is a time of
humility; a time to make by hand, if possible,
the necessary items. The number of *star* quilts
made often marks respect and love for the
deceased. They also add to the prestige of
the family. At the memorial feast, the quilts,
sometimes numbering fifty to a hundred, are
displayed in ceremonial structures called
boweries. During the course of the memorial feast, the quilts are given to the guests
of the family as thanks for their participation in the ceremony.

Star quilts also have entered the political arena, with gifting to politicians and elected tribal, state, and federal officials. An unforeseen act of possible reciprocity is enacted when a tribal group or tribal officials gives a *star* quilt to a political figure. The *Lakota Times* featured Senator Lawrence Pressler thanking a political *tiospaye* for receiving a *star* quilt: "Your beautiful quilt is one of our most cherished possessions."[6] Also pictured is Senator Tom Daschle, who held a "victory feed" at the Pine Ridge, Rosebud, and Cheyenne River reservations. At Rosebud, he was given a *star* quilt by the Vietnam Veterans' Association. This is the Sioux way of enmeshing politicians. Daschle is expected to reciprocate the gift in his subsequent legislative actions. When a bill is introduced in Congress to abrogate Indian treaties, tribal advocates should, perhaps, refer to this ultimate gift and expect proper decisions. But perhaps the Lakota metaphor of "giving to honor" is too subtle for the political arena.

In the important contemporary powwow circuit and in the recently proliferating Sun Dances, giving of *star* quilts has become an established component of ritual exchange, particularly in Sioux communities. Quilts are often given to the singers or drum groups as an means of thanking the musicians for excellent performances or for singing an honor song. Often, however, the singers may, in turn, offer these quilts for sale in order to obtain gas money to return home.[7]

The proliferation of *star* quilts as ceremonial items and their use in the honorific aspects of reservation and larger society events have led to an increased demand on quilters. The last twenty years also have seen an explosion of interest in quilts and quilting within non-Native communities and a corresponding interest by non-Natives in

*A*s *star* quilts have become increasingly more important to the ceremonial and ritual activities in contemporary Lakota Sioux and Dakota Sioux life, so has the influence of women in the maintenance of these traditions. As Patricia Albers observes at Fort Totten, a Dakota reservation:

> An area where women's influence had grown was in the social networks that organized and supported ceremonial activity on the reservation. Women were primarily responsible for building what the Dakota called "collections," that is, an accumulation of gifts to be distributed at these give-aways. . . . Most of these items were . . . reproduced directly by female labor, as in star quilts— one of the most prestigious goods in ceremonial exchanges.[8] [Others were] purchased through female incomes. Since women made most of the contributions to give-aways, it was their prerogative to decide to whom gifts would be given in the social networks that linked the Dakota at Devil's Lake to Indian people from neighboring communities in Canada and the United States. Through this activity a number of women gained considerable prestige and renown not only at Devil's Lake but on other reservations as well.[9]

This status has resulted in the saying often heard at social gatherings: "Women are the carriers of culture."

Buffalo Skull Star Quilt, c. 1993

Maker unknown (Sioux), Rapid City, South Dakota. 68.5 x 70.5 inches. Collection of Michigan State University Museum

The buffalo skull is a prominent image in this Sioux star quilt. White Buffalo star quilts, in tribute to the rare and sacred white buffalo, have also become popular in recent years.

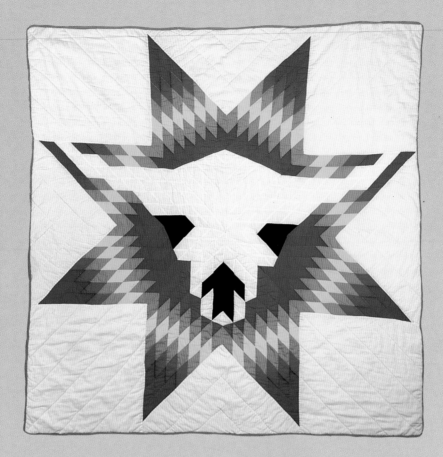

Eagle Head Star Quilt, c. 1993

Maker unknown (Sioux), Rapid City, South Dakota. 72.75 x 85 inches. Collection of Michigan State University Museum

This star quilt depicts an eagle head surrounded by eight tipis. The eagle is among the most popular images incorporated into Sioux quilts.

acquiring Sioux quilts. This has enabled some Sioux quilters to substantially augment their household income through sales of quilts both to other Sioux and to outside audiences.

This burgeoning demand also have fostered the establishment of economic organizations on reservations to help supply quilts needed for ceremonial uses and also to provide a means of income. As early as 1983, a cottage quiltmaking industry was founded on the Cheyenne Reservation. The *Lakota Times* reported:

> This organization was a dream of two women, Marcia O'Leary and Deleen Kougl, a dream come true. The business provides opportunities for many women from the reservation to use not only their talents but to also incorporate years of tradition and heritage into present day use through designing and creating hand-quilted star quilts and other hand-made products.[10]

Another quilt business, founded in 1985 on the Sisseton-Wahpeton Reservation by a church-based economic grant program, specialized in decorator pillows.[11] Meanwhile, at one of the border towns adjacent to the reservations, a factory has been recently established to manufacture "Dakota quilts." Unfortunately, the factory does not employ any Indians and is simply trying to capitalize on the growing popularity of *star* quilts in the marketplace.[12]

Though quiltmaking activities have been initiated for economic development on many Lakota Sioux and Dakota Sioux reservations, many of these endeavors have relied primarily upon outside funding and they have not had a great economic impact on the lives of women. It remains to be seen if the market will sustain these new cottage craft industries. The majority of tourists in the Black Hills near Sioux reservations are interested only in buying Indian trinkets—tomahawks, beaded belts, and headbands made in Hong Kong—and are not willing to purchase the higher priced yet authentic locally handmade quilts and other crafts. However, the adaptations of the *star* motifs to lower priced items such as sofa pillows, baby buntings, purses, and carrying bags seem more marketable. Within the context of the community, though, the making and giving of quilts have had a great impact on traditional systems of economy and prestige.

The Hawaiian Quilt

Research Project

by Elaine Zinn

The Hawaiian Quilt

Among the many types of quilts made in Hawaii, those done in the appliquéd whole cloth style, referred to simply as Hawaiian quilts, are the best known and, in recent years, have become almost worldwide symbols of Hawaii. Their dynamic, bold designs bring forth images of exotic flowers or plants growing in tropical rain forests. They also serve as visual records of Hawaii's places, events, and people, primarily the royal Hawaiian families.

The designs, construction techniques, and colors of Hawaiian appliquéd quilts are unlike those used in the majority of American quilts. Designs are cut from one piece of fabric that is folded in eighths. Generally, two colors of cloth are used, one for the appliquéd design and a contrasting value or hue for the background. Row after row of quilting stitches echo out from the appliquéd design like gentle ocean waves.

Hawaiian quilts are a unique blend of two diverse cultural traditions: American quilt-making and the ancient Hawaiian art of making *kapa* (cloth made from the inner bark of mulberry and other native trees). For years kapa was the primary cloth used for a wide variety of purposes. Cottons and other materials, along with new traditions of clothing and bed covers, were introduced to Hawaiians by Europeans and Americans. The earliest record of the teaching of sewing skills to Hawaiian women is dated April 20, 1820, and reports of an exchange aboard a sailing ship bringing the first New England missionaries to the Hawaiian Islands. Some researchers now believe the Hawaiian women were taught sewing and perhaps quilting skills at an even earlier date by wives of sea captains who stopped in Hawaii during their voyages across the vast Pacific Ocean.

A resurgence in Hawaiian quilting began in the late 1970s along with the explorations

Kapa Pohopoho (Scrap Quilt), 1997

Made by members of Ka Hui Kapu Apana O Waimea, Waimea, Hawaii. 70 x 70 inches. Collection of Michigan State University Museum

and interests in other traditional Hawaiian arts, such as the *hula* (dance), kapa making, wood carving, and feather work. As increasing numbers of people from around the world traveled to the islands during the 1980s, a global interest in Hawaii and Hawaiian quilting grew. Hawaiian quilters shared their quilting art with students enrolled in classes throughout the Pacific, Asia, America, and Europe. On the islands, quilting was taught at city and county parks and in recreation programs, museums, hotels, and churches.

In 1985, Mealii Namahoe Richardson Kalama, well-known Hawaiian quilter and quilting teacher, was awarded a National Heritage Fellowship by the National Endowment for the Arts, Folk Arts Program. At about that same time, Hawaii Craftsmen, an organization of island artists, produced the film *The Hawaiian Quilt—A Cherished Tradition*, featuring Mealii Kalama and other Hawaiian quilters. The film premiered in

New York City in 1986 at the first Great American Quilt Festival sponsored by the Museum of American Folk Art. The premiere was attended by an entourage of Hawaiian quilters led by the First Lady of Hawaii, Jean Ariyoshi. A very precious quilt, believed to be a gift to the last reigning monarch of Hawaii, Queen Lili'uokalani, was one of seventeen Hawaiian quilts in a special exhibit at the festival. Hawaii and corporate sponsor GTE also hosted an evening event during the festival complete with a luau, Hawaiian music, and hula.

In 1988, KawaiaHa'o Church in Honolulu opened its meeting hall for an exhibition of forty-five Hawaiian quilts and demonstrations by more than a dozen quilting instructors, an event sponsored by the Kalihi-Palama Culture and Arts Society, Inc. (KPCAS). In 1990, Kokusai Art of Japan hosted an exhibition in Japan of fifty of the finest Hawaiian quilts from Hawaii's museums and from individual contemporary quilters.

Lynn Waihe'e, Hawaii's
former First Lady, and Mealii
Kalama view "**Lili'uokalani's
Fans and Kahili**", the first quilt
documented by HQRP c. 1990.
Mrs. Waihe'e served as honorary chair of the HQRP from
1990 to 1994.

Hawaiian quilting at her mother's knee, shared their excitement. With the KPCAS Board of Directors' approval, the Hawaiian Quilt Research Project (HQRP) to document the islands' remarkable style of quilting was under way.

Akana and this author soon invited others to join: Lee Wild and Peggie Ehlke of the Mission Houses Museum; Gussie Bento, coordinator of the Kamehameha Schools; Bernice Pauahi Bishop Heritage Center; and Laurie Woodard, museum collections manager of the Friends of Waipahu Cultural Gardens Park. The group set seven objectives for the project:

1. To research and record the history, designs, and traditions of Hawaiian quilts and *Hawaiian flag* quilts created before Hawaii's statehood in August 1959;

2. To research and record the history and traditions of Hawaii's quiltmakers;

3. To research and record the patterns, layouts, and styles of Hawaiian appliquéd quilts and *Hawaiian flag* quilts;

4. To foster conservation, preservation and the maintenance of the tradition of Hawaii's unique quilt heritage;

5. To increase public awareness and appreciation of Hawaiian quilts;

6. To encourage the art of Hawaiian quiltmaking; and

7. To engage in education about Hawaiian quilts and quilting through exhibits, lectures, and other activities.

After several months of viewing forms and reports of several state documentation projects, the group adapted the guidelines and documentation forms of the California Quilt Heritage Project.

History of the Hawaiian Quilt Research Project

*A*lthough the quilts themselves are documents of Hawaiian history, there is no recorded history about the origin of the Hawaiian-style quilts and their traditional designs. By systematically recording the history of quilts found in private and public collections, Elizabeth A. Akana and this author hoped to find links to the origin of the Hawaiian quilt and its designs, as well as information relating to family quiltmaking traditions. Not long after the KawaiaHa'o quilt show, the two presented their vision of a Hawaiian quilt documentation project to KPCAS Executive Director Wendell Silva. Silva, who is part Hawaiian and whose own mother learned

Quilt Days

*B*y 1990, the HQRP was ready to hold its first Quilt Day. Modeled after similar ones orga-

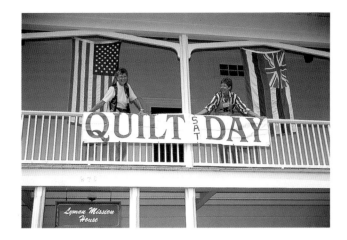

A typical Quilt Day for the Hawaiian Quilt Research Project (c. 1990) begins with hanging the banner. Next, volunteer Harriet Yamaguchi checks for seams in the fabric of a quilt before measuring, and the photographer prepares to document a Hawaiian flag quilt. Using a small textile magnifying glass, volunteer Sue Chang counts stitches to record information on HQRP data forms, completed by volunteers who examine and record the necessary documentation.

nized by other states, the Hawaiian Quilt Day was designed as an opportunity for quilters and quilt owners in a community to bring in their quilts to be documented. The HQRP's steering committee spent many hours forming committees, training volunteers, and securing, mostly through donation, the supplies and materials needed. Lynn Waihe'e, Hawaii's first lady, graciously agreed to serve as honorary chair of the HQRP.

It was fitting that HQRP's inaugural Quilt Day, August 11, 1990, was held in conjunction with the Honolulu Academy of Arts' showcase of Kokusai Art's Hawaiian quilt exhibition upon its return from Japan. The first three quilts documented that day came from the collection at Washington Place, the official residence of Hawaii's governor and his family. The first two were identical designs, *Lili'uokalani's Fans and Kahili*, and the third, created by Mealii Kalama, was *Crown Flower*, inspired by the favorite flower of Hawaii's last reigning monarch, Queen Lili'uokalani.

People came from many parts of the island—including three generations of one family—with one, two, three, and sometimes even four quilts. Each quilt was carefully photographed by the official HQRP photographer, Albert K. Y. Chang. Textile specialists from the University of Hawaii and the Pacific Regional Conservation Center at the Bishop Museum and other volunteers formed teams of three to examine each quilt and record information, including multiple measurements, fiber content of each fabric (including the batting), condition, and number of quilting stitches per inch. In addition, volunteers interviewed quilt owners about the history of the quilts and their makers.

Quilt Day activities included an opportunity for people to view and trace Hawaiian quilt patterns loaned to the project and to "talk story" (a Hawaiian phrase for sharing or telling stories) with Hawaiian quilters who were demonstrating the art of appliqué or quilting. Attendees were given information about the tradition and history of Hawaiian quiltmaking and about how to care for and store their quilts.

At the close of the first Quilt Day, the HQRP had documented forty-two quilts: thirty Hawaiian-style appliquéd quilts, six *Hawaiian flag* quilts, five outline embroidered quilts, and one piece of kapa. In addition, a new cadre of volunteers was born. For instance, several members of the Pearl Harbor Hawaiian Civic Club who brought quilts had "adopted" the event as a service project by the time the next Quilt Day was held on O'ahu. Subsequently, they organized a new Hawaiian Civic Club at Kapolei and have continued to assist with each Quilt Day.

Between August 1990 and May 1996, the HQRP documented quilts at twenty-six Quilt Days, plus quilt collections at almost all island museums and historical societies and family quilt collections. The HQRP also coordinated two Hawaiian Quilt Festivals to inform the public about the project. The first, a one-day "minifestival" in 1995, was held at the Honolulu Academy of Arts' Linekona Arts Center. Approximately nine hundred people attended the free programs, which included lectures and demonstrations, an exhibit of contemporary quilts by Stan Yates and Elizabeth Akana, pattern tracing, and a display of the new HQRP photo panels. The twelve panels, designed by Peggie Ehlke, illustrate the purpose and activities of the project and are displayed at Quilt Days and at other quilt-related events.

In 1996, a second Hawaiian Quilt Festival was held at the Neal S. Blaisdell Center. This time, admission fees helped raise operating funds for the HQRP. Some eighteen hundred people attended the two-day event, which included an exhibit of forty Hawaiian quilts, quilting workshops, a merchant's mall, lectures, demonstrations, a pattern tracing, fashion show, and a silent auction.

Computerizing the Data   Data collected on each Hawaiian-style appliquéd and *Hawaiian flag* quilt registered in the project have been entered into a custom-made program containing 205 data fields for each quilt. Forty-three fields hold data on the quiltmaker and her family gathered by oral interview; 162 fields are dedicated to data on the quilt, including general description, measurement, condition, materials, construction, and binding. *Hawaiian flag* quilts have additional fields for data unique to that type of quilt.

Color slides of documented quilts are being placed on CD-ROM disks, and plans to add black-and-white photographs of quilt patterns are under way. At this time, there are no plans to add images of the quilters.

Pattern Documentation   Before the HQRP started there were few public collections of patterns. One of the largest existing collections was developed by Helen Gascon, a home economist with the University of Hawaii Cooperative Extension Service, who taught ethnic cooking and Hawaiian-style appliqué quilting to women whose husbands were stationed at military bases during the 1960s and 1970s. Most of her students completed at least one quilt before their "tour of duty" was over.

When she first taught quilting classes, Gascon had only one pattern. She sought more and received a windfall in the form of a trunkful of patterns from a woman moving to Florida. Friends also donated patterns. Gascon gave copies to the Wai'anae Library on O'ahu, where the collection now totals more than three hundred patterns and is available for tracing by the public, as well as by those researching pattern origin, variety, distribution, and ownership.

As part of the registration process, HQRP volunteers began making tracings of quilt patterns, a time-consuming process. After tracing some one hundred patterns, and realizing that they couldn't provide adequate archival storage for the tracings, the volunteers switched to photographing the patterns. From there, images will be scanned into a computer database.

Findings to Date   As of November 1996, the 902 quilts in the HQRP database included 754 Hawaiian-style appliquéd quilts, 97 *Hawaiian flag* quilts, 35 outline embroidered quilts, and 16 pieced quilts. Though the HQRP plans a thorough analysis of the data in 1998 and 1999, there have already been some interesting findings.

The first surprise was the existence in Hawaii of whole cloth quilts with designs worked primarily in red outline embroidery stitches. Embroidered with Hawaiian flowers and other motifs, the quilts appeared at the first Quilt Day and at several held since. Already a grant received from the Quilter's Guild of Dallas has enabled HQRP to conduct more in-depth research on this quilt type.

Originally, the HQRP did not intend to register patchwork quilts, but when owners bring pieced quilts along with Hawaiian-style quilts by the same maker, they are also recorded. Preliminary assessment indicates that pieced quilts often were made and used

This **Hawaiian Flag Quilt**
(*early 1900s, 69 x 83 inches*)
*was made for Margaret
Ferguson, whose daughter,
Llewellyn Gray Owens, donated
it to the collection of the
Daughters of Hawaii. The date,
quiltmaker, and place where the
quilt was made are all
unknown.*

by families as utilitarian quilts while the Hawaiian appliquéd quilts were stored away to be displayed on special occasions.

Names of people written on the quilt patterns may provide clues to the creator of the pattern or the person who shared that pattern from her collection. After photographing six hundred quilt patterns, HQRP staff noted that certain designs appeared in more than one collection and on more than one island. This indicates that, contrary to the belief by some, patterns were widely shared.

Many quilt owners registering their quilts do not know the name of the design, the maker of the quilt, and/or when the quilt was made. Quilt owners also have names for their quilts that are quite different from quilts with similar designs registered by the HQRP, in Hawaiian quilting books, or in the pattern collection at the Wai'anae Library. Despite the efforts of the knowledgeable project personnel, approximately half of the quilt designs in the database remain "unknown."

The value of the Hawaiian Quilt Research Project was brought home to many residents on Kaua'i in the aftermath of Hurricane 'Iniki on September 11, 1992. The hurricane's violent wind, rain, and mud whipped through the island, damaging thousands of homes and cherished possessions, including Hawaiian quilts. Some island families, realizing how precious their quilts were, donated them for future safekeeping to the Kaua'i Museum, which suffered only minor structural damage during the storm. Those whose quilts were lost or damaged relied upon the HQRP records to help verify their insurance claims.

This graphics database will greatly facilitate research. Pattern names can be analyzed by looking at quilts with similar designs but different names or by categorizing the names themselves, such as those signifying royal emblems and places or plants, winds, or rains associated with particular locations. Quilt dating may be possible by documenting changes in design layouts or in patterns of quilting over time. Particular pattern designs may be identified with different islands or areas where certain quiltmakers developed their own design or quilting style.

Future of the Hawaiian Quilt Research Project As these preliminary assessments indicate, much of the history of Hawaii's quilting legacy has been lost. Yet much can be pieced together from further analysis of the oral, written, and graphic data gathered on the quiltmakers and the quilts. The HQRP Board of Directors has set short- and long-term goals to be reached by the year 2000. When the database reaches a thousand quilts, the HQRP will begin an extensive review of the collected data. Plans include a forum, led by a quilt scholar, to involve Hawaii's scholars in the fields of anthropology, folk culture, and history in the analysis and interpretation of the data. At the conclusion of this process, HQRP hopes to produce a book and a quilt exhibition. With more quilts yet to be documented and new volunteers to be trained, the project will undoubtedly continue into the twenty-first century.

Part III
Strengthening Community

$\mathcal{S}$tars of Honor:
The Basketball Star
Quilt Ceremony

by C. Kurt Dewhurst and Marsha L. MacDowell

The quilt ceremony is about honoring people . . .

in this manner, they show support for a loved one. They bring

their most highly prized possessions to the giveaway. Translated

from the past to the present Native American culture, giveaways

reflect the depth of family pride exhibited toward their family

members. When you are honored, you know you are held in

high esteem by the family.— Spike Big Horn[1]

One of the most distinctive uses of quilts in Native communities occurs as part of the annual high school boys' and girls' basketball tournaments in Montana,[2] when *star* quilts are given away by team members from high schools on the Fort Peck Reservation to individuals who, in some way, have contributed to the basketball season. These have become important occasions not only for the athletes and their families but also for the entire community. The basketball tournament *star* quilt ceremony is a public statement of tribal heritage that reinforces the tradition of honoring respected and loved individuals.[3] As witnesses to the ceremonies and frequent recipients of the quilts, non-Natives participate in an event that increases their awareness and understanding of those values and beliefs.

In the northeast corner of Montana's Big Sky country lies Fort Peck Reservation, home to six thousand of the ten thousand enrolled members of the Assiniboine and Sioux tribes. Each tribe is composed of various bands: the Sioux include Sisseton/Wahpetons, the Yanktonais, and the Teton Hunkpapas; the Assiniboine bands include the Canoe Paddler and Red Bottom.[4] Both tribes have a long history of cooperative coexistence and unity in the face of encroaching non-Native settlement in the region.

In 1871, the Fort Peck Indian Agency was formed to serve Native peoples living in this region, with government boarding school programs initiated in 1877. The reservation's first missionary schools were established by the Presbyterians and the Mormons in the early twentieth century.

According to many oral and written accounts, it was at these schools that quilting was first introduced to Native women. Although many patterns were learned, the *star* has become perhaps the most popular. Anthropologist Nancy Tucker identifies the pattern as arriving at the Fort Peck Reservation through contact with the Dakota Presbytery missions. She reports how Nellie Clark "recalled bringing a *star* quilt back from a Presbyterian school she attended in South Dakota in about 1908," and one Lorena Sheilds "remembers her mother, Louise Red Lightning, working on *star* quilts with the Dakota Presbytery women at Fort Peck between 1915 and 1920."[5] Catherine Spotted Bird gives yet another account: "The late Nina First of Fort Kipp, Montana, went to a church mission meeting in South Dakota in the 1920s . . . [where she] saw the *star* quilt for the first time and brought it back."[6]

Star quilts, sometimes also called *morning star* quilts or *star* blankets, have become a central feature of numerous giveaway ceremonies in the community and hold special meaning for both those who make them and those who receive them as gifts. *Star* quilts are made to honor military veterans, dignitaries, and for giveaways at powwows, baby-naming ceremonies, and funeral ceremonies, where they are draped over the casket before being given to officiating clergy and pallbearers. Quilts are also used to honor individuals who have demonstrated achievements in academic or athletic pursuits.

The *star* quilt itself has become a popular symbol of Sioux and Assiniboine identity. *Star* quilt designs now appear on powwow posters, as part of dance regalia, and even on T-shirts and baseball caps. But on the Fort Peck Reservation, it is the *star* quilt's link to the long-standing tradition of honoring ceremonies that is most significant.

Basketball Star Quilt, 1996

Made by Rae Jean Walking Eagle (Assiniboine/Sioux), Brockton, Montana. 77.5 x 87 inches. Collection of Michigan State University Museum

Nearly all quilts made for the high school basketball star quilt ceremonies in northern Montana are done in variations of the star pattern, often incorporating a pieced or appliquéd basketball. This quilt is made of satin, a material popular on the Fort Peck Reservation.

Top left: Family members often work right up to the last minute to complete quilts for the honoring ceremony at the district basketball tournament in 1996. Here, Kurt Dewhurst interviews Judy and Ben Johnson as they work on quilts made for their son Terrence.

Top right: Shortly before the ceremony commences, team members and their families gather to view quilts, to make final decisions about recipients, and to organize the procession. In this photo, Golden Walking Eagle shows off the star quilt he will use to honor a member of one of the opposing teams.

Above: Star quilts are carefully spread on the gymnasium floor as the honoring ceremony begins.

Above: Recipients of a quilt in honor of their son embrace quilter Judy Johnson. Star quilts are placed around the shoulders of the receiver.

The Origin of a Tradition

The basketball *star* quilt ceremony sprung from an act of honoring at a 1947, Brocton, Montana, basketball game. Tessie Four Times, grandmother of one of the players, expressed her pride in her grandson by wiping the sweat from his back with a shawl and then casting the shawl on the floor for anyone to pick up. This act can be traced to a Native custom of honoring those in battle.[7]

Years later, during discussions at a Red Eagle Presbyterian Ladies' Aid Society meeting in early 1964, it was suggested to again honor Brockton players in this way. Along with other women in the community, the group began making *star* quilts in preparation for a giveaway at an upcoming game. In February 1964, during the halftime of the last game of the Class 2-C District Basketball Tournament in Sidney, Montana, members of the Brockton team carried those *star* quilts into the gym and spread them on the floor. Then each team member gave a quilt to the coaches from each school participating in the tournament, as well as to other honored individuals. Every year since, the ceremony has been repeated at the district level tournaments and, when teams advanced in tournament play, also at the divisional and state levels. As each ceremony requires the production of new quilts, almost every member of the community has become involved in one way or another.

The importance of *star* quilts is evident on a year-round basis at Brockton High School, where Native language instructor Viola Spotted Bird teaches a quiltmaking class for students and teachers. *Star* quilts hang on the gymnasium walls along with plaques listing the honorees. Athletic team booster clubs raise funds by selling lapel pins of team members photographed in front of *star* quilts. The school yearbook, *Ho-Tanka*, or *Big Voice*, carries a feature on the tournaments and ceremonies.

The 1996 Basketball Tournament Quilt Ceremony *R*egardless of the number of wins or losses during regular season games, every Montana high school boys' team plays in the season-end state tournament. In 1996, the boys' basketball team at Brockton High School, although ending the season with more losses than wins, prepared for its upcoming play-off games while family and friends prepared for the quilt ceremony by beginning to make or commission *star* quilts. Each team member presents at least one quilt to someone he chooses to honor for his sportsmanship, character, or some special act that deserves recognition. Team members keep the name of each person they want to honor to themselves until the ceremony, some-

times finalizing their decision only moments before the event.

During the week immediately before the game, Brockton High School teachers Paul Westberg and Kathy Nielsen oversee the Star Quilt Extravaganza, in which all the students create a *star* quilt design on paper. Designs are posted on a classroom wall and votes are cast for the most innovative or beautiful designs.

On game day, the Brockton team arrives at Sidney High School wearing warbonnets, as is the tradition for tournament games. Although the game ends in their defeat, they quickly turn their attention toward the following evening's *star* quilt ceremony.

The night of the event, Leland Spotted Bird, the master of ceremonies, joins the group to supervise the order of the procession and carefully record the names of the parents, player, and honoree. When the last game before the championship game has only five minutes left, the group starts toward the gymnasium. Flanked by parents, elders, and other family members and holding quilts over folded arms, team members form a processional line, with team captains first, followed by players in order of seniority, and then cheerleaders and managers.

Each family spreads its *star* quilt out on the floor in front of them. With more than twenty spectacular quilts, the gym is soon transformed into a visual display. Spotted Bird explains that the quilts cannot be presented directly to a player because the state high school amateur athletics rules do not allow athletes to accept gifts worth more than $15. However, the quilt can be given to the parents of the player to be honored, which also honors them for their parenting role.

Spotted Bird then announces the honorees, and when the final quilt is presented, a recording of an honor song is played. As

Made by Sybil Lambert (Sioux), Brockton, Montana. 85.5 x 71.5 inches. Collection of Michigan State University Museum

he describes the meaning of the song for the crowd, the Brockton team, their parents, and honorees join hands and circle the floor in an honor dance.

Conclusion   The tradition of holding basketball tournament *star* quilt ceremonies has now spread to all three Fort Peck Reservation high schools, all of whom play in leagues that are primarily non-Native. The much-anticipated events attract sellout crowds filled with the parents and families of players as well as community members.

Through this ceremony, Sioux and Assiniboine have found a creative way to carry on a decades-old tradition. As old buffalo robes have been replaced by beautiful *star* quilts filled with love, comfort, and respect for those they honor, the basketball court has become a contemporary stage for an honoring ceremony that respects the coming of age, the passage of life, and the timelessness of Native values.

$\mathcal{H}$ow Yupik Women Spoil Their Cloth: The Seal Party Quilts of the Nelson Island Eskimos

by Ann Fienup-Riordan

Nelson Island sits six hundred miles west of Anchorage, on the Bering Sea coast of Alaska. Today, close to two thousand Yupik Eskimos make their homes there, divided among five villages ranging in size from two to six hundred people. Each community supports a cash economy, and families have access to many aspects of Western technology, including television, snowmobiles, telephones, electricity, and, in some cases, running water. In many ways, though, these men and women still live a subsistence life comparable to that of their forebears. A primary occupation of Yupik men is fishing and sea mammal hunting, and women devote weeks to processing the catch. Yupik dancing and traditional ritual distributions remain important parts of community life. Although most young and middle-aged community members are bilingual, Yupik continues to

be a child's first language and is the primary language of village residents over fifty.

Imagine a "typical" Eskimo family—peaceful hunter, wife, and child surviving on their own in an inhospitable homeland. This well-known stereotype, however, originated in the Central Canadian Arctic and does not apply to the Yupik Eskimos of Alaska, who are anything but typical. Far from merely surviving, their environment provides them with a wealth of resources, including seals, walrus, belugha whales, both oceangoing and fresh-water fish, waterfowl, small mammals, moose, musk oxen, bears, berries, and greens. Although the low-lying coastal plain is treeless, every spring the rivers wash down an abundance of driftwood that the people traditionally used to build semisub-terranean sod houses and elaborate ceremonial paraphernalia. Yupik families do not live in isolated igloos. Rather, during the

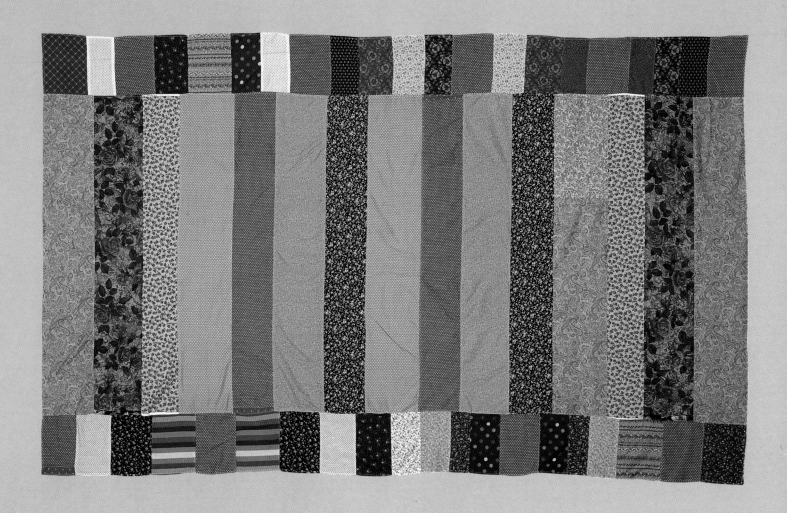

Nelson Island "seal parties" are held in connection with annual seal harvests. Strips of fabric, distributed to community members, are then used to make quilts and quilt tops, which are given out during the winter dances held later in the year. This quilt top (60.5 x 100 inches) by Martina Lawrence was made from fabric distributed in 1996. Collection of Michigan State University Museum

winter ceremonial season people gather into communities running as large as three to four hundred residents.

I asked a Yupik friend, Julia Nevak, to tell me what I should say about the colorful quilts found today in every home on Nelson Island. She smiled and said, "Tell them how Yup'ik women spoil their cloth!" I smiled back, remembering the first seal party I'd seen so many years ago and how surprised I was to see women tearing up whole bolts of cloth and throwing the pieces into the air as gifts to their neighbors. Even before I saw the colorful quilts they made from these strips, I was a convert.

I first came to the village of Toksook Bay on Nelson Island in May 1974, sent out from Anchorage to help with an economic development project. I soon found that the pottery project I had come to help with was in disarray. The people I spoke with, however, told me not to despair, that I had come at the best time of the year, that the seal parties were about to begin.

I'd never read about seal parties nor even heard of them. As I soon learned, seal parties were given when the men and boys of the village brought home their first bearded seals of the season. The festivities were full of excitement and lots of fun, as not only was the meat and blubber of every man's first-caught seal given away, but lots of other things were given away as well.

They began the next day—three parties in a row. I was just up and having a cup of tea when a little girl came to the door and said to come quick. There, right next door, a woman was standing on her porch throwing diapers and packs of gum into the waiting hands of a large group of women. She also threw strips of cotton cloth, which were carried by the wind in every direction. I joined the fun and followed the group to the next house for a repetition of the event, noticing that not all the same women attended and new women joined the group. I asked about this later and was told that when a woman gives her seal party, her relatives could not attend; only nonrelatives received the gift of meat.

At the turn of the century, seal parties, or *uqiquq* (from *uqur*, which means oil or fat, literally "one that is provided with oil"), were standard practice all along the Bering Sea coast of southwestern Alaska, and they are still common in many coastal communities today. With the introduction of trade goods in the early 1900s, crackers and a teaspoonful of tea were added to the distribution, growing to the elaborate disbursements of store goods that accompany the gift of seal meat on Nelson Island today.

The island women do not remember a time when they did not include strips of cloth in their seal parties. Cotton drilling and calicos were popular materials at the Tununak trading post from the 1800s on. In the 1940s, a woman could get twenty-five cents for a handwoven grass basket, enough to buy a yard of cloth. Women from fish camps on the southern side of the island would walk twenty miles over the mountains and back to attend Mass in the Tununak church, bringing their baskets with them and taking home cloth, tea, and matches in return.

In preparation for a seal party on Nelson Island today, the seal is brought inside the house, placed on big pieces of cardboard on the floor, and cut across the stomach right down to the meat. The skin is removed together with the fat, and the fat is cut into strips two feet long and four inches wide, bordered on one side by a thick piece of skin. The women then cut the meat into pieces to pair with the fat.

After the seal is divided, the store-bought goods are also cut up, cloth strips are torn, string is cut, boxes of cookies and tea are opened, and packs of gum are undone. Then the party begins. Katie Moses described the seal party as she remembered it when she was little:

> I'd run to invite ladies. All excited, they would jump and leave whatever they were doing, even hot tea. The seal party comes first. With good hunting they are continuous day after day. It is a belief that women celebrate the first mukluk [bearded seal] of the spring so their husbands and sons who catch their first seal will gain as successful hunters. It symbolizes the sharing of thankfulness. During the springtime, the village comes alive with living sounds. The bright sun beats down, reflecting on the white snow, blinding the people at the same time and tanning anybody who is enjoying the springtime. Rushing to the house where the husband caught a mukluk, you would think that the women are racing on the Fourth of July. Usually the women want to get the best position.[1]

The women gather outside the hostess's home. Everyone has either an enamel pan or a plastic or tin bucket, which they place at the porch entrance. The goods to be distributed come originally from the outside, the male domain, and enter the inside, the

Women reaching for cloth thrown during a Toksook Bay seal party, 1977.

female domain, for preparation. Their distribution both extends and redefines relationships within the village, between men and women and between families, as raw seal meat (the new, harvested food) and canned tuna (the prepared, processed food) are temporarily juxtaposed and then one after the other thrown into the air.

When everyone is gathered, the porch door opens and the hostess begins to throw hunks of blubber into each bucket. The blubber is followed by the distribution of large chunks of meat, one piece for everyone, with the better parts as well as the leftovers given to older women. While men are excluded from the seal party, small children gather round hoping for edible tidbits. Later in the day, girls will play at diminutive seal partying, with shreds of cloth, bits of cracker, and pieces of rock.

Following the seal come pieces of salmon soaked in seal oil, dried fish, squares of sealskin leather, pieces of string or colored yarn measuring about five inches long (these will be tied to fish hooks as bait), *giluq* (strips of dried seal gut, twenty of which can be sewn together to make a waterproof rain parka), and strips of cotton cloth, as long as the width of a bolt and about six or seven inches wide.

But that is not all. Following these staples come, in no apparent order, candy and cigarettes, candy cigarettes, plastic beads, an occasional Frisbee, disposable diapers, needles, gum, bars of soap, apples, more strips of cloth, toilet paper, and Mexican hats. Soap powder and loose tea also are scooped from big boxes and given to the waiting women, who neatly hold out the hem of their loose-fitting cotton dresses, pour in the powder or tea leaves, gather them into a knot and tie it tight with one of the pieces of string. There is laughter and mounting confusion as the giveaway gets

going. Of everything given there is always too much, and the hostess throws the extra in the air in a random direction. Things keep hitting people in the head. I talked to one girl who had just given her first seal party. She said that the oldest women had advised her to close her eyes while the women tried to attract her attention with their "Me! Me!" gestures. Women snap things up quickly and pop them into the large front pockets of their dresses with a wonderful grace. When there is nothing left to throw, each woman picks up her bucket and walks home.

The seal party offered a wonderful window into how the women of Nelson Island still thought about and acted on their concept of what it means to be related. Even more exciting, I found the seal party not an isolated relic of traditional culture but rather part of an annual cycle of ritual distribution. Its immediate counterpart on Nelson Island is the men's and women's exchange dance (*kevgiruaq*), in which men and women are said to "fight through the dance."

On the first night of the exchange dance, all the women in the village pair up as married couples, one woman taking the part of the husband and the other the part of the wife. Then, together, the women dance a multitude of gifts into the community hall and on the following morning give them out to the men of the village. The men perform for the women on the following evening, and the next morning the women receive their gifts in turn. The entire sequence of dances and gift-giving takes hours and hours, as everyone in the community has a turn on the dance floor. The particular dance performed is always the same, but each couple vies with the others to make its rendition particularly hilarious.

Even if one knows nothing about Yup'ik cultural configurations, the exchange dance is still a splendid and exuberant performance to behold. Seen in the light of the seal party, its eloquence is apparent. Whereas in the seal party gifts are thrown out the doors of individual houses, in the exchange dance gifts are danced in the door of the community hall. In the seal party, these gifts consist of strips of cloth and bits of string and bits and pieces of every conceivable household commodity. In the exchange dance, whole cloth and full skeins of yarn are given. In fact, many of the goods distributed during the midwinter dance contain, in abundance, the stuff of seal party gifts. Even the order in which the goods are given replicates the order of the seal party distributions. Nelson Islanders recognize this parallel, with some younger women voicing how this was one of the important things about dancing: "We get what we need for the spring, which is soon!"

After the dance, when the servers have finished the initial distribution of gifts of obviously equal value, such as twenty one-pound cans of Crisco, the floor is opened to choice. Each woman, going from eldest to youngest, has her pick of what remains. The first things chosen are the long, colorful pieces of cloth, from six to twenty feet in length and stretched out by the servers, as they were by the dancers when they were presented, so that everyone can admire their length and pattern.

As many goods leave the store and begin the cycle of reciprocity at the winter dance, others end their journey. Among the most valued are the quilts and bedspreads made of strips of cloth from seal parties gone by. Parents give these *ulit* (blankets) in the name of their children, and they are specifically directed to elders or honored guests.

The strips of cloth given at the seal party are a miniature of the bolt of cloth spread out for display during the dance, in a part-for-whole relation to it. The patchwork quilt that

reappears during the succeeding dance distribution is a qualitative transformation of the bolt. In the same way, the gut parkas worn by ocean hunters and by the shaman during spiritual hunting trips are constructed from strips of dried gut distributed in the seal

Women distributing seal meat during a seal party at Tununak on Nelson Island, 1980.

Boys presenting gifts at the exchange dance, including a folded **Seal Party Quilt**, Nelson Island, c. 1980.

parties. What is introduced into the exchange system—bolts of cloth, rolls of gut—during the winter dancing will be taken apart, cut, and distributed for the spring seal party. Alternately, the articles that exit from the cycle during the winter distribution—such as quilts and rain parkas—are a fabrication from seal and seal party parts. Here seasonal and ritual cyclings are equated with movement between taking apart (cutting and tearing) and fabrication.

A woman routinely tears the length of cloth that she receives in the midwinter exchange dance into strips for her spring seal party distribution. With the strips of cloth that she herself has collected from the various seal parties, she fabricates a simple pieced cover to give away during the next year's exchange dance. If all that was required was a cover for the bed, the Yupik people have certainly taken a circuitous route to ensure its provision. Their worldview, their whole cultural mode of being, has been put on stage along with the dancers, acted out, and so reestablished and reaffirmed. Instead

of a moral on the order of "never the twain shall meet," the Yupik celebrations seem to imply that that which is separated (socially, physically, and, as we shall see, metaphysically) will in the end be reunited.

Although village elders are given the preferred position and choicest gifts in both the seal party and exchange dance distributions, the result is honor without wealth. The older women redistribute the gifts they receive within their families. Cloth and diapers go to their daughters and daughters-in-law (and ultimately to their grandchildren), and candy goes directly to the children.

Age is doubly honored. The older matrons are given as their due that which they will dispense with the magnanimity appropriate to their years. Thus, a social as well as biological and historical cycling is apparent. The goods exchanged between the women of different families are used to delineate the hierarchy of sharing among the women of each individual family. But the goods do not stop here. With circularity appropriate in a culture caught up in cycling, the seal party guests are given gifts not to be used in the recipients' own seal parties but redistributed in a different form through the winter gift-giving. Cloth given to the older women in the seal party thus reemerges as a quilt in the midwinter dance, sewn together to celebrate the grandchildren. The goods recycle through time, reconstituting social ties and illustrating a dynamic structure of life or reproduction.

Let me relate several more experiences to show how this point of view pervades village life today. In spring 1978 I revisited Nelson Island while pregnant with my first child. My Yupik friends proceeded to teach me the elaborate set of dos and don'ts that still accompanies pregnancy and childbirth in the village. I was to sleep with my head toward the door. As soon as I got up every morning, I was to run outside as fast as I could. Only then might I come in, sit down, and drink tea. In fact, any time during the day that I left the house I was to do it quickly without stopping in the doorway. If I were to pause in my exiting, the baby was sure to get stuck during delivery.

This series of prescriptions draws an obvious parallel between the womb in which the unborn baby lives and the house in which the expectant mother resides. Analogically, the throwing of gifts out of the house through the doorway at the time of the seal party is comparable to their birth. Analogous relationships exist between the progress of the souls of the human dead and the return of gifts into the community hall at the time of the exchange dance. Imagery of birth and rebirth pervades the Yupik system of symbols and meanings—the finality of death everywhere averted, in both action and ideal.

Another anecdote helps clarify this cultural framework. When I returned to Toksook Bay with my newborn daughter in the fall of 1978, she was immediately named. The older woman who had been my teacher while I lived on the island had a cousin who had drowned not three weeks before. No sooner had my daughter and I come into the village than she came to where we were staying and gave my daughter the name of her dead cousin. Then, in every house in which we visited, people would ask me what my daughter's name was. When I told them, they would laugh and say such things as, "Oh, he's come back a *kass'aq* [white person]!" or "He always did want to learn English!" or "To think now he has red hair!"

All this verbal play on the baby's name was a kind way of welcoming my daughter into their midst. But, equally important, these endearments were wonderfully explicit expressions of the belief that in the newborn child the soul of the recently dead is born again. In the Yupik world, no one ever finally passes out of existence. Rather, through the naming process, the essence of being human is passed on from one generation to the next.

The cycling of human souls is especially important in light of the traditional belief that the souls of seals must be cared for by the successful hunter so that they, too, will be born again. Seals as well as other animals are believed to give themselves to humans voluntarily. Yupik people do not view this as a necessary response on the part of the seals but as an intentional act in which they willingly approach the good hunter in the ritual of the hunt. When the seal is "killed," it does not die; rather, its *unguva* (life) retracts to its bladder, where it remains until returned to the sea the following season. In the past, during the annual Bladder Festival, Yupik hunters and their wives inflated and feasted on the bladders of seals and other animal guests. After they had properly hosted them, they pushed the bladders down through a hole in the ice so the souls of the seals might be born again.

Through these events the circle is complete. As do the seasons cycle, so do whole bolts and bits of cloth. Human and animal souls likewise are continually in motion. The birth of a baby is the rebirth of a member of its grandparental generation. The death of the seal means life to the village. The "spoiling of cloth" by Yupik women is both the end of the bolt and the beginning of a quilt, a gift valued many times over. The same people and the same seals have been on this earth from the beginning, continually cycling and recycling between birth and rebirth. Through this cosmological circuit, a life-celebrating system is put forward, a celebration of life each Nelson Island quilt embodies.

The Quiltmakers

of Akwesasne

by Alex Jacobs (Mohawk)

Akwesasne means "land where the partridge drums." When the Mohawks first came to this area they could hear the sound of many partridge in the woods, as the area was abundant in wildlife. The Mohawk people came from older villages in the area. Downriver was the ancient site of Hocheloga, near Montreal, that was resettled as Kahnawake; upriver was Oswegatchie, near Ogdensburg, a Mohawk/Oneida community. Situated at the point where small rivers merge into the larger St. Lawrence River, Akwesasne was chosen for its abundant natural resources for hunting and fishing and as a strategic area on navigable waterways that could be protected. Elders say their ancestors settled this area long before the Europeans; the village of Akwesasne became known as St. Regis only after Jesuit missionaries built a church there in the 1600s. Mohawks fished at Akwesasne in the summer and followed

deer into the Adirondack Mountains during the winter. Europeans mistakenly thought they, not the Mohawk, "settled" the site because of the Mohawks' annual migration.

Akwesasne became a refugee center as many Iroquois, Algonquin, and Abnaki passed through or settled there, and many of their descendants, carrying their clan names, still live in Akwesasne. The Adirondacks, or "Bark Eaters," were an Algonquin tribe displaced by the Iroquois migration to northern New York. The Iroquois call themselves *Haudenosaunee*, or The People That Build. Their palisaded long-houses were distinctly different from the round and scattered wigwams of the Algonquins. Mohawks call themselves *Kanienkehake*, or People of the Flint.

Akwesasne remains a strategic area, with many competing jurisdictions, including an international border running through the center of the community. The community

*O*ne of the ways the Akwesasne adapted to year-round settlement and the restrictions of border jurisdictions was for the men to find employment outside their community. Over the last century, Mohawk and Iroquois men found work in the emerging steel and iron industry. Known as skywalkers—ironworkers specializing in high-rise steel construction—they constructed many of North America's tallest structures and bridges. Life at Akwesasne was altered by the emphasis on wage work and travel and by wage earners spending long periods away from home, in cities and other areas. Although working on high-rise steel is still a traditional occupation of Mohawks, this is changing; children of the ironworking generations now have many more options available.

The building of the St. Lawrence Seaway in the 1950s further dramatically changed life in the Akwesasne community. Heavy industry, lured by cheap hydroelectric power, brought scores of non-Natives into the area and created pollution, which has had devastating effects on fishing, hunting, gathering, and farming.

was first divided between the United States and Canada during the American Revolution and the War of 1812; tales of the division are rich with references to spy intrigues between the border countries. The establishment of the border clearly affected all Mohawk people, as multiple allegiances were demanded on either side.

Challenges to allegiances continue to this day. As recently as 1990, the Mohawks of Akwesasne, Kahnawake, and Kanesatake/Oka were surrounded by the Canadian Army, Ontario and Quebec provincial police, the Royal Canadian Mounted Police, and New York state troopers after disputes over unregulated gambling led to the Mohawk Civil War. During this time, the Mohawks of Kanesatake attempted to stop the village of Oka from expanding a golf course into a Mohawk burial ground. A mishandled attack by the Quebec police led to the involvement of the Canadian Army. Kahnawake blockaded the Mercier Bridge in Montreal, and numerous road blockades went up across Canada in support of the Mohawks.

After the region's original divisions were made and reserves established, the annual migration to different hunting and fishing sites subsided and the Mohawks established year-round residences at Akwesasne. While hunting and fishing continued to be activities to provide food, the Mohawk turned to other seasonal occupations, including farming. Crops were planted and harvested, houses and barns were raised, families in need were aided, and old people who had no one were assisted by what can be called mutual aid societies—groups of women and men bound together by clan, family, and community ties. Iroquoian societies are matrilineal, so that a clan is received from the mother's side. Women, therefore, ran clan business and directed the work of the mutual aid societies. Women also owned the land, the gardens, and the tools; men were needed at planting and harvesting times. Even today, from season to season, family gardens sometimes serve larger clan groups.

The various changes in political borders, economic conditions, employment opportunities, educational structures, and environmental conditions imposed upon the Akwesasne community greatly affected the Mohawk and some left their traditional practices behind. Yet others, despite all the drastic changes, quietly retained, and even strengthened, many of their traditions. A community alarmed at losing natural resources made a special point of maintaining and restoring traditional language, arts, and practices.

Elders tell of days in the 1930s, during the Roosevelt administration, when programs were started to encourage people to utilize their knowledge and traditional skills. Men were put to work cutting lumber and clearing areas for campgrounds and recreation. Men also worked at painting, carving, or woodworking, and women worked at quiltmaking, basketmaking, and other traditional arts. My own mother, Sarah Billings Jacobs, recalls a woman, Annie Swamp Lazore, who led the National Youth Authority (N.Y.A.) quiltmaking program at Akwesasne in the 1930s. Annie's mother, Josephine Swamp, was a major quiltmaker of the time.

Today, two long-standing forms of Mohawk traditional arts—basketmaking and quiltmaking—have seen a resurgence. The Mohawk women of Akwesasne have long been known for the making of sweetgrass and black ash splint baskets. Local Algonquins made baskets and other utensils out of birch bark. Using natural materials, including the abundant sweetgrass found in

the wetlands by the river, Iroquois women made corn washers, berry baskets, and sewing baskets. Men mainly produced the pack baskets used to carry heavy items on a person's back.

Women basketmakers would travel by wagon or boat to local tourist or commercial sites where they would sell or trade their work for such items as the calico they used to make long dresses and yoked blouses. Basketmakers are now finding their work being recognized by a wider community as a valuable artistic and cultural expression. Baskets are now finding increased

In addition to using techniques and designs of their own cultural groups, Native quilters borrow designs and patterns from other groups. Here, Alex Jacobs holds the Hawaiian-style appliqué quilt made by his mother, Sarah Jacobs (Mohawk).

visibility in museums, galleries, and private collections.

Quiltmakers and basketmakers often hail from the same families, and some artist are skilled in both. The tradition of quiltmaking within the community resembles other kinds of folk culture or heritage. Women are not in the "business" of quiltmaking, it is more a family tradition passed between generations. Most elder women learned quilting at a young age but were unable to quilt much while their children were young. After retirement or when their children were grown, they had time to quilt again.

Some of the younger generation are now learning quiltmaking and fabric work. Occasionally, programs may be funded to duplicate the sewing bees or a group of women related by family or work just decides to get together and work fabric. In the more traditional districts, homemakers' associations do such group, communal, and community work.

Not everyone takes up the sewing—it is realized that the young women have to like it and want to do it. Some decide to participate when they see the pride the community has for the quiltmakers. Others realize their mother or grandmother will never have the time to create all the quilts and pieces that family members want and will take it upon themselves to carry on the tradition. Some see quiltmaking as an opportunity to assist their family in earning extra income as an alternative to jobs at reservation or local stores. They then recognize the values of traditional arts and see it as more than a pastime or hobby.

Quilts represent many things to the Mohawk people. The elder women say they quilt to keep their hands and minds occupied; it's work they enjoy doing. In addition to making blankets to keep their family

warm, they make baby and wedding quilts to give away. Their daughters and relatives are quick to point out the importance of quilt and fabric work in their own lives and in the lives of the extended families. The daughters feel the importance of the tradition and remember growing up surrounded or influenced by the colorful fabric, the gathered women, their mother working alone, and the intimate warmth of the finished and functional quilts. They remember each piece of fabric, from whose clothing it came, and when it was worn. The cloth may represent years and generations of clothing worn by family members; the patterns may also come from their families. Such treasured family heirlooms are usually not sold.

When women are asked what the best or most fun part of quilting is, their answers include arranging the patterns, creating a new design or pattern, when the top cover is done, when the actual quilting is started and the piece starts to look finished, and —the most obvious and said with humor—when it is finally done. They comprehend the time and effort put into the work and express amazement at the time and patience demonstrated by some well-known quilters; some of the elder women may take one or two years to finish a particular piece, and the actual quilting can take a month or more. Women also talk of the memories inherent in each design, pattern, and piece of material and the event or season a particular piece was created for. They muse how years ago, quilting was a way to recycle old clothing by a generation loath to throw away usable material. Referring to both the time invested and the many times they prick their fingers with needles, they also laugh about all the blood spilled for their craft, art, and family.

In Akwesasne, local and district groups of women organize various weekly, monthly, and seasonal socials and events for fund-raising, mainly in Snye and Cornwall Island. One such event—the annual Akwesasne Freedom School Quilt Auction—has apparently taken over many of the old social aspects of quilting and sewing bees. It has become the single biggest fund-raising event for the Freedom School, which serves Mohawk children from kindergarten through sixth grade and emphasizes Mohawk culture and language. The Freedom School, which receives no direct governmental funding, serves mainly those of traditional Iroquoian Longhouse beliefs; Akwesasne community members often are teachers and do the cleaning and cooking.

The Freedom School Quilt Auction was started in 1979. Each family with children enrolled in the school must supply a quilt for the auction. Held on the first Saturday in August, the auction is an all-day event and includes a display of the quilts and other crafts, traditional foods, and much socializing. As word of the event has spread, prices have risen. The auction represents a happy mix of individual, family, and community pride with the practicality of fund-raising, marketing, and interaction with individuals outside the community.

Women, men, and families from the community, not just those associated with the school, donate quilts and fabrics for the auction. The number and beauty of the quilts speak of the community's pride.

Because the auction demands a lot of energy during a short amount of time, some organizers would like to see even more fund-raising events occur throughout the year. Other suggestions include taking orders all year long or only during the winter months. Some talk of establishing a shop in which to sell material, notions, quilts, and other fabric work.

Most Mohawk women usually do not make enough "extra" quilts to sell, either as bed covers or as art. For those few who do sell their quilts, the market prices for their work vary greatly depending on where they sell it. If sold from the homes, prices can be quite low. In selling through a store or outside the community, prices more closely match the time and effort spent on each quilt. Today at Akwesasne, visitors can find quilts at Thanksgiving and Christmas sales; during winter carnivals and midwinter ceremonies; and during spring and Easter sales. Some women bring items for sale and take orders when they attend the Kateri Tekakwitha conferences.

Most women do not consider their work as art. The idea that quilts may be hung as decoration still astounds people who say that their quilts are meant for bed coverings, for keeping people warm. Yet some women have taken to quilting as an art form and a means of expression, and some of the quilts made for the auction are so beautiful and meaningful that community members bid to keep them "at home."

Recent quilt designs have increasingly incorporated traditional Iroquois symbolism: the tree of peace, turtle and other clan motifs, the eagle, and the three sisters (corn, beans, and squash). Some quilters become well known for specializing in one pattern. These symbols are also sometimes used in a contemporary fashion, occasionally with traditional quilt designs of Amish, Hawaiian, Sioux, and other cultural groups. Sheree ("Peachy") Bonaparte, who is new to quiltmaking, is one such artist who uses stylized and realistic Iroquoian symbols in overall innovative designs to convey important cultural and political messages. Quilters also may use fabric much like a painter uses paint and a stretched canvas,

At the Freedom School Quilt Auction of 1996, quilts are hung on clotheslines for visitors to review before the auction begins. The activities of the day also include sales of other crafts and traditional food. As the auction begins, quilts offered for sale are held up while the auctioneer encourages bidders, who are assigned numbered signs to raise in the air. Many community members gather for this important local event.

resulting in a mix of traditional and contemporary expression.

Prior to the 1990 Mohawk Civil War, the use of Iroquois traditional symbols on quilts was rare. By incorporating traditional Iroquoian symbols in their work, quiltmakers are bringing a healing process to everyone who sees their work. The recent political violence still has an effect, and the use of Iroquois symbols offers a gentle but firm reminder of what people believe in and are fighting for.

Today, quiltmakers of Akwesasne are a diverse group of women. They reflect the differences at Akwesasne—Longhouse or Christian, American or Canadian, traditional or progressive—yet they share a common history. These women, through love and affection, determination and sheer willpower, quietly go about the business of bringing pride and affirmation to their families and to an entire community. They are to be honored.

Quilts and the Hopi Baby-Naming Ceremony

by Marlene Sekaquaptewa (Hopi)

and Carolyn O'Bagy Davis

R ecords of missionaries and government school matrons indicate that quilting was first taught to Hopi women beginning in 1887, when the first government school was started in Keams Canyon on the eastern edge of the Hopi Reservation. By contemporary North American standards, a century of quilting would be considered a long-established tradition as today's Hopi women are second- and third-generation quilters, many creating a unique blending of piecework and Hopi cultural images. But by Hopi standards, quilting is a recently introduced art form.

The Hopi people live on the southern edges of Black Mesa in northeastern Arizona. Eleven Hopi villages are located on First, Second, and Third Mesa. Another village, Moencopi, is located about forty miles to the west. The Hopi have inhabited this dry, forbidding country for a millennium— the Hopi village of Oraibi on Third Mesa is considered to be the oldest continuously inhabited community in North America. Using pottery and tree ring dates from roof beams, archaeologists have dated this village's origins to A.D. 1150. The Hopi people of today are generally thought to be descendants of the ancient cliff-dwelling people, the Hisatsinom, who lived in northern Arizona and the Four Corners region for more than two thousand years.

A deeply religious people, the Hopi have retained their culture and religion to a degree not found in many other Native American peoples despite four centuries of pressures from outside groups. Traditional religion and dances remain part of an intricate year-long ceremonial cycle. Hopi society is matrilineal and organized through extended families or clans. Life is hard in this dry country with freezing winters and scorching summers, and early government Indian agents found the area forbidding and

This 1923 photo shows Walpi village on First Mesa, originally settled about 1700.

ing also is purchased, although many Hopi women still sew their dresses and aprons.

The arrival of Anglo teachers and missionaries to the Hopi country in the late 1800s soon resulted in a gender switch in Hopi textile and clothing production. In government schools, it was widely held that every young woman should master the domestic arts, including quilting, sewing, nutrition, and other home crafts. An 1890 government report on Rules for Indian School stated: "The girls must be systematically trained in every branch of housekeeping and in dairy work; be taught to cut, make, and mend garments for both men and women; and also be taught to nurse and care for the sick."[2]

Early records for the Moqui Indian Training School, the government school established at Keams Canyon, list quantities of garments that the female students had produced during the school year. James Gallagher, superintendent of the school, wrote in 1887 that "The matron has been employed with the sewing machine in making dresses for the girls."[3] That year the girls' sewing room manufactured 1,471 garments. Many Hopi boys were also involved in the sewing classes. They were trained in tailoring and often worked to stitch the uniforms worn by the Indian school students.

Converting the Indians to wearing "citizens' dress" rather than traditional Native costume was a strong priority of the early Indian agents. By 1900, Sarah E. Abbott, field matron for the Keams Canyon School, noted that in addition to the more than five hundred garments stitched in sewing class, the girls had pieced and quilted thirty-three quilts.[4]

One teacher accurately commented that she did not think that any of the Hopi girls had ever held a needle before in their lives—probably a very true assessment as

unappealing.[1] They could not comprehend the attachment of the Hopis to their land, but the Hopi are agricultural, and their ties to their land are closely integrated to their ceremonies and daily life.

Quilting Comes to Hopi

The Hopi also have a long textile tradition. In addition to growing many varieties of corn, beans, squash, and melons, Hopi cotton cultivation and textile production can be dated back eight centuries. By the sixteenth century, they were the major producers and distributors of cotton in the Four Corners area. During the long winters, the Hopi men, farmers in summer, spun and wove cotton fibers into lengths of fabric to be used in clothing and ceremonial garments. Much of the weaving of ceremonial dress took place in kivas, underground ceremonial chambers, while everyday clothing was woven and stitched by the men in their homes.

Hopi men still weave wedding and ceremonial garments, but few families grow cotton. Most cotton for spinning is purchased on large spools and must be respun in preparation for the weaving. Everyday cloth-

Corn has played an important role in Hopi life, and images of corn often appear in many Hopi arts. Marlene Sekaquaptewa (Hopi) of Hotevilla, Third Mesa, Arizona, used corn as the quilting pattern in this Irish chain quilt entitled "**Hopi Corn**" (1996, 59 x 78.5 inches). Cornmeal and cobs of corn are used in Hopi baby-naming ceremonies in traditional ways to ensure a long life and strength for the baby. Quilts are given to babies along with their clan names. Collection of Michigan State University Museum

"Martha's Sewing School." Martha Moser Voth, wife of Mennonite missionary H. R. Voth, taught Hopi women to sew in her weekly sewing and quilting bees held at the Mennonite Mission Church at Oraibi, Arizona, c. 1893.

historically Hopi women did not produce their clothing; that was a job for the men. When H. R. and Martha Voth established a Mennonite mission at Oraibi in 1893, Martha immediately began holding sewing circles and quilting bees in her home. She noted: "Their clumsy efforts caused a great deal of merriment," and furthermore, "The men thought it very funny that the women should learn to sew."[5]

The painted pottery and woven baskets that are the traditional crafts of Hopi women have long been recognized as an enduring and prized art form, displayed today in many museums and art galleries. And so it was not long until Hopi women mastered the skills of fabric design and quiltmaking. Not

only did they integrate the skill into their required domestic achievements at school, they embraced quilting into their daily lives, passing the craft and passion for quilting on to their daughters and granddaughters.

Quilting was also a popular way early missionaries attracted people to the churches, an enticement to convert the Hopis to Christianity. During the long quiet hours of stitching, church lessons were given, with an ultimate goal of obliterating the traditional religion. Because only a few quilting squares would be distributed at a session, most quilters returned each week for more lessons and more fabric squares for their quilts.

In later years, quilting bees were generally made up of women, but in the early years of the 1900s the churches held quilting bees for the men. Many of today's Hopi quilters recall their fathers attending evening quilting sessions at the mission churches. One quilter remembered her father quilting every Thursday evening, as she often went along to thread needles. For many years, she saved a quilt that her father had pieced of old wool and denim squares until it eventually wore out.

Jacob Hamblin, a missionary from the Church of Jesus Christ of Latter-Day Saints (the Mormons), first visited the Hopi villages in 1858. Hamblin brought several Hopis back to Utah to various Mormon settlements to see productive farms and spinning and grinding mills. In the 1870s, the Mormons were invited to settle near Moencopi, with the provision that they build a spinning mill. In 1879 at nearby Tuba City, Mormon missionary John W. Young built a woolen factory measuring ninety by seventy feet and holding 192 spindles. Eventually, female members of the church taught quilting in the women's Relief Society meetings.

Nine-Patch Quilt, 1996

Made by Pearl Nuvangyaoma (Hopi), Second Mesa, Arizona. 39 x 42 inches. Collection of Michigan State University Museum

Nuvangyaoma's quilt is pieced with patches sent to Hopi missions by White Cross women, a group affiliated with the American Baptist church.

Trip Around the World Quilt, c. 1995.

Made by Frieda Yoyhoeoma (Hopi), Sipaulovi, Second Mesa, Arizona. 60 x 93 inches.

Abigail Johnson was a Baptist missionary, a "mission Mary," who went to Polacca in 1902 and later served at Second Mesa. She held weekly quilting bees for men and separate gatherings for the women, giving out 3½ by 5½-inch White Cross blocks to piece together a quilt top. (The White Cross is a support and outreach extension of the American Baptist church. Members rolled bandages and stitched quilts to be sent off to Indian and foreign missions. They also cut squares from donated material and cutaway sewing scraps in their weekly meetings, tying them into small, stacked bundles to be sent out to Indian mission churches across the country.) Native quilters had to have a true artist's eye to piece together a cohesive design from the wildly assorted colors and fabrics. Nevertheless, over the years, many beautiful quilt tops were stitched with these postcard-sized quilt blocks.

Although the Oraibi Mission Church was destroyed in the 1940s by a fire caused by lightning, the quilting bees continue at Mennonite churches in Kykotsmovi and Bacavi, and mission churches today are still the recipients of boxes of these bundled White Cross blocks.

Hopi Today Today, second- and third-generation quilters live in every village on the Hopi mesas. Quilting bees are a weekly activity among the women at the mission churches and community centers, and quilts are often displayed at local village craft shows. Not surprisingly, quilts have become part of Hopi life and ceremony. Quilts are often the favored gift to celebrate a wedding or birthday. When a daughter or son leaves home to attend school or work off the reservation, he or she carries a quilt as a remembrance of home and family. Hopi women use quilts to chronicle important events within their family and community, just as quilters across the country instinctively stitch a quilt to mark a noteworthy occasion and give a tangible token of their regard and affection.

Quilts have also been integrated into some beautiful Hopi ceremonies, most notably the baby-naming ceremony. When a Hopi baby is born, infant and mother are secluded inside their home for twenty days. Traditionally, the house was kept dark during this time with a blanket draped in front of the door and coverings hung over the windows. At harvesttime or well before the birth of the baby, two perfect ears of white corn would be selected and set aside. These mother ears will be placed next to the baby in the bassinet or cradle and will stay near the infant until the naming ceremony takes

place. Later, they will be saved as a spiritual memento of the child's birth.

Early every morning, the paternal grandmother comes to the new mother's home to care for the mother and child. Every fifth day there is a ritual hair washing and bathing with yucca soap. The new mother observes a ritual fast for twenty days, eating no meat, animal fat, or salt. A special dish of whole cobs of corn cooked in water mixed with cedar leaves is always available to be offered to close friends who come to visit.

Before dawn on the twentieth morning, the infant's paternal grandmother and female relatives gather at the home for a ritual washing and blessing of the baby. Each woman brings a small jar of water that is used to wash the mother's hair. Next, fresh water is poured into the basin to symbolically bathe the mother. Then the baby is bathed in clean water, with all of the women

ritually helping. After the baby is dressed, his or her face is rubbed with white corn-meal. The paternal grandmother then sits with the baby on her lap and wraps the child with a quilt that she has purchased or stitched for her new grandchild. After wrapping the baby with the quilt, she strokes its breast with the mother ears of corn and repeats a blessing. She says a prayer for the child to live a long life in good health and strength, and with her blessing she offers a clan-associated name to the child.

After the grandmother's blessing, family and friends are invited to offer a blessing and give a name to the baby. A gift of a quilt accompanies the offered name, and some-times, if there are a lot of family and friends participating, the baby almost disappears under a mountain of quilts in this warm and endearing celebration. In earlier times, the child's father or godfather wove a special

Above left: Rita Nuvangyaoma (Hopi) of Sipaulovi on Second Mesa, Arizona, holds her log cabin quilt.

Above right: Miriam Torivio (Hopi) of Sunlight Mission on Second Mesa, Arizona, with one of her quilts.

blanket for the child and the child received only one wrapping. Older women recall that as quilting became more prevalent in the Hopi villages, a quilt was substituted for, and by the early 1900s had replaced, the handwoven blanket. By the 1930s, accounts of the naming ceremony show multiple gifts of quilts as common practice. Today, it is not uncommon for a baby to be given eight or ten clan names and quilts.

After the blessings and the gifts, the baby is taken by the mother and the paternal grandmother to the eastern edge of the village to greet the morning sun. The child is presented and prayers are said to *Taawa* (the Father-Sun) to ensure the child's growth in good health under his watchful presence. The mother and grandmother repeat the names given to the child, and, after the last blessing, mother, grandmother, and child return home for a ritual feast of special foods.

For this meal, the father's family butchers a sheep that is cubed and cooked in a stew with hominy. The mother's family contributes great quantities of *piki* bread, a wafer-thin bread made of blue cornmeal, and *pikami*, a traditional corn pudding. This pudding, an essential part of the feast, is made of white cornmeal ground to a fine powder. Sprouted wheat that has been dried and ground is stirred in with a greasewood stirring stick, then sugar and boiling water are added. The pudding is poured into a large metal container and put in an underground oven to bake overnight. Huge quantities of pikami are prepared to feed the anticipated crowd of friends, family, and other villagers.

After the blessings a crier stands on a rooftop welcoming everyone in the village to the home to eat. The oldest male in the home takes a small bit of food outside and ritually offers it to the spiritual leaders and ancestors, and more prayers are given ask-ing for guidance in the life of the new infant and the eventual blessing of more children for the family. Before the meal begins a pinch of corn pudding is dipped into the hominy stew and then placed in the honored baby's mouth, and the grandmother says, "This is the food we eat." Then the other family and guests are served. When the paternal relatives have eaten and are ready to leave, the mother and maternal relatives present them with gifts of piki and pastries, a sort of ritual payment for giving a name. Any other leftover foods are given to the paternal mother-in-law.

Many Hopi women, especially the older ones, feel strongly that observing the baby-naming ceremony is one of the most important things that can be done for Hopi society. Names are very important among the Hopi people; a name gives an identity. Names given at the naming ceremony always have a clan association, and the child will generally become known by one of the names offered. At other times in a Hopi's life other names may be given, all very important to the identity of the individual. The naming ceremony honors a new life and incorporates that young one into the family, but on a larger scale the ceremony also reaffirms the membership and responsibility of each individual within the Hopi community. With its emphasis on family responsibilities, the blessings, and consumption of special foods, all made with the life-giving corn, the baby-naming ceremony is endowed with parallels that mirror the larger role of the individual within Hopi culture. Hopi belief does not distinguish between the temporal and the spiritual world. The name given to a Hopi enters the child into an already established pattern; the clan system brings him into that life and prepares him to be known as a Hopi when he goes into the next world.

It is of no small consequence that the quilt is an integral part of the ritual. A gift of a quilt is a literal gift of warmth, as well as a symbolic blessing. Long after the naming ceremony, a quilt endures as a tangible piece of love and a link to the extended family members who will always be a part of the child's life. Children are treasured by the Hopi people, and on any trip to the Hopi mesas a visitor will see beautiful Hopi babies wrapped in handmade quilts, gifts from this important ritual that wrap them within the circle of an ancient and tightly integrated community.

Just as quilts are an important marker to the beginning of life, quilts also are often used for burials. Many Hopis observe traditional practices, where a family makes all of the last arrangements, and a quilt is often used as a burial shroud. This wrap will carry the deceased into eternity.

Quilting Techniques and Designs. In spite of the general lack of sophisticated quilting supplies, such as generous lengths of new fabric, patterns, and quilting tools, Hopi women—and a few men—are avid quiltmakers. Living far from towns and lacking well-paying employment means that many Hopi quilters must work with what they have at hand. Like other quilters living in rural areas, Hopi use worn-out clothing and various scraps of fabric to fashion beautiful and graphic quilt tops. Secondhand or worn-out clothing is unstitched and used as a filler or batting in the quilt. As quilt patterns are scarce, hand-drawn patterns are passed from quilter to quilter. Today, baby quilts are pieced in patterns traditionally used by many quilters, such as the *pinwheel*, *log cabin*, *spools*, or *lone star*. Many quilts feature images of Hopi symbolism, such as kachinas, rattles, lightning bolts, bows and arrows, and clan motifs. These designs are appliquéd, embroidered, or painted on the quilt blocks. On First Mesa, where there is a strong ceramic tradition, quilt blocks often have pottery motifs. A great-granddaughter of the famous historic potter Nampyeo stitches dazzling quilts painted with images of pottery designs created by her talented ancestor.

The butterfly is another important motif that is often pieced, painted, or appliquéd onto quilts. Today, the Butterfly Dance is popular in many Hopi villages, but the butterfly has always been an important symbol of Hopi ritual, and butterfly images can be seen on prehistoric pictographs, pottery, and ancient kiva murals. Consequently, it is not uncommon to see a variety of butterfly images on Hopi quilts. The appliquéd pattern butterfly with black buttonhole stitching is most popular with older quilters. Other quilters paint butterflies on their quilts. One notable quilt had butterflies painted on each quilt block, their wings decorated with Hopi pottery designs.

Unfortunately, not many old Hopi quilts still exist. Of necessity, they are generally used until they wear out. Still, the Hopi quilt heritage is long and full, and many exciting quilts continue to be created from rudimentary materials. A Third Mesa quilter, for example, recently pieced a quilt in an *Irish chain* pattern, quilting the Hopi corn image in the solid middle blocks. Pottery designs are incorporated into many First Mesa quilts, and some quilters from Second Mesa have created a quilt with images of their Sun clan or the Hopi Butterfly Maiden painted and appliquéd on quilt blocks. These wonderful blendings of ancient Hopi culture and traditional quilting heritage continue the long quilting tradition on the Hopi mesas, expressing the eloquent skills of the Hopi quiltmakers.

Butterfly Quilt, 1996

Made by Lawrence Wester (Hopi), Hotevilla, Third Mesa, Arizona. 39 x 47.25 inches. Collection of Michigan State University Museum

Butterfly dances are held annually in many villages, and butterflies are popular motifs on quilts, including those given at Hopi baby-naming ceremonies.

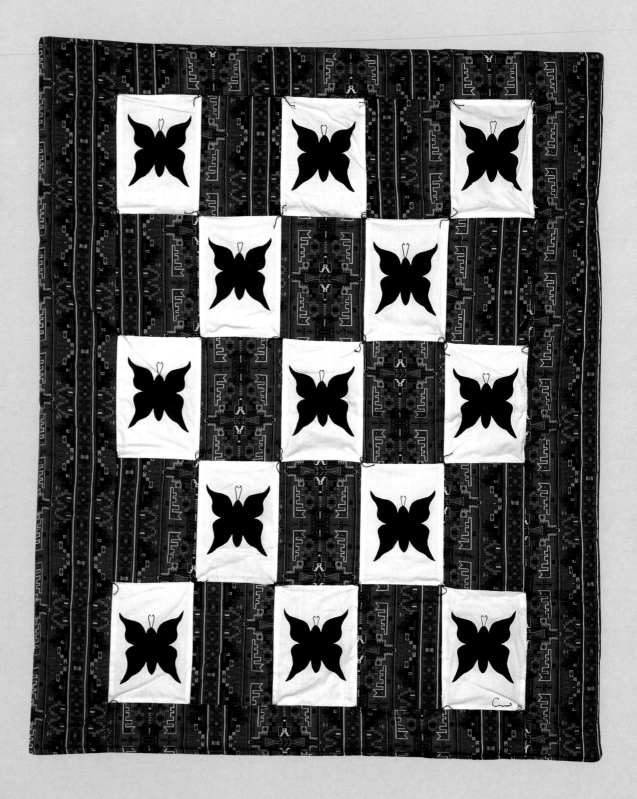

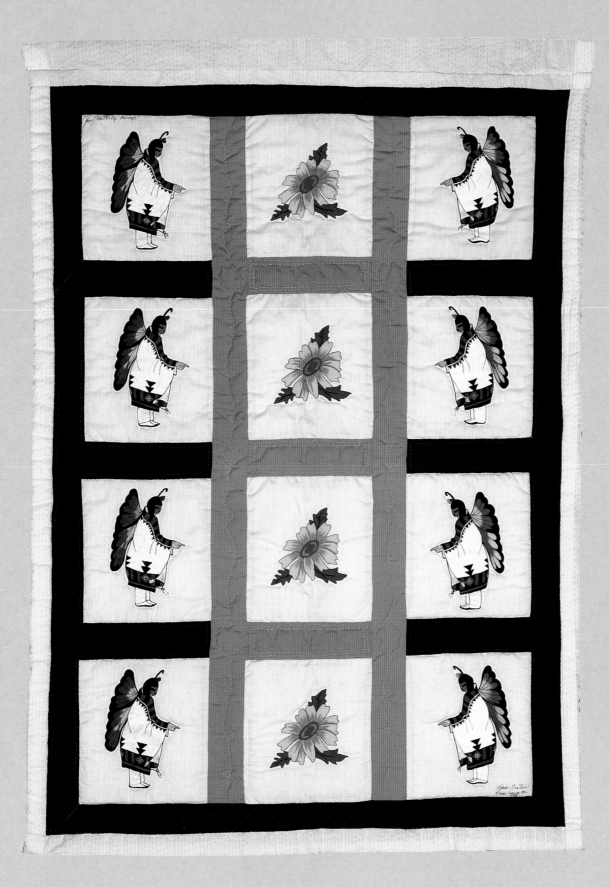

Butterfly Maiden Quilt, 1996

Made by Karen Tootsie (Hopi), Keams Canyon, Arizona. 35.5 x 50.5 inches. Collection of Michigan State University Museum

This baby quilt carries images of the Butterfly Maiden, a traditional symbol on the Hopi mesas.

Part IV
A Native
Aesthetic

Rosebud Quilts:
Building a Museum Collection, Creating an Exhibition

by Emil Her Many Horses (Sioux)

In March of 1988, I started collecting quilts from the women of the Rosebud Lakota Sioux Reservation, located in south-central South Dakota. As director of the Buechel Memorial Lakota Museum, I had proposed to develop a collection of quilts for a traveling exhibition titled "Rosebud Quilts and Quilters." The exhibition would travel throughout South Dakota as part of the state's 1989 centennial celebration, with grant support from the South Dakota Arts Council and the Rosebud Educational Society.

The quilt exhibition would feature *star* quilts, one of the favorite items used in the traditional giveaways held by the Lakota people. The giveaway is a public way of honoring others, particularly relatives.

This c. 1930 photo of Mrs. Frank Four Horses (Sioux) on the Rosebud Reservation, South Dakota, shows her draped in a pieced quilt.

DETAIL ON PAGE 164:
Rebecca Horned Antelope (Sioux) at a giveaway held in her name on the Rosebud reservation, South Dakota.

dings. They also may be held to honor a veteran, someone named to a powwow committee, or an individual or team winning a sporting tournament. One of the most elaborate giveaways marks the memorial of a deceased family member. The year following the death, the family begins to gather material items—handmade *star* quilts, shawls, Pendleton blankets, articles of clothing, towels, dishes, utensils, luggage (footlockers are a favorite), fruits, and many other items. In the old days, it was even common to give away horses.

Everyone is welcomed by a host family to these memorial giveaways and feasts (or dinners) but especially those individuals who helped the family through its period of mourning. Once the traditional feast is completed, the giveaway begins. First, any food left over from the dinner is distributed so people will have something to eat later. Specially invited guests usually are given *star* quilts and blankets in memory of the deceased relative. Then the family members will attempt to show their gratitude by giving a gift, no matter how small, to all who are present. Although the pain of losing a loved one does not cease, the memorial giveaways help the family deal with its grief. It is a final letting go of the deceased family member.

While the *star* pattern seems to be the most popular among the Lakota women, how the pattern developed or how quilting was introduced to the Lakota community was not as important to me as how the quiltmakers learned to make the quilts themselves. One story illustrates this how and why: When her sister could not find anyone to make a quilt for her giveaway, Genevieve Moore, a well-known beadworker, offered to help. After making that first quilt, she has been making them ever since.

There are a number of different reasons for having a giveaway. One such occasion is a naming ceremony, when an individual receives a traditional Lakota name, usually a handed-down family one but sometimes a new name. Lakota names are generally only used when the individual is publicly honored, when a song is sung to celebrate that individual. When the name has been used in the Honoring Song, the family shows its appreciation by giving away material items, again in honor of the person whose name was used.

Giveaways often recognize rites of passage, such as births, graduations, and wed-

An *unidentified Lakota quilter works outside her tent on a patchwork quilt with star blocks, c. 1930.*

Many of the quiltmakers were taught by an elder within the family or learned from observing other family members. Standards for accomplishments are high. Pauline Whirlwind's mother-in-law made her take apart her first quilt three times: "She said if you want to be a good quilter, you've got to do it right."[1] Whirlwind not only makes her own quilts but also helps other quiltmakers in creating their *star* quilts.

Lakota women on the Rosebud Reservation often combine their artistic abilities to make the colorful *star* quilts. Some create quilt tops and may or may not do their own quilting. Others prefer to only do the quilting. Both groups are highly talented and extremely fast in their ability to create a quilt. Woman may barter back and forth and exchange their services in order to have enough quilts at their own giveaways.

Once I started collecting I realized I was also receiving a highly educational experience. Pearl Spotted Tail often threatened to make me sit down and quilt with her and her daughters, to learn exactly how much work is involved. She creates quilts for her own giveaways and also sells quilts to others. Spotted Tail's unique color sense has made her quilts highly marketable, and she has sold enough to help pay for her chil-

CLOCKWISE FROM TOP LEFT:

Warbonnet Star Quilt, c. 1988

*Made by Genevieve Moore (Sioux),
Parmelee, South Dakota. 72 x 86 inches.
Collection of Buechel Memorial Lakota Museum*

Lone Star Quilt, c. 1988

*Made by Pauline Whirlwind (Sioux),
Upper Cut Meat, South Dakota.
72 x 98 inches. Collection of Buechel Memorial
Lakota Museum*

Four Corner Star Quilt, c. 1988

*Made by Pearl Spotted Tail (Sioux),
Parmelee, South Dakota. 86 x 90 inches.
Collection of Buechel Memorial Lakota Museum*

dren's college education; however, the price garnered never reflected the amount of work that was involved.

She uses earth tone and pastel colors in combination with any other unusual colored fabric she can obtain. When asked how she came up with her color combinations, she replied, "It's simple. All you have to do is go outside and look around you. You see colors all around you." In an interview by a local newspaper Spotted Tail also said: "When I walk in the mornings, I think of my stars. . . . When I walk in the evenings, I see quilt colors in the sunsets."[2] One unusual quilt with a background of silver gray and a *star* pattern in shades of red and dark blue was inspired by her nephew John's pickup truck: silver gray with maroon-and-red trim. There is only one color—black—that Spotted Tail does not like to use. She associates that color with death.

Many quiltmakers have mastered piecing and quilting to the point that they can make a quilt in a day or two. Spotted Tail may cut the pieces for a quilt in the morning, sew the quilt top together in the afternoon, and stretch the top on a quilting frame in the evening. By the next day, she completes all the quilting and binds off the edging.

When I first approached Marie Good Shield, a quiltmaker who has seven quilts in the Buechel Museum collection, to reproduce certain quilts for the exhibition, I had some difficulty describing what I wanted. Realizing my difficulty, Marie pulled out two spiral-bound notebooks. On each page, she had drawn the pattern of each style of quilt she made, with each diamond colored in by pencils. All I had to do was write my name at the bottom of each page and she would make that quilt.

Several of Good Shield's quilts are her own unique patterns, including a *veterans* quilt, which has the American flag design worked

within the *star* pattern. *Veterans* quilts are commonly given by families to members of the local American Legion posts to honor both living and deceased loved ones who served in the military. Veterans are highly honored among the Lakota people as a new form of the old warrior societies. Those who have been wounded in battle are especially respected; they have the right to wear a red eagle feather to signify their bravery.

Nellie Star Boy Menard is another quilt-maker represented in the Buechel Museum's collection. In addition to being a talented quiltmaker, Menard is well known for her beadwork, quillwork, and Fancy Dance shawls. Her more than eight hundred shawls are worn by Fancy Shawl Dancers across the United States and Canada.

Menard is very proud of her family. Along with her daughter, Marina LaDeaux, she constantly prepares quilts for giveaways honoring family members. In 1995, Menard was awarded the National Heritage Fellowship by the National Endowment for the Arts in recognition of her quiltmaking skills and activities in a ceremony held at the White House. In appreciation of this honor, Menard gave First Lady Hillary Rodham Clinton, the presenter, one of her hand-tied Fancy Dance shawls. In addition to the First Lady, tribal officials, clergy, and elected officials have been honored with gifts made by Menard.

Because I had attended several giveaway ceremonies held by Nellie Menard and her family, I was very familiar with Menard's artistic gifts, and I asked her to consider making quilts for the collection. Her many patterns include ones using Lakota religious symbols, such as pipes, tipis, and eagles, and colors representing the six directions in which prayers are offered. Nine Menard quilts—one in each pattern she makes—are now in the Buechel collection. One has the

Lone Star Variation
Quilt, c. 1988

Made by Marie Good Shield (Sioux), piecer, and Pauline Whirlwind (Sioux), quilter, St. Francis and Upper Cut Meat, South Dakota. 78 x 82 inches. Collection of Buechel Memorial Lakota Museum

Veteran's Quilt, c. 1988

Made by Marie Good Shield (Sioux), designer and piecer, and Carla Running Horse (Sioux), quilter, St. Francis and Parmelee, South Dakota. 76 x 82 inches. Collection of Buechel Memorial Lakota Museum

star pattern done in rainbow colors set on a red background. I had seen quilts done in this style draped over the chair of several family members during their naming ceremony, when the two parties involved in the naming ceremony become members of each other's family. Once the ceremony is over, the quilts were given to those respected individuals who were asked to bestow the name upon her family members.

Madeline Green is another quiltmaker who has taken quiltmaking to a new level of art. Her wonderful sense of color, quality of workmanship, and the fact she prefers to use satin make her quilts highly sought after. For many years, Lakota grandmothers would take pieces of satin and make a quilt

with elaborate embroidery work on it for their first grandchild. My own grandmother made just such a quilt for her first great-grandchild. Today, Green's satin baby quilts are very popular among the Lakota people to celebrate new births. She claims: "It takes me twice as long to work with cotton material than it does to work with satin."[3]

Green's quilts also are used to honor the deceased. As it is not considered proper to speak of death, when a person dies the family often will cover the coffin with a *star* quilt, thus sending their loved one into the spirit world draped in a colorful *star* quilt. It is an act of love.

Green often complains that when she makes a large quilt, the quilting frame takes

Sioux quiltmaker Pearl Spotted Tail of Parmelee, South Dakota, hopes her **Crazy Horse Star Quilt** (1996, 57.5 x 58 inches) in a tipi design will help others learn about her people. She feels it is important to remember her ancestors, including Crazy Horse, and honors him in this pattern.

Eagle Star Quilt, c. 1988

*Made by Nellie Menard
(Sioux), designer and piecer,
and Carla Running Horse
(Sioux), quilter, Rosebud and
Parmelee, South Dakota.
82 x 98 inches. Collection of
Buechel Memorial Lakota
Museum*

**Rainbow Star Quilt,
c. 1988**

*Made by Nellie Menard
(Sioux), designer and piecer,
and Carla Running Horse
(Sioux), quilter, Rosebud and
Parmelee, South Dakota. 82 x
98 inches. Collection of Buechel
Memorial Lakota Museum*

up her whole living room, leaving no room
to sit. The purple *broken star* quilt she made
for the collection was 88 by 102 inches.
Green made two other satin quilts in the *star*
pattern for the collection. One had a white
background, sunburst colors for the star, and
scalloped edging. When asked to make a
third, she asked, "Any color?" I replied, "I
don't have a green one." "Any design?" she
asked. "Just as long as it's different from the
rest," I told her. She then made one of the
most beautiful quilts in the collection—a
mint green quilt with sunburst colors in the
pattern called *double star*.

Rosebud quiltmakers create unique patterns while maintaining high levels of craftsmanship. One, Gloria Crazy Cat Black
Spotted Horse, often made small quilted

purses with *star* patterns using unusually
small diamonds. When asked to make a
quilt for the Buechel collection, she created
a colorful *sampler* quilt of twenty blocks with
stars of different colors.

Black Spotted Horse also is known for her
purses with miniature *eagle star* patterns. The
background color of these purses was usually aqua and sunburst colors for the diamond pieces not forming the eagle. Using
her purse design as inspiration, she made
another beautiful *sampler* quilt for the collection, each of the twenty blocks showing a
different variation on the *eagle star*. Each of
the sampler quilts had taken a month to
make.

Of all the quilts in the collection, one I
find especially unique by Marie Looking

Satin Double Star, c. 1988

*Made by Madeline Green
(Sioux), Okreek, South Dakota.
88 x 98 inches.
Collection of Buechel Memorial
Lakota Museum*

**Sampler Star Quilt,
c. 1988**

*Made by Gloria Crazy Cat
Black Spotted Horse (Sioux),
St. Francis, South Dakota.
74 x 86 inches. Collection of
Buechel Memorial Lakota
Museum*

Horse is red and white with a *star* design best described as a combination of the *drunkard's path* and the *mariner's compass* patterns. The *star* is not made of diamonds but in a design that some people call a *crazy* pattern. Quilt tops of this sort are very common at giveaways, usually given to elder women. Such generosity honors the person for whom the giveaway is held. The Lakota consider it appropriate to give away items they value highly. It is believed they will always receive back that which they have generously given away. What better way could you honor a loved one than to give away what you value?

On opening night, I stood outside the gym listening to visitors' responses to the exhibition. When the doors opened I heard a gasp; seeing this array of thirty-two quilts literally took the visitors' breaths away. I was especially satisfied by the faces of the quiltmakers themselves. They were so proud of their creations. I watched an elderly Lakota woman walk silently around the display of quilts, then I asked, "Wouldn't you like to have all these quilts for a giveaway?" She smiled and shook her head "Yes."[4]

To my regret, I was unable to collect an example from each of the many quiltmakers on the Rosebud Reservation, and I was unable to collect more than one example from some quiltmakers with large repertoires of patterns. I do feel very fortunate to have been able to collect the quilts and to document the quiltmakers of the Rosebud Reservation for the Buechel Museum. Each quiltmaker and quilt has their own unique story to tell.

Hawaiian Quilting:

A Personal Remembrance

by Linda Moriarity (Native Hawaiian)

My grandmother's sewing room was a small room attached to the washhouse and outdoor shower. It had sash windows on two sides, propped up with sticks, and a small walk-in closet where she stored her gardening tools and a myriad of tins containing feather pelts, thread, assorted pieces of cloth, quilt patterns cut from butcher paper, and rolls of dried *lauhala* (*Pandanus* sp.), the leaves of the hala tree, for weaving and repairing floor mats. Two small wood tables in the sewing room were stacked with projects in progress, a lauhala hat partially woven, a feather hat *lei* attached to a propped-up pillow, and countless stacks of island fabric, in some sort of order, waiting to be pieced into a patchwork quilt. There was also an old treadle Singer sewing machine with a basket of mending on the side. Not unlike other Hawaiian women of her generation, she was a homemaker, which meant that she made

most everything she used in her home. Mother of nine children, her name was Catherine Puakou Scharsch Morgan, and she was half Hawaiian and half German and French. Her mother, Kulia Kaalo Scharsch, was pure Hawaiian and well known on the island of Kauai for designing and sewing Hawaiian-style quilts.

As a child I spent all of my days with my grandmother, who was then in her early seventies, while my parents worked. A good portion of that time was spent in her sewing room. Our day usually started at around seven in the morning with the rooster crowing in the chicken coop in the backyard. We had breakfast, cleaned up, put on our wide-brimmed lauhala hats (which she wove), and went outside to do the daily chores. We fed the chickens, ducks, and the few cats that hung around the house. She watered the plants and weeded around her flowers, especially the white ginger, bushes of roses

A *series of* **Hawaiian Flag Quilts** *is hung on the stage of Lihue Parish Hall during the 1933 exhibit of the Mokihana Club on the island of Kauai.*

L-669-3-1-33

and jasmine, and vines of stephanotis and *pakalana*—all those sweet-smelling flowers that she loved so much. She would pick flowers as she worked her way around the yard, sticking them in her hair or pinning them to her hat. Sometimes she would pick enough to make a lei for my mother to wear to work or to give to a friend. Daily we would pick up the large leaves that fell from the two tall breadfruit trees in the yard. Some days we would pick the fruit using a long stick with a sharpened sickle attached to the top end. There was always weeding and pruning to be done. Near midday, when the sun was too hot for my grandmother, we washed our faces with cool water from the outside faucet, hung up our hats, and went into the house for lunch. After that my

grandmother went to her sewing room, where she settled down for the better part of the day.

Depending on her mood and the urgency of completing a project, she would choose from the range of crafts she did so well—feather lei making, lauhala weaving, embroidery, quilting, or stitching a garment on the machine. Of these, I would say she excelled in quilting, in the Hawaiian style, a skill she learned from her mother. On the days she worked on her quilt, she first dusted the room, wiping down the surface of the table and placing a clean white sheet on the work area. She then took out the quilt, which she had carefully wrapped in a sheet, and unfolded the section where she had left off. If she was appliquéing the pattern onto the

Hawaiian Flag Quilt, c. 1915

Made by Catherine Puakou Scharsch Morgan (Native Hawaiian), Kapaa, Kauai, Hawaii. 67 x 69.75 inches. Collection of Linda Moriarity

It was customary in many Native Hawaiian families for women to make flag quilts for the males. Morgan made this quilt as a gift for her son Arthur, who received it after his marriage.

**Lily Hawaiian Appliqué
Floral Quilt, c. 1920**

*Made by Catherine Puakou
Scharsch Morgan (Native
Hawaiian), Kapaa, Kauai,
Hawaii. 77.5 x 85.75 inches.
Collection of Linda Moriarity*

backing, she would usually fasten an embroidery hoop to the immediate area. If she was quilting, she would not use any aids except for a thimble. I sat next to my grandmother and watched her quilt, helping by threading the needle or putting a knot at the end of the thread. I was always amazed at how cleverly she somehow hid the knot inside the quilt batting. I would examine her quilt and not find a single knot.

During her lifetime, my grandmother, as did her mother before her, designed and made a quilt for each of her children. She gave the quilt to them when they left home or got married. These quilts were cherished and carefully cared for. Hawaiian quilts were never used daily were but kept in special trunks, wrapped in soft cloth and only taken out for special occasions. My grandmother took her quilts out for an "airing" several times a year, placing them on her bed and opening all the windows to let in the fresh air. During the holidays, particularly Christmas, she would place a quilt on her bed for a couple of weeks. No one was allowed to sit on the quilt—it was out for display. Quilts remain in families and are passed on from one generation to the other. The last quilt she completed was for me, her first granddaughter. The quilt, *Roselani* (*Heavenly Rose*), is a rose pattern in a medium pink on a white background.

Quilting in Hawaii was first introduced by the missionary women in 1820. As the story goes, a sewing bee was held on the brig *Thaddeus* for a group of Hawaiian women of the royal order. With limited English, this was their first lesson in sewing. They were given bits of cloth to sew together from the remnant bags of the missionary women, and from this the patchwork quilt originated. Traditional Hawaiians produced a cloth called *kapa*, made by beating strips of the inner bark of the paper mulberry (*wauke*) and then felting them together to produce large sheets. These sheets were then dyed and stamped with intricate designs and used as bed coverings (*kapa moe*) and clothing. Often the kapa moe were scented with fragrant perfume derived from leaves and flowers. There was also the native tradition of plaiting lauhala and other reeds and grasses to produce sleeping mats, floor mats, and baskets. Fine sleeping mats were intricately woven with softly plied fibers nearly resembling silk, with the overall design of the weave producing subtle yet striking symmetrical patterns. As the traditional cloth and covers had an overall design element, the piecing together of small pieces of fabric to produce a "patched" design must have seemed strange to the early Hawaiian women.

A great deal of thought and skill went into producing the kapa moe to ensure the cloth

My grandmother's quilting group met at what we called the Hawaiian church across the street from her house, actually a Congregational church with a large Hawaiian congregation. Of the group of three to five women, all Hawaiian, my grandmother was the oldest in her late sixties. The others were about ten years younger. She was also the most experienced quilter and usually designed the quilt and cut the pattern. They all worked on appliquéing and quilting, set up on the large covered porch of the church. First, they swept the porch and then put down a lauhala floor mat on the area where they would be working to help keep the quilt from getting dirty. They were always careful never to bring any food near the quilt, and they washed their hands clean before sewing. As most of the women were older, they preferred to work on the porch because of good natural light. I never recall them working inside the church hall, which was rather dark. My grandmother's sister, Eileen Smith, who at this writing is ninety years old, remembers that as a child her mother and a group of women would meet at their home and spend a part of the day quilting together. She said the ladies would come to their house before she left for school and would remain until the early afternoon. Her mother always had her thread many needles before she went off to school as the ladies, all middle-aged and older, had trouble with this. Eileen said this was a routine task before school most mornings and by the time she returned home in the afternoon they were gone. The ladies usually brought poi and dried fish and crackers for lunch. They collectively worked on quilts for each other's families, often making the same design in different colors. An example is the breadfruit, or 'ulu, pattern which was very popular as an appropriate quilt design for males.

ments of function and design. The Hawaiian quilt was first documented around 1858 when the prince of Hawaii was born. As part of the presentation of gifts, women made colorful quilts in his honor. In contrast to the patchwork quilts that had become the standard blanket, the Hawaiian-style quilt gave the women an opportunity to create and express themselves individually. Furthermore, with the westernization of Hawaii and the availability of more fabrics and color, it is reasonable that the women would want to use a whole piece of fabric, like the whole sheets of kapa, rather than pieces of remnants. For the time and effort involved in making a quilt, why not use a whole, new piece of cloth?

For most Hawaiian women, quilting was "pickup" work, a project to work on when they had time after cleaning the house and caring for the children. It was a chance to have some quiet time alone as well as engage in some creative endeavor. It was also, at times, a shared activity among friends. In many cases, groups of women formed through association with churches, benevolent societies such as the Ka'ahumanu Society, or an extended family network would undertake a quilting project. Collectively, they planned and sewed a quilt for a particular event, for sale, or for a family member. My grandmother made Hawaiian quilts on order for a number of prominent families on Kauai. She was also a member of the Ka'ahumanu Society, and their local auxiliary would occasionally get together several mornings a week to work on quilts sold as fund-raisers for their group. This money went to buy food for the families of women who were sick or destitute. The group would visit Hawaiian women in the hospital and then deliver boxes of tinned

Catherine Puakou Scharsch Morgan (1882–1961) was born on the island of Kauai to a full-blooded Hawaiian mother and a German/French father.

was soft and smooth next to the skin and the design appropriate. It was therefore natural for the Hawaiian women to quickly grasp the Western fabrics and sewing techniques and adapt them to traditional ele-

food and *poi*, a starchy staple of the Hawaiian diet, to their homes. Sometimes my grandmother would bring them a big pot of stew or some fish that my father had caught.

Inspiration for quilt designs came from many factors: personal experiences and perceptions, the natural environment, historical and current events, and respect for the royalty. Following the overthrow of the Hawaiian monarchy and annexation by the United States came a proliferation of quilts depicting the Hawaiian flag and the coat of arms. Concerned that they would not be able to keep their flags, Hawaiians preserved them in quilts such as *Ku'u hae aloha* (*My Beloved Flag*). Interestingly, these words were often incorporated into the quilt design. My grandmother made two *flag* quilts in her lifetime, one a pattern from her mother, the other a maroon-and-yellow quilt in honor of Queen Ka'ahumanu. Other patterns relating to the island royalty included designs of the king's flower vase, the palace chandelier, and architectural details of the king's house.

Most popular were quilts of flowers, flower leis, bouquets of flowers, and plants that had definitive leaf patterns, such as the breadfruit and pineapple. Favorite floral patterns in early quilts included the rose, carnation, and lily. Usually, the designs and color were a close facsimile of the flower and plant itself. In our family, my grandmother and great-grandmother each made several quilts of *breadfruit* design and the *Hawaiian flag* for their sons while creating floral designs of *baby rose*, *stephanotis*, and *calla lily* for their daughters.

Most quilters gave names to their quilts, and over the years, famous quilts took on personages. Just as Hawaiians compose songs expounding on the beauty of a place,

quilt designs are likewise so inspired. *Na Molokama* is a quilt patterned after the majestic waterfall at Hanalei. *Kuahiwi Nani O Haleakala* (*Beautiful Mountain of Haleakala*) refers to the island of Maui.

Many quilt designs appeared in dreams. My own grandmother related such an experience, when a dream gave her the vision for a quilt. The following morning she got up and immediately sketched the design, developing the pattern by the end of the day. All quilt designs are very personal. Some are shared as a gesture of love and friendship while others, which may have hidden or dual meanings, are not. Certain popular patterns, such as the *breadfruit*, have many variations in design.

In addition to the predominant design, the subtle pattern formed from stitching enhanced the overall quilt. These varied with the maker and ranged from conventional straight or diagonal lines, plaids and circles or diamonds, which were repeated throughout the quilt, to following the pattern in freehand quilting. The latter involved stitching lines within, without, and parallel to the outline of the design and filling the inner spaces with scrolls and other interesting patterns. Some quilts combine the two techniques. Kauai women used a *turtle* quilting pattern, unknown to the other islands. My grandmother created a *stephanotis* design of royal blue on white, appliquéing with a red cross-stitch and quilting in a combination of following the pattern with the design and a diagonal pattern outside of it. This stunning quilt reflects the range of diversity and creativity of quilting in Hawaii. I was fortunate to share those days with my grandmother in her little sewing room, when she had time to indulge in the joy of creating something beautiful for her family.

$\mathcal{C}$ontemporary

Native Quilt Artists

by Margaret Wood (Navajo/Seminole)

A tree bursts through and breaks apart a government building. The eagle atop the tree regally surveys the flying pieces of destruction. With images drawn from historical traditional iconography and contemporary life, Native quilter Alice Olsen Williams visually comments on recent incidents critical to Mohawk sovereignty in her quilt titled *The Tree of Peace Saves the Earth*. It was inspired by the Oka Incident, in which Mohawks near Oka, Quebec, stood up against local and national Canadian law enforcement in an effort to preserve some sacred sites from commercial development. Williams pieced the gray Canadian Parliament building, then cut it apart to show it—the symbol of organized dominant culture—being destroyed by the Tree of Peace, a significant symbol in Mohawk culture. Williams is among a growing number of quilters breaking with more traditional use of patterns, fabrics, uses, and forms.

Sometimes called quilt artists or art quiltmakers, they generally create quilts intended to be hung on walls as art. Other artists are moving outside their regular artistic medium within the quilt format, creatively incorporating new fabrics, techniques, and images into existing patterns or inventing entirely new patterns.

The work of many contemporary Native quilt artists incorporates motifs, activities, places, and stories drawn from their own tribal background. For instance, a Navajo adapts rug or basket patterns to her quilts; a Cherokee woman uses appliquéd figures dressed in dance regalia; and a Warm Springs quilter renders in fabric a coyote tale. Some draw on pan-Indian or specific design motifs of other tribes, as when a Mohawk woman completes a Hawaiian pattern quilt, an Ojibwa quilter uses fabric printed with scenes of Inuit life, or a Choctaw makes a *thunderbird*-pattern baby quilt. As quilters of mixed blood produce art expressing their various tribal identities and as quilters come in contact with those from other cultural backgrounds, the blending and borrowing of tribal motifs increase.

For the vast majority of quilters, quilting is a labor-intensive activity done for reasons other than economics. Among most Native quilters, though, where excess financial resources are a rarity, quilting solely as an artistic expression is a luxury many cannot afford. Native artists usually choose art forms that offer more promise of financial return. Among quilters in general, only a few, such as Nancy Crow and Jinny Beyer, have become nationally known and financially successful, with their work shown in prestigious galleries and museums and commanding increasingly higher prices in the world art market. However, these artists derive most of their income not from the sale of quilts but from peripheral activities, such as lecturing, workshops, book writing, fabric design, and the sale of printed cards and calendars.

A few Native quilters from various parts of the country are beginning to gain recognition in the art world, producing very different quilts even while sharing common tribal heritages. The following vignettes illustrate representative backgrounds, motivations, frequent themes, and techniques used by these Native quilters.

Bernyce K. Courtney As a child in eastern Oregon, B. K. Courtney (Wasco/Tlingit) started doing beadwork. As an adult, she worked for years to revive the tradition of Tlingit basket weaving. Then, in 1986, she started making quilts. To learn this new medium, she read books, took quilting classes, and turned to her seamstress mother and sisters for advice.

Her first quilt was an original design based on a traditional beadwork pattern, which she later recognized as being similar to the traditional quilt pattern *trip around the world*. Now most of her quilt designs are drawn from either tribal beadwork or basket patterns. Courtney uses bright solid colors in her quilts, a dramatic change from the tans and browns of the natural materials used in her baskets. Her work incorporates machine piecing, hand quilting, and, occasionally, some appliqué, beadwork, and fabric on which she hand-printed basket designs.

Conrad House Multimedia artist Conrad House (Navajo/Oneida), a resident on the Navajo Reservation in northeastern Arizona, works with beadwork in paintings on canvas and collage boxes and also has worked with leather, ceramics, and glass. Recently, approximately half his work has been devoted to quilted wall hangings.

House designs the quilts, which are then machine pieced and tacked by John Bridges. The first quilt House designed was a baby quilt made of scrap corduroy and hand stitching, a gift for a sister who didn't even have a baby at the time.

House considers his quilts "paintings without the paint," the color being the fabric. Based on Navajo handwoven chief's blanket designs with Amish and Pueblo Indian influences, his most recent works include hand-appliquéd animals, such as horses, mountain sheep, and turtles. He mainly works in denim but also uses art canvas left over from painting canvases he stretches himself. House remembers his mother making utilitarian quilts of denim saved from parts of worn-out jeans. He and Bridges are currently working on a wall hanging made of satin.

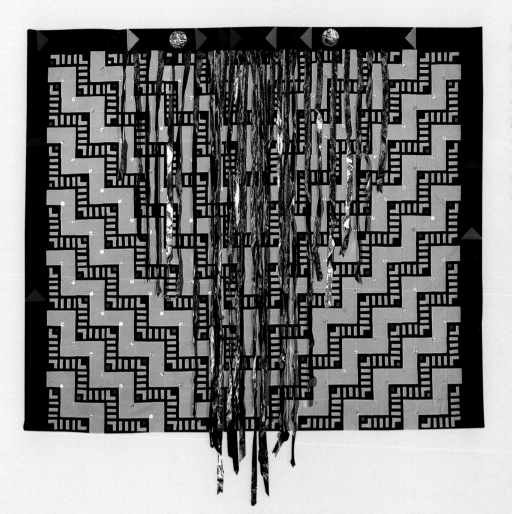

In this innovative **Wasco Button Blanket Quilt** (1996, 81 x 78.5 inches), Bernyce K. Courtney (Wasco/Tlingit), of Warm Springs, Oregon, incorporates design elements from a Wasco sally bag (a twined woven carrying bag) and the buttons used on a Tlingit button blanket. She says of her quilting, "I am honoring this culture but the culture is comforting me."

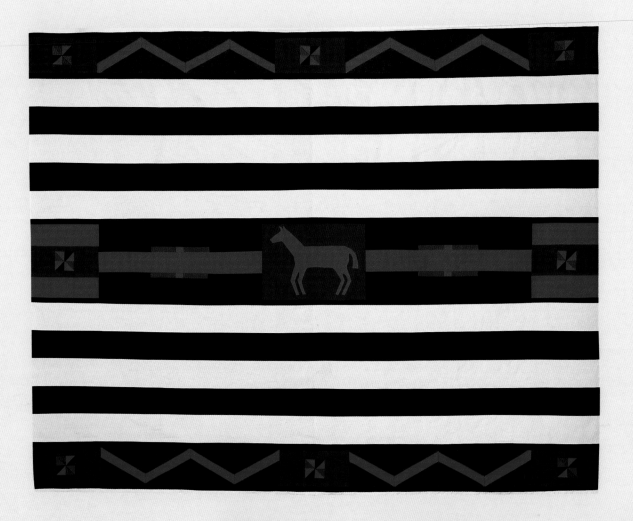

Conrad House (Navajo/Oneida) of St. Michaels, Arizona, situated an appliquéd horse in the center of a pieced Navajo rug design for his **Horse Chief's Blanket Quilt** (1995, 71 x 56 inches). Though House does not quilt his textile pieces, his work is influenced by the colors used by Amish quilters and his childhood memories of the patchwork quilts made by his family. Collection of Michigan State University Museum

Life Between Sunsets, 1985

Made by Bernyce K. Courtney (Wasco/Tlingit), Warm Springs Reservation, Oregon. 44 x 63.75 inches. Collection of Michigan State University Museum

In this quilt, Courtney blends her interest in her dual heritage by using traditional Wasco and Tlingit imagery and colors in her art.

Jennifer Emerson-Tsosie

𝒥ennifer Emerson-Tsosie (Navajo) of Flagstaff, Arizona, earns her living producing clothing and quilts reflecting Native American themes. In 1987, she made her first quilted wall hanging, an original design inspired by a handwoven Navajo Ganado Red rug. Typically, this rug combines deep red mixed with black, gray, and white in an intricately detailed design. Tsosie's grandmother, who has woven Navajo rugs ever since she can remember, also provides inspiration for some of Tsosie's quilts. Other quilt ideas come from her silversmith husband's jewelry designs.

Tsosie's quilts and wall hangings are mostly machine pieced and appliquéd of cotton and satin fabrics; sometimes they are enhanced with beadwork. She also uses both hand and machine quilting. Tsosie gains much personal satisfaction from her quilt work and takes great pride in her careful craftsmanship.

For House, the quilt medium allows a great deal of spontaneity, boldness of color, and variety of textures and patterns.

Alice Olsen Williams

𝒯he work of Alice Olsen Williams of Ontario, Canada, reflects the mixed heritage of her Anishnabe (Ojibwa) and Norwegian backgrounds. Her Anishnabe mother was a seamstress and beadworker from whom Williams learned beadwork, embroidery, knitting, and sewing. Williams remembers exactly when she became a quilter. In the summer of 1980, a friend persuaded her to take a four-week quiltmaking course, which met once a week for two hours. By the time Williams finished her first class project, a small wall hanging featuring the traditional *honeybee* pattern, she was hooked. She always loved sewing and fabrics and, over the years, had accumulated a collection of yardage used to make clothing for her children. Quilting put both her sewing skills and the scraps to a new use.

At first, Williams made quilts in traditional patterns, including *shoofly*, *Dresden plate*, and *bear paw*, but after four years she started making original designs. She loves building pictures with fabrics; many of her themes deal with the environment, the land, and the sacredness of life. She uses her hand-quilted, hand-appliquéd pictorial work to educate people about the dominate culture and her Anishnabe culture. Williams also teaches quiltmaking to students and community members as an artist-in-residence at a Canadian university.

Conclusion

𝒮ince the late nineteenth century, Native quilters have shown their work in tribal exhibitions

Ganado Red Quilt, c. 1989

Made by Jennifer Emerson-Tsosie (Navajo), Flagstaff, Arizona. 60 x 84.5 inches. Collection of Michigan State University Museum

"Ganado"-style Navajo rugs, highly regarded for their stark graphic designs, were originally made for sale at the trading post in Ganado, New Mexico. Emerson-Tsosie uses crosses or plus designs in her "Ganado Red Quilt" to convey the conflict in her life between Christianity and the Native American religion.

This pictorial quilt, named **"The Tree of Peace Saves the Earth"** (1990, 65 x 68 inches), was created by Anishnabe quiltmaker Alice Olsen Williams of Curved Lake, First Nation, Ontario, Canada. Inspired by the "Oka Incident" at Oka, Quebec, where Mohawks stood up to local and national Canadian law enforcement officials, the quilt depicts a tree, rooted on a turtle's back, bursting through and breaking apart the Canadian Parliament building. An eagle sits atop the tree, and war clubs are buried beneath the turtle and roots. Collection of Michigan State University Museum

and displays held in conjunction with pow-wows, venues that presented and judged quilts as women's handicrafts. In the 1970s and 1980s, when various national juried Native arts and crafts shows began to regularly include textile divisions or separate categories for quilts, things started to change. With ribbons and prize money available, quilt designs became more original and workmanship improved.

Museums and galleries have started including Native quilts as art in exhibits and in permanent collections. As more tribal museums and Indian-controlled galleries open around the country, Native quilters are being invited to exhibit in these new venues.

Native quilters also are benefiting from increased multicultural awareness, as the larger quilting community recognizes minority and ethnic quilters. Books and magazines are devoting more attention to the work of Native quilters.

This is a very exciting time. As quilts receive more recognition as art and their market value increases, production of art quilts will continue to rise. For quilters in general, and Native quilters in particular, many more opportunities for exposure, critical recognition, and financial rewards exist than ever before. Native quilters are finally beginning to receive the recognition they have long deserved, boding well for the new millennium.

Three Profiles

Mealii Namahoe Richardson Kalama

by Elaine Zinn

Mealii Namahoe Richardson Kalama (January 3, 1909–July 29, 1992) was one of Hawaii's most widely beloved Hawaiian quilters. Lavonne Richardson, sharing memories of her grandmother, recalled: "Quilting and Hawaiian values were a very important part of her growing up, and the way in which she learned about them would have significant influence on her personality and how she would eventually influence others throughout her entire life."[1] As the *mo'opuna kuakahi*

(the first-born grandchild), Mealii was given to her grandparents to raise:

> I recall the story Granny would often tell about how many a time she could be found lying under the quilting frame, looking up, listening to the women above "talk story" in Hawaiian, and watching them sew for hours and hours.
>
> When she was thirteen, Mealii came to Honolulu to live with her mother and to attend school, but she returned to Hilo during her summer vacations. She had so missed the quilting sessions while she was away at school that she attempted to do some stitching on a quilt while her kupuna (grandmother) was away from the frame. Spotting the uneven stitches, kupuna offered to teach Granny how to quilt, but stitching was not the first lesson. "You must first create designs," she was told, "but you will not find them in books." Kupuna sent her into the backyard to cut out a pattern of the 'ulu (breadfruit tree) chosen as a lesson based on the dual meaning of 'ulu. As a noun,

Mealii Kalama, Native Hawaiian quilter from Oahu and recipient of a National Heritage Fellowship presented by the National Endowment of the Arts, named this 1982 quilt *"Ka U'i O Meali'i"* (The Beauty of Meali'i) (102 x 102 inches). The design depicts the blossoms of the bombax tree and also incorporates Kalama's logo, the tight curve of an unopened fern leaf.

it refers to the tree that provides a staple food, and as a verb, it means "to grow." Granny was taught that her work on the breadfruit pattern was important because through the work, she would grow and thus gain in wisdom and never hunger for it. While the pattern she created that day had the leaves and the fruit the 'ulu represented, there was not a flower. "Ina aole pua aole hua ke kuma, "she was told. "If there is no flower, there is no fruit on the tree."

This was Granny's initial hands-on experience in learning how to quilt and another of a great many lessons on the value of life, nature, and people that she would learn and eventually teach to others. Granny was sixteen at the time, and in this one experience alone, she learned not only the mechanics of quilting but the deeper, underlying meaning to the craft as well—creativity, appreciation of nature, the things that sometimes go unnoticed. Oh yes, and certainly this is when she began to develop that never-ending patience that was one of her character traits—for she did complete that first quilt of the 'ulu pattern, having to do many, many stitches over and over again and taking more than a year and a half to finish.[2]

For twenty-six years, Mealii Kalama was supervisor of recreation for the City and County of Honolulu. For all but one of those years she taught Hawaiian quilting on a volunteer basis at the Papakolea Playground and then at Kawaiaha'o Church, where she was first director of music and then ordained a lay pastor in 1977. She trained hundreds of quilters in the Hawaiian style of quiltmaking. Her work gained such distinction over the years that she was honored by the National Endowment for the Arts' Folk Arts Program as a recipient of the 1985 National Heritage Fellowship. In nominating Mealii for this fellowship, Dr. Robert E.

Potter wrote:

In all of this teaching, she communicated her deep understanding of the Hawaiian values of love, sharing, and concern for nature to her students, regardless of their ethnic background, religious affiliation, or socio-economic status. Her classes represented the broad spectrum of humanity which makes up Hawaii's population.

It is Mealii's combination of skill and love that she imparts in her quilts that have made them works of art. Her beautiful quilts exude a spirit of peace and grace to all who are fortunate to own one or view them. All of her quilts have a distinctive signature, which some of her students call the "Kalama swirl." In explaining her "logo," she would tell a story her kupuna told her about the young shoot of a Hawaiian fern which bends over toward the ground as it first starts growing and then later straightens up.

It shows humility, looking first at the earth and giving thanks for its sustenance. Then later, it looks up to the heavens and the sun and gives thanks for light and life. Out of humility comes the design. "The patterns must be flowing. All nature has a gratefulness," Mealii would point out to her students. "Not even the coconut tree stands straight. It bows its head in the breeze. All nature acknowledges its Creator. And all designs must show that flowing gracefulness of nature. All must acknowledge the breeze and the air. All must display growth, ulu."[3]

Washington Place, the official residence of Hawaii's governor, displays a quilt designed by Mealii depicting the crown flower, the favorite flower of Queen Lili'uokalani, the last monarch of Hawaii.

Laurence Rockefeller commissioned Mealii to design thirty quilts, each eight feet square, for the Mauna Kea Resort, the first large hotel on the Kohala coast of the Big Island, which opened in 1965. The women at the church basted and appliquéd her original designs (a task she did not find creative), but it was Mealii who spent hundreds of hours quietly quilting more than a million tiny stitches in each quilt . . . then donating her commission to the church as part of her tithe. The Kamehameha Schools, the private school for boys and girls of Hawaiian ancestry, proudly displays their school quilt designed by Mealii Kalama at the school's annual song contest and again a few months later at high school graduation ceremonies.

Her quilt *Ka U'i O Meali'i*, designed for a granddaughter in 1982, was exhibited at the 1986 Great American Quilt Festival, an event sponsored by the American Folk Art Museum in New York City as part of the celebration for the Statue of Liberty rededication. In 1995 and 1996, one of her early quilts, *Kukui O Lono* (*Lamp of Lono*), made in collaboration with other women in her family in 1921, was included in the traveling exhibition of quilts titled "Gatherings: America's Quilting Heritage," sponsored by the American Quilt Society. Mealii Kalama and several of her quilts also are featured in the film *The Hawaiian Quilt—A Cherished Tradition*, produced by Hawaii Craftsmen, and in Hawaii Public Television's national television series *Hawaiian Quilting*.

Margaret Wood

by Carla Roberts (Eastern Delaware)

Margaret Wood stitches together layers of fabric and layers of time to create contemporary art quilts that reinterpret American Indian traditions. Wood brings her Navajo/Seminole heritage to bear as she transforms the Seminole tradition of patchwork into fiber arts of distinction. Although not a weaver in the traditional Navajo Way, Wood weaves together stories past and present to translate timeless messages into contemporary thought.

Margaret Wood describes *Rusty Maize* as a "crazy quilt with a message." The quilt developed from a collection of fabrics she accumulated over a decade that all featured the color rust. That rusty color is also the tone of the southwestern landscape where Wood grew up, as well as the deep red-brown skin of the Native peoples of her homeland. *Rusty Maize* reinterprets the *Navajo wedding* basket form as well as its counterpart in Pima culture, the *man in the maze* basket. Both basketry forms embody the concept of a pathway—a pathway to the light, to the

Margaret Wood (Navajo/Seminole) of Phoenix, Arizona, created this "**Rusty Maize Quilt**" (76 x 80 inches) in 1994. She explains: "For about ten years I collected rust prints. I kept scraps of other projects and bought small pieces of rust-colored prints I liked, thinking I would make a log cabin quilt some day. Then one day I realized that my work was all nontraditional and I would be bored working on a log cabin."

center, the good path, the righteous path, the middle path.

Wood talks of the quilt as a kind of map. The viewer enters the path—representative of the path of life—at the upper left corner along the black, white, and red stairstep pattern of the *Navajo wedding* basket design. In traversing the path, the way becomes less distinct as the colors disintegrate and the pathway forks. For Wood, this symbolizes the choices that must be made in life when there is not always a clear, strong path to follow. Through many permutations, the path leads back to where it began, but we sense that this path is probably not just a circle but a spiral. Though the path seems to lead back to the beginning, it is actually spiraling upward.

In its title, *Rusty Maize* also reminds us of the symbol of maize—corn, the life-sustaining grain of this Western Hemisphere that links so many of the indigenous cultures of the Americas. Corn images point the way, leading us in the four directions from south to east, north to west. Each corn symbol is designed from patchwork squares of red, yellow, black, and white, colors that in combination simulate flesh tone. Thus, the corn images remind us of our relationship to one another in this journey of life.

In the center of *Rusty Maize* a montage includes a *tree of life* design. Symbolic variations of the *tree of life* occur in many cultures throughout the world. However represented, the *tree of life* teaches the strength of walking the middle path, in between good and evil, with integrity and balance and in harmony with others. *Rusty Maize* is truly a *crazy* quilt with a message for all of humanity.

*N*ellie Star Boy Menard

by Laurie N. Anderson (Sioux)
and Marsha L. MacDowell

In 1995, Nellie Star Boy Menard was honored as a recipient of the National Heritage Fellowship awarded by the National Endowment for the Arts. This recognized her mastery of Lakota arts, particularly quiltmaking, regaliamaking, and beadwork; her lifelong role as educator both within her own Lakota Sioux community and to a wider non-Native public; and her tireless participation in the maintenance of family and community traditional culture.

Born in 1910 on the Rosebud Reservation in South Dakota, Menard learned many of her skills under the tutelage of her grandmother, Helen Leads the Horse, during the four-day *Hunka* ceremony, the Sioux girls' coming-of-age ceremony. She learned quilting, including the *star* pattern, from her mother, Grace Runs Clothes, when she needed quilts for the memorial feast giveaway after her son died.

Menard attended the Rosebud Boarding

School and Flandreau Indian School, where her talents for artistic excellence were already in evidence. One of her blanket designs for a Pendleton blanket was accepted for production by the famous Pendleton Woolen Mills, and some of her beadwork designs were published in Carrie Lyford's *Quill and Beadwork of the Western Sioux.*[1]

After graduating in 1929, Menard began her teaching career as an art instructor at the Rosebud Boarding School. From 1937 to 1942, she started and ran an arts and crafts shop in Rosebud before moving to Browning, Montana, where she served as the manager of the Northern Plains Arts and Crafts program from 1943 to 1946. Then Menard moved back to South Dakota to head the Sioux Indian Museum in Rapid City, where she worked until her retirement in 1972. She continues to serve as a teacher and consultant in special workshops and programs on Indian culture at various South Dakota colleges.

Over the years, Menard has given away scores of quilts; she also has been the recipient of many to honor her. Shortly after receiving the National Heritage Award, Nellie Star Boy Menard also received the South Dakota Living Indian Treasure Award. The latter award, along with a *star* quilt, was presented to Menard at a powwow held in conjunction with the Northern Plains Tribal Arts Market in Sioux Falls. In addition, Menard has received Superior Performance Awards from the U.S. Indian Arts and Crafts Board and is featured in the fourth edition of *Indians of Today*, the *Encyclopedia of American Indians*, *Album of American Indians*, *Sioux of the*

**Crazy Star Quilt,
1994–95**

*Made by Nellie Star Boy
Menard (Sioux), Rosebud,
South Dakota. 79 x 96 inches.
Collection of Michigan State
University Museum*

Rosebud, and the 1976 bicentennial edition of *Community Leaders and Noteworthy Americans.*

Within her own Rosebud community, Menard is a respected elder, known and held in high esteem. Quiltmaker Lula Red Cloud, who as a teenager lived with the Menard family for several years, remembers the generous and patient mentoring she received from Nellie. Like countless others, Red Cloud learned from Menard not only the technical skills associated with a craft but also a broad spectrum of traditional knowledge about Sioux history and culture.

Despite her years of full-time employment and the fact that she raised thirteen children—ten of her own and three grandchildren—Menard has prodigiously produced a wide variety of traditional art forms. She is proficient in tanning, quillwork, cross-stitching, fingerweaving, featherwork, dressmaking, and crocheting but is perhaps best known for her beadwork, dance shawls, and quilting. Just as her mother and grandmother taught Menard her basic craft skills, Nellie has passed them on to her children, grandchildren, and now even her great-grandchildren.

She has made and mostly given away hundreds of the colorful flat fringe shawls used mostly by the women of the Fancy Shawl Dress Dancers. Her beadwork and quilts have been sold in shops and galleries around the world, but more often Menard makes them for giveaways in honor of community leaders and loved ones for achievements such as high school and college graduations, for birthdays, for welcoming new babies, for service in the military, for participating in funeral ceremonies, and for memorial feasts to honor the memory of a

Dance Shawl, 1994

Made by Nellie Star Boy Menard (Sioux), Rosebud, South Dakota. 56.5 x 64.5 inches. Collection of Michigan State University Museum

deceased loved one. Menard also has presented quilts to political, civic, tribal, and religious leaders to honor their work; Hillary Rodham Clinton, Pope John Paul, and U.S. Senator Tom Daschle have all received quilts made by her.

Nellie Menard's creativity in developing original designs is highly evident in her *star* quilts. Even when using patterns that are commercially available, she will choose and put together colors that are highly original. The idea for her *crazy star* quilt came about when Menard showed her grandson pictures of different quilts she had made. Menard shares: "My grandson said, 'Grandma, make all those together in one quilt,' and so I made it. . . . It was his idea that I put that together." She presented the finished quilt to him upon his return home from military service; a variation of the quilt is in the collections at the Michigan State University Museum.

Native Quilting

Research and Exhibition

Project

by C. Kurt Dewhurst and Marsha L. MacDowell

Project History

For more than a decade, Michigan State University (MSU) Museum staff has been conducting field, museum, and archival-based research on Native Hawaiian and North American Indian quiltmaking traditions. In the course of the work, two other organizations—the Smithsonian Institution's National Museum of the American Indian (NMAI) and Atlatl (a national service organization for professional Native artists)—joined MSU Museum as major collaborators for the purpose of developing an exhibition.

The Native Quilting research and exhibition project first began as a natural extension of the MSU Museum's long-standing research, exhibition, and public programs related to folk and traditional culture. It also reflected the museum's commitment to develop research and public program projects in collaboration with organizations and members of cultural groups, including many Native American tribal groups, in Michigan.

In 1984, the Michigan Quilt Project was established at the museum to specifically survey, document, preserve, and present information on Michigan's quilts, quilters, and quilting traditions. A primary vehicle used by MSU Museum staff for identifying quilts was the establishment of Quilt Discovery Days, held in collaboration with a variety of local organizations in more than thirty-five sites. Community members were encouraged to bring in their quilts for a statewide inventory and enjoy an opportunity to share their quilts and quilt stories with others. Museum staff and volunteers photographed quilts and quilters, recorded information about quilts and quilters on inventory forms, and, where possible, audiotaped stories about quilts and quilters. It was during this initial survey that two historical Odawa quilts were documented.

Subsequently, an investigation was

begun into the quilting activities of Ojibwa, Odawa, and Potawatomi, Michigan's major tribal groups. Through the various activities of the Michigan Traditional Arts Program, contacts and relationships had been established with many Native Americans around the state, and it was these individuals, in particular basketmakers and quillworkers, we first turned to for information about quilting. Sure enough, nearly all we contacted either were quilters themselves or knew quilters. We quickly realized that we simply had not previously thought to ask about quilting.

By 1990, we curated a program component on contemporary Ojibwa, Odawa, and Potawatomi quilting for the annual MSU Museum Festival of Michigan Folklife, a major state festival held every August on campus. Textile artists demonstrated quiltmaking and discussed their work with festival visitors. It was at this point that the seeds of our first major organizational collaboration were planted.

Fred Nahwooksy, at that time the community services coordinator at the National Museum of the American Indian (NMAI), attended the festival and suggested the possibility of a national exhibition on American Indian quiltmaking. Nahwooksy recognized the potential of this project meeting the mission statement of NMAI so clearly articulated in its literature:

> The National Museum of the American Indian is an institution of living cultures dedicated to recognizing and affirming to Native communities and the non-Native public the historical and contemporary culture and cultural achievements of the Native peoples of the Western Hemisphere by advancing—in consultation, collaboration, and cooperation with Natives—knowledge and understanding of Native cultures, including art, history and language, and by recognizing the museum's special responsibility to protect, support, and enhance the development, maintenance, and perpetuation of Native culture and community.

Though we were aware of Seminole, Native Hawaiian, and Sioux quilting traditions, we were not aware of existing research on quilting in other Native communities. However, based on our experience in Michigan, we hypothesized that, like us, the question of whether Natives quilted had simply not been asked by many scholars. We also were interested in seeing how quiltmaking in Michigan possibly fit into a larger tradition of Native quilting. Encouraged by Nahwooksy, we began field research in selected communities across the country and, at the same time, initiated discussions with other NMAI staff about preparing an exhibition.

As we continued our fieldwork, we began contacting colleagues engaged in research on quilts and Native American culture. We also contacted curators of museums with significant textile or Native American holdings and visited selected collections. By 1992, our preliminary findings included evidence that quiltmaking traditions indeed existed in nearly all the tribal communities sampled. We found that within Native communities, quiltmaking was firmly linked to tribal aesthetics and customs. We found little written or photographic documentation of the quiltmaking traditions, regardless of the longevity, pervasiveness, or importance of quiltmaking within the community. We did find, though, an abundance of oral narratives of the historical and contemporary use of quilts.

During this research phase, we interviewed Margaret Wood, a Navajo/Seminole quilter who lives in Phoenix, Arizona, and at that time a board member of Atlatl. She immediately saw a match for Atlatl's mission: "To promote the vitality of Native American art by heightening awareness of indigenous aesthetics and modes of expression, creating an informational network for Native American artists, and enhancing the economic development of Native American arts." In 1993, Wood joined us and NMAI staff to confirm the collaborations and to begin planning the continued research phase. Shortly after, another key consultant, Linda Moriarity, joined to represent the Native Hawaiian perspective. In addition to being part of a family of Native Hawaiian quilters, Moriarity had extensive experience researching and presenting Hawaiian folklife.

Together, the team agreed to involve as many Native people as possible in all phases of the project. Wherever possible, we would ensure a first-person Native voice was present in the interpretation of the material and would seek creative ways of returning gathered information to the home communities. A set of goals established for the exhibition helped the team develop a focused research plan for the next two years:

1. To acquaint visitors with information about the diversity of traditions found within any culture;

2. To challenge visitors to consider quiltmaking as a Native American/Native Hawaiian art form;

3. To encourage visitors to examine the variety of meanings that an object might have depending on the context of its origin and use;

4. To motivate visitors to discern the differences and similarities in quiltmaking traditions among Natives and non-Natives;

5. To show how Native quiltmaking tradi-tions reflect tribally specific and pan-Indian cultural meanings;

6. To encourage visitors to examine and rethink the ways in which material culture is documented, analyzed, and interpreted;

7. To challenge visitors to consider the ways in which material culture is shaped by cultural contact and the cultural group diaspora;

8. To provoke visitors to see the similarities between various kinds of material culture within a given tribal community;

9. To show how quiltmaking is a living, dynamic tradition within Native communities; and

10. To counter stereotypes about Native American and Native Hawaiian cultural traditions in general, and material culture in particular, as historically depicted through the media.

We began by staging a series of American Indian Community Quilt Discovery Days at tribal events and museums; using a field team to document significant quilting activities in selected communities; and working together to promote the project and to seek funding sources. Where we could, our respective organizations contributed staff time and services. It also was agreed that we would remain curators and primary field-workers of the project and that the field collections of research materials, including quilts, would be housed at the Michigan State University Museum. NMAI agreed to appoint a project manager to coordinate NMAI internal resources and to assign the community services coordinator as a liaison to the project. Clara Sue Kidwell and Danyelle Means have served in the former capacity, with Fred Nahwooksy and Keevin Lewis in the latter.

The collaboration has remained intact since, though not without changes in the plan. The sometimes conflicting start-up activities of the newly established NMAI, changes in project personnel, searches for funding, and the coordination of a complex and widespread group of individuals working on the project forced us to alter timetables, goals, and scope of the work. At times, the lack of consistent, predictable funding and the fact of many creative personalities in the project made for stretches of moderate, sporadic, and, occasionally, duplicate activity; at other times, the changes brought forward exciting new opportunities and information that were incorporated into the project.

Despite these challenges, the project continued to garner enthusiasm—perhaps most importantly among Native peoples—wherever research and planning occurred. The collaborations also enabled and sustained a number of creative, innovative research strategies. NMAI participated in the sponsorship of four Quilt Discovery Days, modeled on those held as part of the original Michigan Quilt Project, at the National Hoop Dance Contest in Phoenix, Arizona, the Oneida Nation Museum in Wisconsin, the Museum at Warm Springs at the Warm Springs Reservation in Oregon, and the powwow at the opening ceremonies for NMAI's George Gustav Heye Center in New York City. NMAI also sponsored team documentation of quilting activities at selected sites. These activities included the basketball *star* quilt honoring ceremony of the Brockton High School Boys' basketball team on the Fort Peck Reservation in Brockton, Montana; a baby-naming ceremony at a powwow at Lakes Andes Yankton Sioux Reservation in South Dakota; the weekly meeting of the sewing club at the Tsali Manor Senior Citizens Center on the Cherokee Reservation in North Carolina; the Akwesasne Freedom School Quilt Auction on the St. Regis

Mohawk Reservation in New York; the St. Francis High School commencement ceremony on the Rosebud Sioux Reservation in South Dakota; and at the Ka Hui Kapa Apana O Waimea monthly quilt group gathering on the Big Island of Hawaii. Atlatl included a call for quilt information in its national newsletter, actively recruited quilters to the project, assisted at the Quilt Discovery Days, and helped develop and maintain a roster of contemporary quilters.

With support from an MSU All-University Research Grant and a research leave, as well as a research grant from the Women's Committee of the Smithsonian Institution, the curators, C. Kurt Dewhurst and Marsha L. MacDowell, and two Native American graduate student assistants, Laurie Anderson and Kathy VanDeCar, also were able to conduct field-based research in a number of sites around the country. Visits were made with quilters, quilt owners, and quilt marketers in many settings, including homes, sewing cooperatives, pawnshops, churches, powwows, senior centers, bingo halls, and casinos. Visits were also made to museums and tribal centers with quilt collections and archives of historical photographs. In addition, letters were sent to many quilt scholars (including members of the American Quilt Study Guild and the Alliance for American Quilts), Native American specialists, museums, and to many members of the American Folklore Society's Public Programs Section.

The project's final planned research component occurred in November 1996 when twenty quilters representing a broad array of tribal affiliations, age, experience, and interests gathered in East Lansing, Michigan, for a workshop and public preview exhibition of their work. Coordinated by all three partners, the event was funded by the

Gatherings and Conference Program administered by the Fund for Folk Culture sponsored by the Pew Charitable Trust and by the Preservation and Heritage Programs of the National Endowment for the Arts, with additional support from the Michigan Council for Arts and Cultural Affairs, MSU, the Nokomis Learning Center (a mid-Michigan Native American organization), and the student and faculty Native American associations at MSU. Over the weekend, quilters discussed their mutual needs, challenges, and dreams pertaining to their quilting activities, received feedback from other Natives and the general public regarding their quilts, and heard speakers on quilt marketing, design copyrights, and quilt care. The quilters and their quilts were photographed, and interviews with them were recorded on audiotape.

As the project took shape, the Smithsonian Institution Traveling Exhibition Service (SITES) committed to circulate the major exhibition first at MSU Museum and then at six to eight other venues across the country. Also planned was a smaller version of the exhibit, which will be featured at tribal museums, cultural centers, and community event sites, such as powwows and festivals, in hopes of encouraging local communities to add their own local quilts to the exhibits. The Museum of New Mexico Press in Santa Fe agreed to publish this related book, profusely illustrated with historical and contemporary photographs of quilts, quilters, and quilt-related activities and containing contributions from Native and non-Native authors. Additional support for the book was provided by the Heritage and Preservation Program, National Endowment for the Arts; NMAI, Smithsonian Institution; the Michigan Council for Arts and Cultural Affairs; and MSU Museum.

The research to date has yielded a new museum collection of more than one hundred historical and contemporary Native quilts, thousands of pages of field notes and photographs, approximately one hundred taped and transcribed interviews, and a large body of related documentary material. The research team regularly sought input on why such an exhibition was worth doing, what the visitor should know about Native quilting traditions, and how the collection might best be displayed. It is this material, along with the results of the November 1996 gathering of quilters, that helped form the basis of the final exhibition and this publication.

The multiple levels of collaborations—between the three primary institutions, between artist and field-worker, between staff within each institution and tribally based groups, and so on—had a direct impact on the way the research and exhibition design evolved and eventually was implemented. The Native Quilting project relied on the following principles:

1. Each partner brings significant strengths/insights to the undertaking;

2. The goals of each can be complementary and actually supportive;

3. Multiple perspectives are valued and would be incorporated in the planning and development of the exhibition;

4. One must seek to understand and respect the complex cultural context, often a ceremonial occasion, in which quilts are used/presented to effectively present quilting traditions;

5. The Native voice must be clear and present during all phases of the project to convey the complexity of the nature of quilts in the community; and

6. All knowledge gained/shared should be shared among the partners based on their particular goals/needs.

These principles helped guide the project in formulating strategies for collaborative documentation at ceremonial events and community activities, creating innovative opportunities for documentation, sharing knowledge about communities, and creating long-term relationships with communities.

A key to the collaborations has been conversation. Jim Volkert, assistant director of NMAI, senior exhibit team member, and an early supporter of this project, has said of the process:

> This project is one that has thrived on conversation. Some museum conversations slip into the arcane. This one has not. The process of collaboration between quilters, the Michigan State University Museum, Atlatl, and the National Museum of the American Indian has successfully sought to balance the personal meaning of quilts as instruments of honor for Native people with the public expression of the beauty of the objects.

The fieldwork undertaken in this project has been marked by an open dialogue between researchers, informants, and community members. Where possible, the material gathered has often been shared in some form with its community of origin. For example, the trophy case at Montana's Brockton High School now contains a photo–text display about the fieldwork based on the basketball tournament star quilt ceremony. Conversations also are under way with the staff of the nearby Fort Peck Tribal Museum, a possible site for the smaller traveling exhibition. Project personnel have been in contact with communities that are now beginning or are further exploring their quilt history through local research and exhibition activities.

It is our hope that this exhibition and publication will expand the dialogue on quilting in Native communities. There is much to be learned from those Native artists who make quilts "to honor and comfort."

Acknowledgments

First and foremost, we would like to thank the quilters and their families who welcomed us into their homes and community centers and who were generous in sharing their artistry and stories. Museum, library, and archive personnel and tribal chairpersons and elders provided needed access to papers, collections, facilities, and individuals. While many colleagues sent us information, both solicited and unsolicited, members of two groups, the American Quilt Study Group and the American Folklore Society's Public Sector Folklore Section, were especially generous with assistance. Colleagues at the Smithsonian National Museum of the American Indian, Michigan State University Native American Institute, Museum of New Mexico Press, and Atlatl creatively and consistently assisted when needed at various stages of the project. Lastly, colleagues at Michigan State University Museum, particularly project assistants Laurie Anderson and Marie Gile, collection manager Lynne Swanson, and collection assistants Melanie Atkinson and Pearl Wong, have been instrumental in providing critical research and archival support.

Because this project has been so collaborative in nature, there have been many, many other individuals who have contributed in small and major ways in the research and subsequent development of the exhibition and companion book. It would be impossible to list them all, but those listed below were especially helpful.

Artists: Iris Red Elk Allrunner, James ("Kimo") Balai, Sharon Balai, Doris Benedict, Salli Benedict, Gussie Bento, Mary Big Horse, Gloria Black Spotted Horse, Kathleen Blount, Florentine Blue Thunder, Sheree Bonaparte, Katie Brady, Teresa Brien, Nora Brings Him Back, Leanne R. Buckwheat, Selma Buckwheat, Calico Country Quilt

Guild, Cecil Atkins Carlton, Nancy Martin Comins, Delia Cook, Rita Corbiere, Vicki Cornelius, Bernyce K. Courtney, Myrna Courtney, Barbara Cusick, Melinda Doxtator, Rita Fairbanks, Marietta Four Bear, Alice Fox, Floyd Fox, Eva Gagnon, Pat Courtney Gold, Delores Gourneau, Shirley Grady, Charlie Grinnell, Julia Grinnell, Mary Henio, Marie Horse Looking, Conrad House, Mary J. Ives, Beverly Cook Jackson, Kate Jackson, Sarah Jacobs, Ben Johnson, Judy Johnson, Leda Johnson, Ka Hui Kapa Apana O Waimea, Violet Kaiawe, Deborah Kepola Kakalia, Elizabeth Kimewon, Irene Kubo, Sybil Lambert, Cordelia Leadford, Alberta Lewis, Emmaline McCoy, Carol McFall, Ramona Malnourie, Veronica Medicine, Nellie Star Boy Menard, Archie Miller, Paula Chaca Montoya, Ollie Napesni, Nancy Naranjo, Julia Nyholm, Diane O'Leary, Susan Oliver, Virginia Osceola, Claire Packard, Eraina Palmer, Elizabeth Perkins, Lula Red Cloud, Betsy Rose Rezentes, Carrie Robinson, Marlene Sekaquaptewa, Julia Shigwadja, Harriet Soong, Viola Spotted Bird, Pearl Spotted Tail, Pat Stevens, Carole Stewart, Martha Taylor, Margaret Thayer, Amanda Thompson, Julia Thompson, Judy Toppings, Tsali Manor Senior Sewing Club, Jennifer Tsosie, Ruth Tyler, Vera Tyler, Sheila Wahnetah, Sara Angela Walker, Tillie Walker, Rae Jean Walking Eagle, Lydia Whirlwind Soldier, Paula White, Greta White Calf, Alice Olsen Williams, Caroline Wilson, Margaret Wood, Mary Adair Woodward, Loretta Young, and Marie Young Bear.

Other individuals: George Abrams, Elizabeth Akana, Ken Ames, Loyce Reifel Anderson, Robert Annesley, Jo Allyn Archambault, Nancy Cameron Armstrong, Linda Boynton Arthur, Roy Azure III, Joshua Baer, Deborah Smith Barney, Annette C. Bell, Cuesta Benberry, Barry Bergey, Angela Bianca, Spike Big Horn, Ann Bird, David Blackard, Pearl Broome, Marjorie Cahn, John and Iren Cantlon, Charlene Cerny, Cynthia Chippewa, Varrick Chittenden, Abe Chopper, Robert Cogswell, Donna Dubray Cordier, George Cornell, Dorothy Cozart, Anna Crampton, Marclay Crampton, Mark Cudahy, Marva Dalebout, Carolyn O'Bagy Davis, Minn Dewhurst, Jim Dillon, Don Doll, Joanna Adams Duncan, Pat Dyer-Deckrow, Bonnie Ekdahl, Frank Ettawageshik, Ray Fadden, Pat Ferrero, Ann Fienup-Riordan, Sandi Fox, Gladys Marie Fry, Deb Galvan, Deborah George, Meg Glaser, Sandra L. Goforth, Alan Govenar, Barbara Graymount, Rayna Green, James Griffith, George R. Hammel, Joyce Hammond, Michael Hammond, Karen Hauff, Duane Hekkel, Jill Hemming, Helen Henry, Emil Her Many Horses, Joyce Herold, Cher Hersrud, Rick Hill, Tom Hill, Yvonne Hoag, Teresa Hollingsworth, Norman Hollow, Jonathan Holstein, Maggie Holtzberg, Nancy Hornback, George Horse Capture, Helen Hoskins, Carter Houck, Joyce Ice, Lynne Ireland, Laurie Jensen-Wunder, Deborah Johnson, Tim Johnson, Val Johnson, Suzi Jones, Patricia Keller, Helen Kelly, Clara Sue Kidwell, Stanely Knick, Barbara Lau, Caryl M. Lewis, Kathi Littlejohn, Harry McAnally, James McClurken, John McDaniel, Betty and Harlan MacDowell, Francseca McLean, Chris Martin, Lynn Martin, Peter Mattir, the Rev. Stanislaus Maudlin O.S.B., Peggy Maxwell, Bea Medicine, Gwen Meister, Susan Chippewa Minch, Ruth Montgomery, Paulette Montileaux, Tom Moony, Linda Moriarity, Clydia Nahwooksy, Fred Nahwooksy, Jackson Narcomey, Kathy Nielen, Phil Nusbaum, Nancy Nusz, Earl Nyholm, Karen O'Dowd, Maida Owens, Arnie Parish, Olney Patt, Jr., Beverly Patterson, Molly Perry, Bea Peters, Marla Powers, Jane Przybysz, Laura Quackenbush, Jan Reed,

Arnold Revzin, Carla Roberts, Kim Roberts, Bea Roeder, Jillian Sandrock, Charles Seeman, Dan Sheehy, Julie Silber, Merry Silber, Brother C. M. Simon, S.J., Lou Anna Simon, Fran Soika, Laurie Sommers, Edward Soong, Sandra L. Starr, Linda Taylor, Barb Tazelaar, James Thibeault, Nancy Tucker, Fawn Valentine, Tom Vennum, Minnie Wabanimkee, Merikay Waldvogel, Tammy Walker, Myron Walking Eagle, Dale Weasel, Rick West, Paul Westberg, Ronna Lee Widener, Annie Pulford Wilson, Mary Adair Woo, Cameron Wood, Loretta J. Woodard, Karen Wood Workman, Carolyn Ybarra, Charmaine Young, Shelly Zegart, and Elaine Zinn.

Organizations and institutions: Akwe:kon Press; Akwesasne Museum; Alaska State Library and Historical Collections; American Culture Research Center; American Quilt Study Group; Anchorage Museum of History and Art; Atka Lakota Museum, St. Joseph Indian School; Bishop Museum, the State Museum of Natural and Cultural History; Boynton Photography; Brockton High School; Buechel Memorial Lakota Museum; Bureau of Florida Folklife Programs; *Canada Quilts Magazine*; Center for Native American Studies, Montana State University; Center for Southern Folklore; Cherokee Nation Museum; Clifton Choctaws; Country Stitches; Denver Museum of Natural History; E.A.G.L.E., Michigan State University; Five Civilized Tribes Museum; Fort Peck Tribe; Gonzaga University Library; Hawaii Quilt Project; Heard Museum; Hearts and Hands Media Arts; the Heritage Center, Red Cloud Indian School, Pine Ridge, South Dakota; HIV/AIDS Prevention Education, South Dakota Department of Education and Cultural Affairs; Iroquois Indian Museum; Kamehameha Schools Bernice Pauahi Bishop Estate; Kauai Museum; Mendocino County Museum; Michigan Commission on Indian Affairs; Milwaukee Public Museum; Minnesota Historical Society; the Museum at Warm Springs; Museum of International Folk Art; N.A.I.S.O., Michigan State University; National Anthropological Archives, Smithsonian Institution; Native American Institute, Michigan State University; National Archives Trust Fund, Atlanta, Georgia; National Council on Traditional Arts; Native American Resource Center, Pembroke State University; National Archives; *Native Peoples*; Nebraska Quilt Project; Nebraska State Historical Society; *The New York State Conservationist*; New York State Historical Association; Nokomis American Indian Cultural Learning Center; Northwestern Photographic Company; Oklahoma Historical Society—Library, Archives, and Manuscript Divisions; Oneida Nation Museum; Oneida Senior Center; Plains Art Museum; Public Sector Folklore Section, the American Folklore Society; *Quilters' Newsletter Magazine*; Rocky Mountain Quilt Museum; Roger J. Bounds Foundation; Rosebud Casino; Royal Ontario Museum; St. Francis High School; Sioux Indian Museum; Six Nations Indian Museum; Smithsonian Institution; South Dakota State University, H. M. Briggs Library; Southern Ute Cultural Center; State Foundation on the Arts, Hawaii; State Historical Society of North Dakota; State of Michigan Archives; Takini High School; Thaw Collection, Fenimore House Museum; Tsali Manor Senior Citizens Center; University of Montana Library; University of North Dakota, Special Collections, Chester Fritz Library; University of Washington Press; Western Folklife Center; Wyoming State Archives; and Ziibiwing Cultural Center.

Michigan State University Museum: Erica Adams, Juan Alvarez, Julie Avery, Michele

Beltran, Helena Carey, Ruth Fitzgerald, Francie Freese, Terry Hanson, LaNeysa Harris-Featherstone, Noé Hernandez, LuAnne Kozma, Yvonne Lockwood, Kris Morrissey, Ruth Patino, and Frances Vincent and consultants Dierdre Windsor and Randi Korn.

National Museum of the American Indian, Smithsonian Institution: Peter Brill, Dan Davis, Pamela Dewey, Lee Anne Fahey, Katherine Fogden, Cecile Ganteaume, Gaetana de Gennaro, Johanna Gorelick, John Haworth, Charlotte Heth, Janine Jones, Stacy Jones, Clara Sue Kidwell, Keevin Lewis, Danyelle Means, Dean Moncayo, Marty de Montaño, Fred Nahwooksy, Carol Repkievian, Alyce Sadongei, Carmen Sanchez, Millie Seubert, Susanna Stieff, Russell Tall Chief, Tanya Thrasher, Jim Volkert, and Rick West.

Smithsonian Institution Traveling Exhibition Service: Charlotte Cohen, Josette Cole, Betsy Hennings, Katherine Krile, Jim Rubenstein, and Lee Williams.

Museum of New Mexico Press: Denice Anderson, Jenifer Blakemore, Ron Latimer, Mary Luders, David Skolkin, Susan Surprise, Mary Wachs, and Sydney Webber.

Atlatl: Carla Roberts, Wendy Weston, and Margaret Wood.

Funding sources: Michigan State University All-University Research Initiation Award; Michigan State University Office of Research and Graduate Studies; Michigan State University Office of the Provost; Gatherings and Conferences Program of the Pew Charitable Trust, a program coordinated by the Fund for Folk Culture; Smithsonian Womens' Committee Fund; Special Exhibitions Fund of the Smithsonian Institution; National Endowment for the Arts, Heritage and Preservation Program; and Michigan Council for Arts and Cultural Affairs.

Unless noted otherwise, all quilts were photographed in Lansing, Michigan, by Elbinger Studios, Inc., under the excellent direction of Douglas Elbinger, A.S.M.P., who was assisted by Michael J. Webb, David Woods, Mark Todd, and Chris Bachelder.

Notes

NORTH AMERICAN INDIAN AND NATIVE HAWAIIAN QUILTMAKING

1. Lee S. Wild, "Introduction," in Reiko Mochinaga Brandon, ed. *The Hawaiian Quilt* (Tokyo: Kokusai Art, 1989), 13.

2. Sally Garoutte, "Uses of Textiles in Hawaii: 1820–1850," *Uncoverings* 1985, vol. 6. *Research Papers of the American Quilt Study Group*: 155–56.

3. Mary O'Brien, *Cherokee Quilts* (Tulsa, Okla.: The Mary O'Brien Bookshop, 1996). "According to records of the American Board of Commissioners for Foreign Mission, William Holland ordered domestic gingham, checkered blue and white factory cotton, cotton shirting, dark blue calico, buff calico, pink calico, narrow striped dimity, and assorted remnants for use at the School. . . . In 1831, Holland sold some of this cloth for a quilt; and in 1832 he sold a quilt for $3.50 to help raise funds for the mission."

4. Winifred W. Barton, *John P. Williamson: A Brother to the Sioux* (1919; reprint, Clements, Minn.: Sunnycrest Publishing, 1980), 136, 255.

5. Marsha MacDowell and Ruth Fitzgerald, eds., *Michigan Quilts: 150 Years of a Textile Tradition* (East Lansing, Mich.: Michigan State University Museum, 1987), 83.

6. Patricia Cox Crews and Ronald C. Naugle, *Nebraska Quilts and Quilters* (Lincoln, Nebr.: University of Nebraska Press, 1991), 54–55.

7. Julia Thompson, interview by Alex Jacobs, St. Regis Reservation, N.Y., November 1996.

8. Christopher Martin, *Native Needlework: Contemporary Indian Textiles from North Dakota* (Fargo, N.Dak.: North Dakota Council on the Arts, 1988), 12.

9. Tom Hill, *Patches: The Art of Quilt Making on the Six Nations and New Credit Indian Reserves* (Brantford, Ontario: The Woodland Indian Cultural Educational Centre, 1983), iv.

10. O'Brien, *Cherokee Quilts*.

11. Amanda Seal and Louisa Gibbs to John Ross, 2 April 1864, Papers of John Ross, Collection of the Cherokee Nation Museum.

12. Sandra J. Metzler-Smith, "Quilts in Pomo Culture," *Uncoverings* 1980, vol. 1. *Research Papers of the American Quilt Study Group*: 45.

13. *Bedford Bulletin*, 6 August 1986.

14. Donald Reeves, *Quilts from the Collection of the Oklahoma Historical Society* (Oklahoma City, Okla.: Oklahoma Historical Society, 1978). Thanks to Dorothy Cozart for sharing this reference with us.

15. Fanny Bergen, "The Tapestry of the New World," *Scribner's* (September 1894):n.p. Thanks to Cuesta Benberry for sharing this article with us.

16. Stanley Knick, telephone conversation with Marsha MacDowell, 11 January 1994.

17. Mary Cross, telephone conversation with Marsha MacDowell, 27 September 1994.

18. Charles Burton Thomsen to Joshua Baer, 1989.

19. Reeves, *Quilts from the Collection of the Oklahoma Historical Society*.

20. Merry Silber to Marsha MacDowell, 1995.

21. Shari Miller and Miriam Rich, "Folk Art in the Clifton Community," *Louisiana Folklife* (Special Issue) 8 (March 1983): 17.

22. Adolph L. Dial, *The Lumbee* (New York: Chelsea House Publishers, 1993), 85.

23. Gladys-Marie Fry, *Stitched from the Soul: Slave Quilts from Ante-Bellum South* (New York: Dutton Studio Books, 1990), 79.

24. Veronica Medicine, interview by Marsha MacDowell and Kurt Dewhurst, Harbor Springs, Mich., 21 July 1989.

25. Alice Fox, interview by Marsha MacDowell and Kurt Dewhurst, Sault Ste. Marie, Mich., 9 June 1989.

26. Eva Gagnon, interview by Kathy VanDeCar, Dunseith, N.Dak., 21 November 1994.

27. Mary Woodward, interview by Marsha MacDowell, Tahlequah, Okla., 12 May 1995.

28. Shirley Grady, interview by Kathy VanDeCar, New Town, N.Dak., 9 November 1994.

29. Nellie Star Boy Menard, interview by Marsha MacDowell and Kurt Dewhurst, Rosebud, S.Dak., 18 June 1993.

30. Pearl Spotted Tail, interview by Yvonne Lockwood, East Lansing, Mich., 23 November 1996.

31. Rae Jean Walking Eagle, interview by Laurie Anderson and Kathy VanDeCar, Poplar, Mont., 16 November 1994.

32. Sheila Wahnetah, interview by Marsha MacDowell and Kurt Dewhurst, Warm Springs, Oreg., 23 April 1994.

33. Sharon Balai, interview by Marsha MacDowell and Kurt Dewhurst, Waimea, Hawaii, 2 May 1996.

34. Metzler-Smith, "Quilts in Pomo Culture," 45.

35. Unidentified member of quilt group, interview by Marsha MacDowell and Kurt Dewhurst, Warm Springs, Oreg., 13 May 1994.

36. Emil Her Many Horses, interview by Marsha MacDowell and Kurt Dewhurst, Denver, Colo., 16 June 1993.

37. Mary Woodward, interview by Marsha MacDowell, Tahlequah, Okla., 12 May 1995.

38. Brother C. M. Simon, S.J., interview by Marsha MacDowell and Kurt Dewhurst, Pine Ridge, S.Dak., 17 June 1993.

39. Georgia Rae Easter, "Indian Ingenuity Leads to Unique Quilt Making," *Indians st Work* 1, 18 (1 May 1935). National Archives, RG 435—Records of the Indian Arts and Crafts Board [IACB]. Records Relating to Exhibits and Expositions, San Francisco Exposition, Box 12: Subject Files (Old Box 20), Clippings 1.

40. Barbara Tazelaar, interview by Marsha MacDowell and Kurt Dewhurst, Sault Ste. Marie, Mich., 11 June 1989.

41. Doris Benedict, interview by Alex Jacobs, St. Regis Reservation, N.Y., November 1996.

42. Elizabeth Perkins and Nancy Martin Comins, interview by Alex Jacobs, Akwesasne, N.Y., 7 November 1996.

43. Alberta Lewis, interview by Kurt Dewhurst and Marsha MacDowell, Leupp, Ariz., 6 April 1993.

44. Pearl Spotted Tail, interview by Marsha MacDowell, Rosebud, S.Dak., 25 May 1996.

45. Sharon Balai, interview by Marsha MacDowell and Kurt Dewhurst, Waimea, Hawaii, 2 May 1996.

46. Mary Woodward, interview by Marsha MacDowell, Tahlequah, Okla., 12 May 1995.

47. Veronica Medicine, interview by Marsha MacDowell and Kurt Dewhurst, Harbor Springs, Mich., 21 July 1989.

48. Lula Red Cloud, interview by Danyelle Means, East Lansing, Mich., 23 November 1996.

49. Rae Jean Walking Eagle, interview by Laurie Anderson and Kathy VanDeCar, Poplar, Mont., 16 November 1994.

50. O'Brien, *Cherokee Quilts*.

51. Ibid.

52. Karen O'Dowd, "Indian Influences," *Lady's Circle Patchwork Quilts* 65 (September/October 1989): 32–39.

53. Kate Levit, "The Comfort of Quilts," *Lady's Circle Patchwork Quilts* 79 (January/February 1992): 16.

54. Dorothy Downs, *Arts of the Florida Seminole and Miccosukee Indians* (Gainesville, Fla.: University Press of Florida, 1995), 98.

55. Metzler-Smith, "Quilts in Pomo Culture," 41–47.

56. Deborah Johnson, telephone conversation with Marsha MacDowell, 6 February 1997.

57. Sara Angela Walker, interview by Laurie Anderson, Ethete, Wyo., 21 November 1994.

58. Mary Big Horse, interview by Marie Gile, East Lansing, Mich., 23 November 1996.

59. Downs, *Arts of the Florida Seminole and Miccosukee Indians*, 6.

60. Beverly Cook Jackson, interview by Alex Jacobs, St. Regis Reservation, N.Y., November 1996.

61. Mary J. Ives to Merry Silber, 23 August 1996.

62. Gerald Pete Jemison, "A Portfolio of Iroquois Art and Craft," *The Conservationist* 30, 4 (January/February 1976): 21–28. Thanks to George Hammel and George Abrams for bringing this to our attention.

63. Alice Fox, interview by Marsha MacDowell and Kurt Dewhurst, Sault Ste. Marie, Mich., 11 June 1989.

64. Miller and Rich, "Folk Art in the Clifton Community," 17.

65. Marsha MacDowell, field notes, Oneida, Wis., 15 and 16 October 1994.

66. Ollie Napesni, interview by Yvonne Lockwood, East Lansing, Mich., 23 November 1996.

67. Mary Henio, interview by Kurt Dewhurst, East Lansing, Mich., 23 November 1996.

68. Paula White, interview by Marsha MacDowell, East Lansing, Mich., 24 November 1996.

69. Marsha MacDowell, field notes, Oneida, Wis., 15 and 16 October 1994.

70. Gail Andrew Treschel, "Quiltmaking," in Stephen H. Martin, ed., *Alabama Folklife: Collected Essays* (Birmingham, Ala.: Alabama Folklife Association, 1989), 26.

71. George Horse Capture, "The Frayed Thread of Tradition," in George Horse Capture, et al., *Robes of Splendor: Native American Painted Buffalo Hides* (New York: The New Press, 1993), 61–66.

72. Brother C. M. Simon, S.J., interview by Marsha MacDowell and Kurt Dewhurst, Pine Ridge, S.Dak., 17 June 1993.

73. Karen McMurchie, "The Star Quilt—A Growing Tradition among the Lakota People," *Papers of the 17th Dakota History Conference*, April 11–13, 1985, no. 14, H. W. Blakely, compiler (Madison, S.Dak.: The Karl E. Mundt Historical and Educational Foundation, Dakota State College, 1986), 450.

74. Ollie Napesni, interview by Marsha MacDowell, Rosebud, S.Dak., 25 May 1996.

75. Shirley Grady, interview by Kurt Dewhurst, East Lansing, Mich., 24 November 1996.

76. Sharon Balai, interview by Marsha MacDowell and Kurt Dewhurst, Waimea, Hawaii, 2 April 1996.

77. Christine Faye and Margaret Lovett, *Kauai Museum Quilt Collection* (Lihue, Hawaii: The Kauai Museum, 1991), 8.

78. Sharon Balai, interview by Marsha MacDowell and Kurt Dewhurst, Waimea, Hawaii, 2 April 1996.

79. Harriet Soong, interview by Marsha MacDowell and Kurt Dewhurst, Waimea, Hawaii, 30 March 1996; Harriet Soong, interview by Melanie Atkinson, 24 November 1996.

80. Elaine Zinn, "Hawaiian Quilting," field notes, Center for Folklife and Cultural Studies, Smithsonian Institution, 11 January 1989. Cited in Lori Edmo-Suppah, "Quilters of the Wasco, Warm Springs, Paiute, " *Twanat* 2,4 (December 1995): 8–9.

81. Marsha MacDowell and Kurt Dewhurst, field notes, Shungopavi, Ariz., 7 April 1993.

82. Marlene Sekaquaptewa, conversation with Marsha MacDowell, East Lansing, Mich., 25 November 1996.

83. Barbara Tazelaar, interview by Marsha MacDowell and Kurt Dewhurst, Sault Ste. Marie, Mich., 11 June 1989.

84. Marietta Four Bear, interview by Laurie Anderson, Brockton, Mont., 17 November 1994.

85. Sara Angela Walker, interview by Laurie Anderson, Ethete, Wyo., 21 November 1994.

86. Barbara Tazelaar, interview by Marsha MacDowell and Kurt Dewhurst, Sault Ste. Marie, Mich., 11 June 1989.

87. Mary Big Horse, interview by Marie Gile, East Lansing, Mich., 23 November 1996.

88. Ann Fienup-Riordan, *The Nelson Island Eskimo: Social Structure and Ritual Distribution* (Anchorage, Alaska: Alaska Pacific University Press, 1983).

89. Catherine McKee (Winnebago), interview by Helen Kelley, St. Paul, Minn., 1978.

90. Marla Powers, *Oglala Women: Myth, Ritual and Reality* (Chicago: University of Chicago Press, 1986), 139.

91. Jimmie (Carole) Fife Stewart to Marsha MacDowell, October 1996.

92. Marsha MacDowell, field notes, Muskogee, Okla., 13 May 1995.

93. Powers, *Oglala Women*, 139.

94. Brother C. M. Simon, S.J., with Karin Nelson, "Lakota Star Quilts," A *Report* 11, 2 (San Francisco: San Francisco Folk Art and Craft Museum, 1993), 2.

95. Mary Big Horse, interview by Marie Gile, East Lansing, Mich., 23 November 1996.

96. Lydia Whirlwind Soldier, interviewed by Laurie Anderson, Mission, S.Dak., 15 November 1993.

97. Marsha MacDowell and Kurt Dewhurst, field notes, Warm Springs, Oreg., 23 April 1994.

98. Kathy VanDeCar, conversation with Marsha MacDowell, 1993; Kathy VanDeCar, field notes, Hartford, Conn., 1994.

99. Marsha MacDowell and Kurt Dewhurst, field notes, Rosebud, S.Dak., 26 May 1996.

100. Rae Jean Walking Eagle, interview by Kathy VanDeCar and Laurie Anderson, Brockton, Mont., 16 November 1994; Marsha MacDowell and Kurt Dewhurst, field notes, Brockton, Mont., February 1996.

101. Lula Red Cloud, interview by Danyelle Means, East Lansing, Mich., 23 November 1996.

102. Marsha MacDowell and Kurt Dewhurst, field notes, Warm Springs, Oreg., 23 April 1994.

103. Pat Courtney Gold, handwritten notes, 20 June 1996.

104. Alice Fox, interview by Marie Gile, Sault Ste. Marie, Mich., 7 September 1994.

105. Hill, *Patches*, 22.

106. Information provided by Dr. Joyce Herold, Denver Museum of Natural History, June 1993.

107. Shirley Grady to Laurie Anderson, 1995.

108. Dorothy Reuter, *Methodist Indian Ministries in Michigan 1830–1990* (Lansing, Mich.:

Michigan Area United Methodist Historical Society, 1993), 232.

109. Wild, " Introduction," 13.

110. Mildred Fielder, *Sioux Indian Leaders* (New York: Bonanza Books, 1981), 129.

111. Marsha MacDowell and Kurt Dewhurst, field notes, Warm Springs, Oreg., 23 April 1994.

112. Mylie Lawyer, "Family Work in Two Medicine Camp, Blackfeet Reservation," *Indians at Work* 1, 5 (15 October 1933). National Archives, RG 435—Records of the IACB, Records Relating to Exhibits and Expositions, San Francisco Exposition, Box 12: Subject Files (Old Box 20), Clippings 1. Thanks to Jane Przybysz for sending these and other *Indians at Work* references.

113. Myron Sippi, "Work in the Family Camps at San Carlos," *Indians at Work* 1, 6 (1 November 1933). National Archives, RG 435—Records of the IACB. Records Relating to Exhibits and Expositions, San Francisco Exposition, Box 12: Subject Files (Old Box 20), Clippings 1.

114. Norman Ewing, letter to the Hon. John Collier, 11 April 1934, National Archives, RG 435—Records of the IACB, Miscellaneous Files, 1930–35, Box 1 (Old Box), Board Activities—Arts and Crafts, 1931–36.

115. Hill, *Patches*, iv–v.

116. Florence Lackie Hanes, information provided on Michigan Quilt Project Registry form no. 86.489, 1986, Michigan Traditional Arts Research Collections, Michigan State University Museum.

117. Barbara Tazelaar, interview by Marsha MacDowell and Kurt Dewhurst, Sault Ste. Marie, Mich., 11 June 1989.

118. *New Yorker*, 10 May 1993, 39.

119. *Yankton Daily Press and Dakotan*, 12 February 1994.

120. Sharon Balai, interview by Marsha MacDowell and Kurt Dewhurst, Waimea, Hawaii, 2 May 1996.

121. Gwen Meister to Marsha MacDowell April 1995.

122. Brother C. M. Simon, interview by Marsha MacDowell and Kurt Dewhurst, Pine Ridge, S.Dak., 17 June 1993.

123. Ronna Lee Widener and Bea Roeder, *Master Apprentice: Colorado Folk Arts and Artists, 1986–1990* (Arvada, Colo.: Arvada Center for the Arts and Humanities, 1991), 48–51.

124. Mary Henio, interview by Kurt Dewhurst, East Lansing, Mich., 23 November 1996.

125. *Hopi Quilt Show Newsletter* 1 (Autumn 1996): 2.

126. Richard Vidutis, field notes, Baraga, Mich., 1985.

127. Marsha MacDowell and Kurt Dewhurst, field notes, Cherokee, N.C., 21 June 1995.

128. Marsha MacDowell and Kurt Dewhurst, field notes, Peshawbestown, Mich., 28 July 1989.

129. Helen Kelley, interview by Catherine McKee, St. Paul, Minn., 1978.

130. O'Dowd, "Indian Influences," 32–39.

131. Dolores Gourneau, interview by Kathy VanDeCar, Belcourt, N.Dak., 21 November 1994.

132. *Hawaiian Quilting: From the Collection of Ka Hui Kapa Apana O Waimea* (Kamuela, Hawaii: Ka Hui Kapa Apana O Waimea, 1995), back cover.

133. Marsha MacDowell, field notes, Thoreau, N.Mex., January 1992.

134. *Lands' End Coming Home Catalog* (Christmas edition) (Dodgeville, Wis.: Lands' End, 1992), 34.

135. Margaret Wood, interview by Marsha MacDowell and Kurt Dewhurst, Phoenix, Ariz., 4 April 1993.

136. Sheree Bonaparte, interview by Kurt Dewhurst, East Lansing, Mich., 23 November 1996.

139. Almira Buffalo Bone Jackson to Florence Pulford. Cited in Florence Pulford, *Morning Star Quilts* (Los Altos, Calif.: Leone Publications, 1989), 74.

140. Alice Olsen Williams, notes, 11 October 1996. Michigan Traditional Arts Research Collections, Michigan State University Museum.

141. Sheree Bonaparte, interview by Kurt Dewhurst, East Lansing, Mich., 23 November 1996.

142. Lula Red Cloud, interview by Danyelle Means, East Lansing, Mich., 23 November 1996.

143. Pat Courtney Gold to Laurie Anderson, 1996.

144. Nancy Naranjo to Laurie Anderson, 1995.

145. Mary Big Horse, interview by Marie Gile, East Lansing, Mich., 23 November 1996.

146. Margaret Wood, interview by Lynne Swanson, East Lansing, Mich., 23 November 1996.

147. Ollie Napesni, interview by Yvonne Lockwood, East Lansing, Mich., 23 November 1996.

148. Pearl Spotted Tail, interview by Yvonne Lockwood, East Lansing, Mich., 23 November 1996.

149. Lydia Whirlwind Soldier, interview by Laurie Anderson, Mission, S.Dak., 15 November 1993.

150. Mary Henio, interview by Kurt Dewhurst, East Lansing, Mich., 23 November 1996.

151. Eraina Palmer, interview by Marsha MacDowell and Kurt Dewhurst, Warm Springs, Oreg., 23 May 1994.

152. Deborah Johnson, telephone conversation with Marsha MacDowell, 7 February 1997.

153. Laurie Jensen-Wunder to Laurie Anderson, 30 May 1996.

154. Muriel H. Wright, "Sarah Ann Harlan: From Her Memoirs of Life in the Indian Territory," *The Chronicles of Oklahoma* 39, 2 (n.d.): 304–5. Thanks to Nancy Hornback for bringing this to our attention.

155. Hill, *Patches*, iv.

156. *Detroit News*, 7 October 1938.

157. Marie Young Bear, interview by Laurie Anderson and Kathy VanDeCar, Mandaree, N.Dak., 14 November 1994.

158. Robert J. Schleck, *The Wilcox Quilts in Hawaii* (Kauai, Hawaii: Grove Farm Homestead and Waioli Mission House, 1986), 60.

159. Marsha MacDowell and Kurt Dewhurst, field notes, Pine Ridge, S.Dak., June 1993.

160. Sandra L. O'Brien, ed., *Great American Quilts, 1992* (Birmingham, Ala.: Oxmoor House, 1991). Thanks to Margaret Wood for making the connection between the two pieces.

161. Rose Momsen, letter to Marsha MacDowell and completed American Indian Quilt Inventory Form, March 1995, Michigan Traditional Arts Research Collections, Michigan State University Museum.

162. Wendy Lavitt, *Contemporary Pictorial Quilts* (Layton, Utah: Peregrine Books, 1993), 91–97.

163. Lula Red Cloud, interview by Danyelle Means, East Lansing, Mich., 23 November 1996.

LEARNING THE THREADS: SIOUX QUILTMAKING IN SOUTH DAKOTA

1. D. C. Poole, *Among the Sioux of Dakota: Eighteen Months' Experience as an Indian Agent, 1869–70* (St. Paul, Minn.: Minnesota Historical Society, 1988), 122.

2. Ibid., 64.

3. Minutes of the Fifty-Fifth Annual Convocation of the District of South Dakota, Episcopal Church, 1939, 8.

4. Virginia Driving Hawk Sneve, interview by Laurie Anderson, Rapid City, S.Dak., July 1995.

5. Virginia Driving Hawk Sneve, *That They May*

Have Life: The Episcopal Church in South Dakota, 1859–1976 (New York: Seabury Press, 1977), 85–87, 90.

6. Episcopal Records, Sister Margaret Hawk's Recollections of St. Elizabeth's Episcopal Church, Standing Rock Reservation, ca. 1971.

7. Leonard Bruguier, director of the Institute of American Indian Studies, University of South Dakota, Vermillion, S.Dak., interview by Laurie Anderson, June 1995.

8. Albert Reifel, telephone conversation with Laurie Anderson, August 1994.

9. Nellie Menard, interview by Laurie Anderson, Rosebud, S.Dak., November 1993.

10. Alice Johnson Reifel, unpublished autobiography, ca. 1960–70.

11. Loyce Reifel Anderson, telephone conversation with Laurie Anderson, 17 November 1996.

12. Mark St. Pierre, *Madonna Swan: A Lakota Woman's Story* (Norman, Okla.: University of Oklahoma Press, 1991), 30.

13. Nellie Star Boy Menard, interview by Laurie Anderson, Rosebud, S.Dak., November 1993.

14. St. Pierre, *Madonna Swan,* 40–41, 43.

15. Iris Red Elk Allrunner, interview by Laurie Anderson and Kathy VanDeCar, Wolf Point, Mont., 16 November 1994.

16. Pearl Four Bear, interview by Laurie Anderson and Kathy VanDeCar, Brockton, Mont., 17 November 1994.

17. Tillie Walker, interview by Laurie Anderson, New Town, N.Dak., 11 November 1994.

18. Loyce Reifel Anderson, telephone conversation with Laurie Anderson, 17 November 1996.

19. Ramoná Malnourie, interview by Laurie Anderson and Kathy VanDeCar, White Shield, N.Dak., 10 November 1995.

THE CRAFT OF IDENTITY: QUILTING TRADITIONS OF THE WACCAMAW-SIOUAN TRIBE

1. Brenda Moore, interview by Jill Hemming, Bolton, N.C., 30 September 1994.

2. Priscilla Freeman Jacobs, interview by Jill Hemming, Bolton, N.C., 25 April 1995.

3. James E. Alexander, "Waccamaw Indians History," unpublished document, included in historical documents compiled in 1978 by the Native American Rights Fund, Boulder, Colo., stored at the Bureau of Indian Affairs as file 22930-1949-061. Thanks to Priscilla Freeman Jacobs for bringing this to our attention.

4. Patricia B. Lerch, "Articulatory Relationship: The Waccamaw Struggle Against Assimilation," in James L. Peacock and James C. Sabella, eds., *Sea and Land: Cultural and Biological Adaptations in the Southern Coastal Plain.* Southern Anthropological Society Proceedings, no. 21 (Athens, Ga.: University of Georgia Press, 1988).

5. Patricia B. Lerch, "State-Recognized Indians of North Carolina, Including a History of the Waccamaw Sioux," in J. Anthony Paredes, ed., *Indians of the Southeastern United States in the Late 20th Century* (Tuscaloosa, Ala.: University of Alabama Press, 1992).

6. Shalom Staub, "Folklore and Authenticity: A Myopic Marriage in Public Sector Programs," in Burt Feintuch, ed., *The Conservation of Culture* (Lexington, Ky.: University of Kentucky Press, 1988), 166–79.

7. Hazel W. Hertzberg, *The Search for an American Indian Identity: Modern Pan-Indian Movements* (Syracuse, N.Y.: Syracuse University Press, 1971), 321.

8. Priscilla Freeman Jacobs, interview by Jill Hemming, Bolton, N.C., 25 April 1995.

9. *Kin'lin': Local Heritage Publication of Hallsboro High School* (Whiteville, N.C.: Columbus Board of Education, 1975–81).

10. Rayna Green, "Repatriating Images: Indians and Photography," *Rendezvous* 1, 28 (1993): 151–60.

LAKOTA STAR QUILTS: COMMODITY, CEREMONY, AND ECONOMIC DEVELOPMENT

1. Ella Deloria, *Speaking of Indians* (New York: Friendship Press, 1944).

2. Christian F. Feest, *Native Arts of North America* (London: Thames and Hudson, Ltd., 1992), 151–52.

3. Jeanne Eder, an Assiniboine Sioux scholar, researched the appearance of quilting at the Fort Peck Reservation in Montana and presented the data in the slide show "My Grandmother's Star Quilt Honors Me."

4. Feest, *Native Arts*, 151–52.

5. Patricia Albers and Beatrice Medicine, eds., "The Role of Sioux Women in the Production of Ceremonial Objects: The Case of the Star Quilt," in Patricia Albers and Beatrice Medicine, eds., *The Hidden Half: Studies of Indian Women in the Northern Plains* (Lanham, Md.: University Press of America, 1983), 123–40.

6. *Lakota Times* (now *Indian Country Today*), 15 October 1986, 6.

7. The recycling of quilts through exchange, sale, and gift-giving would be an excellent study of the movement of ceremonial goods throughout the Great Plains in the United States and Canada; the quiltmaker's distinctiveness is also a mark of significance in this transfer.

8. Albers and Medicine, "Role of Sioux Women," 130.

9. Patricia Albers, "The Regional System of the Devil's Lake Sioux," Ph.D. dissertation, University of Wisconsin–Madison, 1974.

10. *Lakota Times*, 15 October 1986, 6.

11. *Institute of Indian Studies New Report* 110 (Vermillion, S.Dak.: University of South Dakota, February 1987), 7.

12. I, as an anthropologist, have been trying to obtain information on this enterprise and have been unable to do so. This situation speaks to larger issues on the place of indigenous anthropologists and on the study of power bases in the dominant society.

STARS OF HONOR: THE BASKETBALL STAR QUILT CEREMONY

1. Spike Big Horn, interview with Laurie Anderson and Kathy VanDeCar, Wolf Point, Mont., 16 November 1994, Michigan Traditional Arts Research Collections, Michigan State University Museum.

2. Documentation of the 1996 District Class 2-C Boys Basketball Tournament and related community activities was conducted by Kurt Dewhurst and Marsha MacDowell, with additional support from Keevin Lewis and Kathryn Fogdon of the Smithsonian Institution's National Museum of the American Indian, 22–26 February 1996. Taped interviews and related documentation are in the Michigan Traditional Arts Research Collections, Michigan State University Museum.

3. Sybil Lambert, interview by Kurt Dewhurst and Marsha MacDowell, Brockton, Mont., 25 February 1996, Michigan Traditional Arts Research Collections, Michigan State University Museum.

4. *Assiniboine and Sioux Fort Peck Indian Tribes: Tribal History and the Fort Peck Reservation* (Poplar, Mont.: Fort Peck Tribes, n.d.).

5. Nancy Tucker, *Experience of Culture Change: Women Star Quilts and the Dakota Presbytery Mission*, unpublished manuscript, 1994, Center for Native American Studies, Montana State University, Bozeman, Mont. The circular quilting pattern refers to the designs of the stitches used to hold the three layers (top, filling, and backing) of the quilt together.

6. Catherine Spotted Bird, "The Star Blanket," *Visitor's Guide to Poplar, Montana* (1995): 21.

7. Sybil Lambert, *History of the Brockton High School Star Quilt Ceremony*, unpublished manuscript, ca. 1993, collected by Kurt Dewhurst and Marsha MacDowell in Brockton, Mont., on 25 February 1996, Michigan Traditional Arts Research Collections, Michigan State University Museum.

HOW YUPIK WOMEN SPOIL THEIR CLOTH: THE SEAL PARTY QUILTS OF THE NELSON ISLAND ESKIMOS

1. Ann Fienup-Riordan, *The Nelson Island Eskimo: Social Structure and Ritual Distribution* (Anchorage, Alaska: Alaska Pacific University Press, 1983), 193–4.

QUILTS AND THE HOPI BABY-NAMING CEREMONY

1. *Annual Report of the Commissioner of Indian Affairs. Report of W. B. Truax* (Washington, D.C.: Government Printing Office, 1875).

2. *Annual Report of the Commissioner of Indian Affairs* (Washington, D.C.: Government Printing Office, 1890), CL 11.

3. *Annual Reports of the Department of the Interior, Indian Affairs. Report of the Commissioner. Report of James Gallagher, Superintendent, Keans Canyon Indian School, September 5, 1887* (Washington, D.C.: Government Printing Office, 1887), 235.

4. *Annual Reports of the Department of the Interior for the Fiscal Year Ended June 10, 1900. Indian Affairs. Report of the Commissioner and Appendixes* (Washington, D.C.: Government Printing Office, 1900), 477.

5. Martha M. Voth from the Moqui Mission, *The Indian's Friend* (monthly magazine of the Women's National Indian Association) (February 1894): 6.

ROSEBUD QUILTS: BUILDING A MUSEUM COLLECTION, CREATING AN EXHIBITION

1. Pauline Whirlwind, interview by Emil Her Many Horses, 1988.

2. Emil Her Many Horses field Collection.

3. Madeline Green, interview by Emil Her Many Horses, 1988.

4. Unidentified Lakota woman, interview by Emil Her Many Horses, summer 1989.

THREE PROFILES

Mealii Namahoe Richardson Kalama

1. Lavonne Richardson, comments at Mealii Namahoe Richardson Kalama's funeral, 7 August 1992.

2. Ibid.

3. Dr. Robert E. Potter, interview with Mealii Kalama, 1984.

Nellie Star Boy Menard

1. Carrie Lyford, *Quilt and Beadwork of the Western Sioux* (Boulder, Colo.:Johnson Books, 1979).

Selected
Bibliography

Agard-Smith, Nadema. *Southeastern Native Arts Director*. Bemidji, Minn.: American Indian Studies Press, Bemidji State University, 1993.

Akana, Elizabeth A. "Documenting Quilts in Paradise." *Lady's Circle Patchwork Quilts*, (November 1995): 12–16.

——. *Hawaiian Quilting: A Fine Art*. Honolulu, Hawaii: The Hawaiian Mission Children's Society, 1981.

Albers, Patricia. "Autonomy and Dependency in the Lives of Dakota Women: A Study in Historical Change," *Review of Radical Political Economies* 17 (1985): 109–34.

Albers, Patricia, and Beatrice Medicine, eds. "The Role of Sioux Women in the Production of Ceremonial Objects: The Case of the Star Quilt," in Patricia Albers and Beatrice Medicine, eds., *The Hidden Half: Studies of Indian Women in the Northern Plains*. Lanham, Md.: University Press of America, 1983, 135.

Alexie, Sherman. *The Lone Ranger and Tonto Fistfight in Heaven*. New York: Atlanta Monthly Press, 1993.

American Indian and Ethnographic Works of Art. San Francisco and Santa Fe: Butterfield and Butterfield, Inc., 1992.

American Indian Art: Form and Tradition. New York: E. P. Dutton, 1972.

The American Indian: The American Flag. Flint, Mich.: The Flint Institute of Arts, 1976.

Baer, Joshua. *Twelve Classics*. Santa Fe, N.Mex.: Joshua Baer and Co., 1989.

Balai, Sharon. *Hawaiian Style Quilting*. Kamuela, Hawaii: Upcountry Quilters, n.d.

Barton, Winifred W. *John P. Williamson: A Brother to the Sioux*. Clements, Minn.: Sunnycrest Publishing, 1919, reprint edition, 1980.

Belland, Merri, and Doris Dyen. *It's Our Way: Seminole Designs*. White Springs, Fla.: Bureau of Folklife Programs, Florida Department of State, 1982.

Benberry, Cuesta. *Always There: The African-American Presence in American Quilts*. Louisville, Ky.: The Kentucky Quilt Project, Inc., 1992.

Bergen, Fanny. "The Tapestry of the New World," *Scribner's* (September 1894): n.p.

Berlo, Janet Catherine, ed. *The Early Years of Native American Art History*. Seattle: University of Washington Press, 1992.

Blackard, David M. *Patchwork and Palmettos: Seminole-Miccosukee Folk Art Since 1820*. Fort Lauderdale, Fla.: Fort Lauderdale Historical Society, 1990.

Brandebourg, Margaret. *Seminole Patchwork*. New York: Sterling Publishing Co., Inc., 1987.

Brandon, Reiko Mochinaga. *The Hawaiian Quilt*. Tokyo: Kokusai Art, 1989.

Brant, Beth, ed. *A Gathering of Spirits*: A *Collection by North American Indian Women*. Ithaca, N.Y.: Firebrand Books, 1984.

Bruchac, Joseph, ed. *New Voices from the Longhouse*: An *Anthology of Contemporary Iroquois Writing*. Greenfield Center, N.Y.: The Greenfield Review Press, 1989.

Burry, Winifrede. "A Native Spirit Sings in the Quilts of Win Burry." *Canada Quilts* (Special Issue) 22, 1, 97 (February 1993): 8–9, 41.

"Canada Quilts Profile: Alice Olsen Williams." *Canada Quilts* (Special Issue) 22, 1, 97 (February 1993): 33–35.

Central Plains Clinic Art Collection. Madison, Wis.: Marshall Erdman and Associates, Inc., n.d.

Coe, Ralph T. *Lost and Found Traditions: Native American Art 1965–1985*. Seattle: University of Washington Press in association with the American Federation of Arts, 1986.

———. *Sacred Circles: Two Thousand Years of North American Indian Art*. Kansas City, Mo.: Nelson Gallery of Art–Atkins Museum of Fine Arts, 1976.

Conforti, Michael, ed. *Art and Life on the Upper Mississippi*, 1890–1915. Newark, Del.: University of Delaware Press, 1994.

Conroy, Mary. *300 Years of Canada's Quilts*. Toronto, Ontario: Griffin House, 1976.

Cozart, Dorothy. "A Century of Fundraising Quilts: 1860–1960." *Uncoverings* 1984, vol. 5. *Research Papers of the American Quilt Study Group*: 41–53.

Crews, Patricia Cox, and Ronald C. Naugle. *Nebraska Quilts and Quilters*. Lincoln, Nebr.: University of Nebraska Press, 1991.

Davis, Hilda J. "The History of Seminole Clothing and Its Multi-Colored Designs." *American Anthropologist* 57 (1955): 974–80.

Dewhurst, C. Kurt, Yvonne Lockwood, and Marsha MacDowell. *Michigan: Whose Story? A Celebration of the State's Traditions*. East Lansing, Mich.: Michigan State University Museum, 1985.

Dial, Adolph L. *The Lumbee*. New York: Chelsea House Publishers, 1993.

Dillon, Mary Evangeline. *Contemporary Southwestern Quilts*. Radnor, Pa.: Chilton Book Company, 1989.

Dilworth, Leah. *Imagining Indians in the Southwest: Persistent Visions of Primitive Past*. Washington, D.C.: Smithsonian Institution Press, 1996.

Doll, Don, S.J. *Crying for a Vision: A Rosebud Sioux Trilogy*, 1886–1976. New York: Morgan and Morgan, 1976.

Downs, Dorothy. *Arts of the Florida Seminole and Miccosukee Indians*. Gainesville, Fla.: University Press of Florida, 1995.

———. "British Influences on Creek and Seminole Men's Clothing, 1733–1858." *The Florida Anthropologist* 33, 2 (June 1980): 46–65.

———. *Miccosukee Arts and Crafts*. Miami, Fla.: Miccosukee Tribe of Indians of Florida, 1982.

———. "Patchwork and Powwows: The Twenty-Fifth Annual Seminole Tribal Fair Story." *Native Peoples* 10, 2 (1997): 50–57.

———. "Patchwork Clothing of the Florida Indians." *American Indian Art* 4, 3 (1979): 32–40.

Dunn, Anne M. *When Beaver Was Very Great: Stories to Live By*. Mount Horeb, Wis.: Midwest Traditions, Inc., 1995.

Easter, Georgia Rae. "Indian Ingenuity Leads to Unique Quilt Making." *Indians at Work* 2, 18 (May 1, 1935). National Archives, RG 435—Records of the Indian Arts and Crafts Board [hereafter IACB] Records Relating to Exhibits and Expositions, San Francisco Exposition, Box 12: Subject Files (Old Box 20), Clippings 1.

Eder, Jeanne Byawin, and Nancy H. Tucker. "My Grandmother's Star Quilt Honors Me." *Plainswoman* 9, 1 (1985): 8–9.

Elsley, Judy. "The Smithsonian Quilt Controversy: Cultural Dislocation," *Uncoverings* 1993, vol. 14. *Research Papers of the American Quilt Study Group*: 119–36.

Evanoff, Betty. "Seminole Indian Patchwork." *Antiques Journal* 30, 10 (October 1975): 50, 51, 56.

Ewing, Norman. Letter to the Hon. John Collier, 11 April 1934, National Archives, RG 435—Records of IACB. Miscellaneous Files, 1930–35, Box 1 (Old Box), Board Activities—Arts and Crafts, 1931–36.

"An Exhibition of Quilts Inspired by the Morning Star Quilts." *New York Times*, Thursday, May 6, 1993, C6.

Farr, William E. *The Reservation Blackfeet, 1882–1945: A Photographic History of Cultural Survival*. Seattle and London: University of Washington Press, 1986.

Fayé, Christine, and Margaret Lovett. *Kauai Museum Quilt Collection*. Lihue, Hawaii: The Kauai Museum, 1991.

Feest, Christian F. *Native Arts of North America*. London: Thames and Hudson, Ltd., 1992.

Ferrero, Pat, Elaine Hedges, and Julie Silber. *Hearts and Hands: The Influence of Women and Quilts on American Society*. San Francisco: The Quilt Digest Press, 1987.

Fielder, Mildred. *Sioux Indian Leaders*. New York: Bonanza Books, 1975.

Fienup-Riordan, Ann. *Eskimo Essays: Yup'ik Lives and How We See Them*. New Brunswick, N.J.: Rutgers University Press, 1990.

——. *The Nelson Island Eskimo: Social Structure and Ritual Distribution*. Anchorage, Alaska: Alaska Pacific University Press, 1983.

Fitzgerald, Ruth, and Marsha MacDowell, eds. *Michigan Quilts: 150 Years of a Textile Tradition*. East Lansing, Mich.: Michigan State University Museum, 1987.

Five Families: Art Exhibition. Pine Ridge, S.Dak.: The Heritage Center, Inc., Red Cloud Indian School in cooperation with the University Art Galleries, University of South Dakota, 1993.

Flecky, Michael, S.J., and Harold Moore. *Photo Album: St. Francis Mission, School, and Community, 1886–1976*. Rosebud, S.Dak.: Rosebud Educational Society, 1976.

Flynn, John. *John Flynn's Feathered Sun: Step-by-Step Workbook*. Billings, Mont.: privately published, 1994.

Fraser, Barbara. "West Coast Indian Art." *Canada Quilts*, (Special Issue) 22, 1, 97 (February 1993): 11.

Frisby, Eleanora. "Passing on the Tradition." *Lady's Circle Patchwork Quilts* 79 (January/February 1992): 30–33.

Gagnon, Gregory, and Karen White Eyes. *Pine Ridge Reservation: Yesterday and Today*. Interior, S.Dak: Badlands Natural History Association, 1993.

Garoutte, Sally. "Uses of Textiles in Hawaii: 1820–1850." *Uncoverings* 1985, vol. 6. *Research Papers of the American Quilt Study Group*: 147–65.

Gebel, Carol Williams. "Quilts in the Final Rite of Passage: A Multicultural Study." *Uncoverings* 1993, vol. 14. *Research Papers of the American Quilt Study Group*: 199–228.

Gildart, Bert. "The Mississippi Band of Choctaw: In the Shadow of Nanih Waiya." *Native Peoples* 9, 4 (Summer 1996): 44–50.

Goble, Paul. *Star Boy*. New York: Macmillan Publishing Co., 1993.

Goforth, Sandra L. "From Kapa to Quilt." *Lady's Circle Patchwork Quilts* 79 (January/February 1992): 38–41.

——. "From Kapa to Quilt." *Lady's Circle Patchwork Quilts* 89 (May 1993): 6–12.

Green, Rayna. *Women in American Indian Society*. New York: Chelsea House Publishers, 1992.

Hammond, Harmony, and Jaune Quick-to-See Smith. *Women of Sweetgrass, Cedar and Sage*. New York: Gallery of the American

Indian Community House, distributed by Atlatl, 1985.

Hathaway, Nancy. *Native American Portraits, 1862–1918*. San Francisco: Chronicle Books, 1990.

Hawaii Public Television. *Hawaiian Quilting*. Television series, program no. 105, 1993.

Hawaiian Quilting: From the Collection of Ka Hui Kapa Apana O Waimea. Kamuela, Hawaii: Ka Hui Kapa Apana O Waimea, 1995.

Hemming, Jill. *The Craft of Identity: Quilting Traditions in the Waccamaw-Siouan Tribe*. Master of arts thesis. Chapel Hill, N.C.: University of North Carolina, 1995.

Hill, Tom. *Patches: The Art of Quilt Making on the Six Nations and New Credit Indian Reserves*. Brantford, Ontario: The Woodland Indian Cultural Educational Centre, 1983.

Houck, Carter. "A Land of Sky and Water." *Lady's Circle Patchwork Quilts* 79 (January/February 1992): 38–41.

Hunt, Gail. *Quilt Works Across Canada: Eleven Contemporary Workshops*. North Vancouver, Canada: Pacific Quiltworks, Ltd., 1996.

Jesse, Kay. "Hawaiian Quilting Revisited." *Quilters Newsletter* (December 1966): 36–39.

Jones, Stella M. *Hawaiian Quilts*. Honolulu, Hawaii: Honolulu Academy of Arts, reprint, 1983.

Kelley, Helen. *Scarlet Ribbons: American Indian Technique for Today's Quilters*. Paducah, Ky.: American Quilter's Society, 1987.

Kimmel, Gerry. *For My Friends*. Liberty, Mo.: Red Wagon, 1992.

Lambert, Sybil. *History of the Brockton High School Star Quilt Ceremony*, unpublished paper, ca. 1993. Michigan Traditional Arts Research Collections, Michigan State University Museum.

Lame Deer, John (Fire), and Richard Erdoes. *Lame Deer: Seeker of Visions*. New York: Washington Square Press, 1972.

Lasansky, Jeannette. "Southwestern Quilts and Quiltmakers in Context." *Uncoverings* 1993, vol. 14. *Research Papers of the American Quilt Study Group*: 97–118.

Leon, Eli. *Who'd A Thought It: Improvisation in African-American Quiltmaking*. San Francisco: San Francisco Craft and Folk Art Museum, 1987.

Levit, Kate. "The Comfort of Quilts." *Lady's Circle Patchwork Quilts* 79 (January/February 1992): 14–16.

MacDowell, Marsha. "Potawatomi, Ottawa, and Ojibway Quiltmaking." Paper read at the American Folklore Society Meeting, Philadelphia, Pa., October 18–22, 1989.

MacDowell, Marsha, and Janice Reed, eds. *Sisters of the Great Lakes: Art of American Indian Women*. East Lansing, Mich.: Michigan State University Museum in collaboration with the Nokomis American Indian Cultural Learning Center, 1995.

MacDowell, Marsha, and Margaret Wood. "Sewing It Together: Native American and Hawaiian Quilting Traditions." *Akwe:Kon Journal* (Special Issue), 11, 3, 4 (Fall/Winter 1994). "Native American Expressive Culture" published in collaboration with the National Museum of the American Indian.

McMurchie, Karen. "The Star Quilt—A Growing Tradition among the Lakota People." *Papers of the 17th Dakota History Conference*, April 11–13, 1985, no. 14, compiled by H. W. Blakely. Madison, S.Dak.: The Karl E. Mundt Historical and Educational Foundation, Dakota State College, 1986.

Manion, P. J. "Navajo Weaver Creates Quilts." *Quilting International* 40 (March 1995): 6–7.

Martin, Christopher. *Native Needlework: Contemporary Indian Textiles from North Dakota*. Fargo, N.Dak.: North Dakota Council on the Arts, 1988.

Metzler-Smith, Sandra J. "Quilts in Pomo Culture." *Uncoverings* 1980, vol. 1. *Research Papers of the American Quilt Study Group*: 41–47.

Miller, Shari, and Miriam Rich. "Folk Art in the Clifton Community," in Shari Miller and Miriam Rich, eds. "Splittin' On the Grain: Folk Art in Clifton, Louisiana." *Louisiana Folklife* 8 (Special Issue), (March 1983): 12–19.

Mori, Joyce. *Appliqué Patterns from Native American Beadwork Designs*. Paducah, Ky.: American Quilter's Society, 1993.

———. *Quilting Patterns from Native American Designs*. Paducah, Ky.: American Quilter's Society, 1993.

Nogelmeier, Puakea. "Hawaiian Crafts," in *Folklife Hawai'i*. Honolulu, Hawaii: The State Foundation on Culture and Arts, 1990.

O'Brien, Mary. *Cherokee Quilts*. Tulsa, Okla.: The Mary O'Brien Bookshop, 1996.

O'Dowd, Karen. "Indian Influences." *Lady's Circle Patchwork Quilts* 65 (September/October 1989): 33–39.

———. "Northern New Mexico." *Lady's Circle Patchwork Quilts* 65 (September/October 1989): 40–49.

Olsen, Kirstin. *Southwest by Southwest: Native American and Mexican Quilt Designs*. New York: Sterling Publishing Co., Inc., 1991.

Olson, Jeanne Field. "Love in Every Stitch: Quilting in Montana." *Montana* 140 (November/December 1996): 18–22.

Penney, David W. *Art of the American Indian Frontier: The Chandler-Pohrt Collection*. Seattle, Wash.: University of Washington Press in collaboration with the Detroit Institute of Arts, 1992.

Porsche, Audrey. *Yuto'keca: Transitions, the Burdick Collection*. Bismarck, N.Dak.: State Historical Society of North Dakota, 1987.

Powers, Marla N. *A Century of Vision: The Star Quilt, A Symbol of Lakota Identity*. Kendall Park, N.J.: Lakota Books, 1990.

———. *Lakota Naming: A Modern-Day Hunka Ceremony*. Kendall Park, N.J.: Lakota Books, 1991.

———. *Oglala Women: Myth, Ritual and Reality*. Chicago: University of Chicago Press, 1986.

Pulford, Florence. *Morning Star Quilts*. Los Altos, Calif.: Leone Publications, 1989.

Quick-to-See Smith, Jaune. *The Submuloc Show/Columbus Wohs: A Visual Commentary on the Columbus Quincentennial from the Perspective of America's First People*. Phoenix, Ariz.: Atlatl, 1992.

"Quilts and the Native Influence." *Canada Quilts* (Special Issue) 22, 1, 97 (February 1993).:6–35.

Rae, Janet, Margaret Tucker, and Dinah Travis, et al. *Quilt Treasures of Great Britain: The Heritage Search of the Quilters' Guild*. Nashville, Tenn.: Rutledge Hill Press, 1995.

Reeves, Donald. *Quilts from the Collection of the Oklahoma Historical Society*. Oklahoma City, Okla.: Oklahoma Historical Society, 1978.

Reno, Dawn. *Contemporary Native American Artists*. Brooklyn, N.Y.: Alliance Publishing, Inc., 1995.

Reuter, Dorothy. *Methodist Indian Ministries in Michigan 1830–1990*. Lansing, Mich.: Michigan Area United Methodist Historical Society, 1993.

Reyer, Carolyn. *Cante ohitika Win (Brave-Hearted Women): Images of Lakota Women from the Pine Ridge Reservation, South Dakota*. Vermillion, S.Dak.: University of South Dakota Press, 1991.

Rush, Beverly, with Lassie Whitman. *The Complete Book of Seminole Patchwork*. Dover Needlework Series. New York: Dover Publications, Inc., 1982.

Schleck, Robert J. *The Wilcox Quilts in Hawaii*. Kauai, Hawaii: Grove Farm Homestead and Waioli Mission House, 1986.

"Seminole Piecing." *Lady's Circle Patchwork Quilts* (July 1986): 33–36.

Shaw, Robert. *Hawaiian Quilt Masterpieces*. Hawaii: Hugh Lauter Levin Associates, Inc., 1996.

———. *Quilts: A Living Tradition*. Southport, Conn.: Hugh Lauter Levin Associates, Inc. 1995.

Simon, Brother C. M., S.J., with Karin Nelson. "Lakota Star Quilts." *A Report* 11, 2. San Francisco: San Francisco Folk Art and Craft Museum, 1993.

Sippi, Myron. "Work in the Family Camps at San Carlos." *Indians at Work* 1, 6 (November 1, 1933). National Archives, RG 435— Records of the IACB, Records Relating to Exhibits and Expositions, San Francisco

Exposition, Box 12: Subject Files (Old Box 20), Clippings 1.

——. *Indians at Work* 1, 2, 6. National Archives, RG 435—Records of the IACB, Records Relating to Exhibits and Expositions, San Francisco Exposition, Box 12: Subject Files (Old Box 20), Clippings 1.

Sneve, Virginia Driving Hawk. *Completing the Circle*. Lincoln, Nebr.: University of Nebraska Press, 1975.

Star Quilt. Bangalore, India: Streleekha, 1995.

Stowell, Cynthia D. *Faces of a Reservation: A Portrait of the Warm Springs Indian Reservation*. Portland, Oreg.: Oregon Historical Society, 1987.

"Talk of the Town: Fancydancer." *The New Yorker Magazine* (May 10, 1993): 38–41.

"That These People May Live"—"*Hecel lena oyate kin nipi kte*" (calendar). St. Francis, S.Dak.: St. Francis Mission, 1992.

Townsend, Louise O. "Kansas City Star Quilt Patterns: 1928–1949." *Uncoverings* 1984, vol. 5, *Research Papers of the American Quilt Study Group*: 131–152.

Treschel, Gail Andrew. "Quiltmaking," in Stephen H. Martin, ed. *Alabama Folklife: Collected Essays*. Birmingham, Ala.: Alabama Folklife Association, 1989, 22–27.

Tribes of the Southern Woodlands. Alexandria, Va.: Time-Life Books, 1994.

Tucker, Nancy. *Experiences of Culture Change: Women, Star Quilts and the Dakota Presbytery Mission*. Unpublished manuscript, 1994, courtesy Center for Native American Studies, Montana State University, Bozeman, Mont.

Vennum, Thomas Jr. *The Ojibwa Dance Drum: Its History and Construction*. Washington, D.C.: Smithsonian Folklife Studies, no. 2, 1982.

Vlach, John M. *The Afro-American Tradition in Decorative Arts*. Cleveland, Ohio: Cleveland Museum of Art, 1978.

Wahlman, Maude S. *Signs and Symbols: African Images in African-American Quilts*. New York: Studio Books, 1993.

Wait, S. E. *Old Settlers of the Grand Traverse Region*. Traverse City, Mich.: 1918, reprinted 1978 by Black Letter Press, Grand Rapids, Mich.

The Waltners. "Sioux Star Quilts." *Quilt World* 12, 1 (January–February): 10–12.

"What's New and News in Quilting." *Quilter's Newsletter* 24, 10 (December 1992): 6.

Whiteman, Roberta Hill. "Star Quilt," in Joseph Bruchac, ed. *New Voices from the Longhouse: An Anthology of Contemporary Iroquois Writing*. Greenfield Center, N.Y.: The Greenfield Review Press, 1989.

Widener, Ronna Lee, and Bea Roeder. *Master Apprentice: Colorado Folk Arts and Artists, 1986–1990*. Arvada, Colo.: Arvada Center for the Arts and Humanities, 1991.

Wittmer, Marcilene. "African Influence on Florida Indian Patchwork." *Southeastern College Art Conference Review* 11 (n.d.): 269–75.

Wood, Margaret. *Native American Fashions: Modern Adaptations of Traditional Designs*. New York: Van Nostrand Reinhold Co., 1981.

Wright, Muriel H. "Sarah Ann Harlan: From Her Memoirs of Life in the Indian Territory." *The Chronicles of Oklahoma* 39, 2 (n.d.): 304–5.

Wyatt, Victoria. *Images from the Inside Passage: An Alaskan Portrait by Winter and Pond*. Seattle: University of Washington Press, 1989, 124.

Zehner, Judy, and Kimberly Mosher. *Quilted Legends of the West*. Bothell, Wash.: That Patchwork Place, 1995.

Zeilinger, Ron. *Lakota Life*. S.Dak.: St. Joseph's Indian School, 1986.

Zinn, Elaine. "Hawaiian Quilting." Field report, Center for Folklife and Cultural Studies, Smithsonian Institution, January 11, 1989. Cited in Lori Elmo-Suppah. "Quilters of the Wasco, Warm Springs, Paiute." *Twanat* 2,4 (December 1995): 8–9.

Photo and Quilt Collections Credits

Quilts from the collection of Michigan State University Museum were photographed by Elbinger Studios, Inc. unless otherwise noted below. Photo credits are given in sequence with photo captions.

p. vi Photo courtesy of the Minnesota Historical Society. p. vii Photo courtesy of the Minnesota Historical Society. p.4 Photo courtesy of Wyoming Division of Cultural Resources. p.6 Collection of the artist Photo: Elbinger Studios, Inc. p.6 Photo by Father Fox, courtesy of Jesuit Oregon Province Archives, Gonzaga University. p.6 Collection of the Roger J. Bounds Foundation, Inc. Photo by Sharon Risedorph, courtesy of Hearts and Hands Media Arts. p.6 Photo by Monroe Killy, courtesy of the Minnesota Historical Society, 1942. p.7 Photo courtesy of Buechel Memorial Lakota Museum. p.8 Photo courtesy of William Maxwell Photographic Collection, University of North Dakota Library. p.9 Photo reprinted from Nebraska Quilts and Quiltmakers by Crew and Naugle by permission of Lincoln Quilters Guild, Lincoln, Nebraska. Copyright 1991 by University of Nebraska Press, courtesy of Nebraska Quilt Project. p.11 Photo courtesy of Oklahoma Historical Society/State Museum of Natural History (Accession #73.83). p.11 Photo courtesy of the Oklahoma Historical Society/State Museum of History (Accession #3876). p.12 Photo courtesy of the Royal Ontario Museum, Canada. p.13 Privately owned. Photo courtesy of Joshua Baer & Company, Santa Fe. All reproduction rights to this image are reserved by Joshua Baer & Company. p.14 Photo courtesy of Nebraska State Historical Society. p.18 Photo: Elbinger Studios, Inc. p.20 Collection of Michigan State University Museum, Photo: Elbinger Studios, Inc. p.20 Photo: Marsha MacDowell, 1994. p.21 Collection of Michigan State University Museum, Photo: Mark Eifert. p.21 Collection Michigan State University Museum. p.24 Collection of Michigan State University Museum p.24 Collection of Michigan State University Museum. p.24 Courtesy of Michigan State University Museum. p.24 Collection of Hana Kangas, Photo: Elbinger Studios, Inc. p.26 Collection of Michigan State University Museum. p.26 Photo by Claude C. Matlock, courtesy of the Historical Museum of Southern Florida. Neg. no. 139-30. p.27 Photo: Katherine Fogden, National Museum of the American Indian, Smithsonian Institution, 1996. p.27 Collection of Michigan State University Museum. p.28 Photo courtesty of Mendocino County Museum. p.29 Collection of Loyce Reifel and Emery G. Anderson. Photo: Elbinger Studios, Inc. p.31 Courtesy of Michigan State University Museum. p.33 (bottom) Photo: Mark Eifert. p.36 Photo: Elbinger Studios, Inc. p.37 Photo: Katherine Fogden, National Museum of the American Indian, Smithsonian Institution, 1996. p.37

Collection of Michigan State University Museum. p.38 Photo by Pam Dewey, National Museum of the American Indian, Smithsonian Institution. p.40 Photo: Katherine Fogden, National Museum of the American Indian, Smithsonian Institution, 1996. p.40 Collection of Michigan State University Museum. p.41 Photo by George Trager, courtesy of the Nebraska State Historical Society. p.42 Collection of Michigan State University Museum. p.42 Collection of Michigan State University Museum. p.42 Private collection. Photo: Elbinger Studio, Inc. p.42 Collection of Michigan State University Museum, Photo: Elbinger Studios, Inc. p.43 Courtesy of Michigan State University Museum. p.45 Photo: Katherine Fogden, National Museum of the American Indian, Smithsonian Institution, 1996. p.45 Collection of Michigan State University Museum, Photo: Elbinger Studios, Inc. p.46 Photo by Kenneth Wright, courtesy of the Minnesota Historical Society. p.46 Photo by Monroe Killy, courtesy Minnesota Historical Society. p.47 Photo courtesy of Minnesota Historical Society. p.47 Photo: J. A. Little, courtesy of State Archives of Michigan, Michigan Department of State, 1909. p.47 Photo courtesy of William Maxwell Photographic Collection, University of North Dakota Library. p.47 Photo courtesy of Minnesota Historical Society. p.49 (left) Collection of Michigan State University Museum, Photo: Mark Eifert. p.49 (center) Photo courtesy of the Buechel Memorial Lakota Museum. p.49 (right) Photo courtesy of Buechel Memorial Lakota Museum. p.50 Photo: Winter and Pond, courtesy of Alaksa Historical Library. p.50 Photo by A. E. Jenks, courtesy of the National Anthropological Archives. p.51 Photo by Don Doll, S.J. p.53 Collection of Michigan State University Museum, Photo: Elbinger Studios, Inc. p.53 Photo: Katherine Fogden, National Museum of the American Indian, Smithsonian Institution, 1996. p. 55 Collection of Michigan State University Museum, Photo: Mark Eifert. p.55 Photo: Katherine Fogden, National Museum of the American Indian, Smithsonian Institution, 1996. p.58 Collection of Michigan State University Museum, Photo: Elbinger Studios, Inc. p.59 Photo courtesy of Department of Anthropology, Denver Museum of Natural History (Accession #6300). p.59 Courtesy of Michigan State University Museum, Photo: Elbinger Studios, Inc. p.59 Photo: Katherine Fogden, National Museum of the American Indian, Smithsonian Institution, 1996. p.60 Photo: Elbinger Studios, Inc. p.62 Collection of the artist. Photo: Elbinger Studios, Inc. p.62 Photo: Katherine Fogden, National Museum of the American Indian, Smithsonian Institution, 1996. p.64 Photo: Courtesy of the National Archives Library. p.65 Photo: Ann Bird, 1989. p.65 Photo: Marsha MacDowell. p.66 Photo: JD Marston Photography. p.66 Photo: James S.

Griffiths, courtesy Southwest Folklore Center, 1980. p.71 Photo courtesy of Betty Cracker Armstrong and the Leelenau Historical Museum. p.72 Collection of Reginald J. Stanley. Photo: Elbinger Studios, Inc. p.72 Photo: Katherine Fogden, National Museum of the American Indian, Smithsonian Institution, 1996. p.73 Photo: Elbinger Studios, Inc. p.74 Collection of the artist. Photo: Marilyn Szabo. p.75 Photo: R.J. Baker Collection, Bishop Museum, the State Museum of Natural and Cultural History. p.76 Photo: Elbinger Studios, Inc. p.77 Collection of Michigan State University Museum. Photo: Mark Eifert. p. 78 Photo courtesy Morning Star Quilts, Leone Publications. p.80 Photo: Elbinger Studios, Inc. p.80 Photo: Katherine Fogden, National Museum of the American Indian, Smithsonian Institution, 1996. p. 81 Photo: Elbinger Studios, Inc. p.81 Photo: Katherine Fogden, National Museum of the American Indian, Smithsonian Institution, 1996. p.82 Photo: Elbinger Studios, Inc. p.82 Photo: Katherine Fogden, National Museum of the American Indian, Smithsonian Institution, 1996. p.83 Photo by Frank B. Fiske, courtesy State Historical Society of North Dakota. p.83 Photo by Frank B. Fiske, courtesy State Historical Society of North Dakota. p.84 Photo courtesy of Kaua'i Museum Archives. p.84 Photo courtesy of Kaua'i Museum Archives. p.85 Photo: Elbinger Studios, Inc. p.87 Photo courtesy of Archives and Manuscripts Division of the Oklahoma Historical Society, Neg. #19521.3. p.88 Photo by Tai Sing Loo; courtesy of the Bishop Museum, The State Museum of Natural and Cultural History. p.90 Photo: Elbinger Studios, Inc. p.94 Photo: Frank B. Fiske, courtesy of the State Historical Society of North Dakota. p.95 Photo: Mark Eifert. p.96 Photo courtesy of Buechel Memorial Lakota Museum, St. Francis, South Dakota. p.96 Photo courtesy of Buechel Memorial Lakota Museum, St. Francis, South Dakota. p.97 Photo: Courtesy of Stella Iron Cloud and Helen Kelley. p.100 Photo: Elbinger Studios, Inc. p.104 Photo courtesy of Jill Hemming. p.108 Photo courtesy of Jill Hemming. p.109 Photo courtesy of Jill Hemming. p.112 Collection of Michigan State University Museum, Accession #1996:130. Photo: Elbinger Studios, Inc. p.112 Photo: Katherine Fogden, National Museum of the American Indian, Smithsonian Institution, 1996. p.114 Photo courtesy of William Maxwell Collection, University of North Dakota Library. p.116 Photo: Mark Eifert. p.116 Photo: Mark Eifert. p.121 Photo courtesy of the Bishop Museum, The State Museum of Natural and Cultural History. p.122 Photo: Shuzo Uemoto. p.123 Photos by Shuzo Uemoto. p.126 Photo: Carl Hefner. p.132 (left) Photo: Marsha MacDowell, 1996. p.132 (center) Photo Marsha MacDowell. p.132 (right) Photo: Katherine Fogden, National Museum of the

American Indian, Smithsonian Institution, 1996. p.138 Collection of Michigan State University Museum Photo: Elbinger Studios, Inc. p.139 Photo: Ann Fienup-Riordan. p.141 Photo: James H. Barker. p. 147 Photo: Marsha MacDowell, 1995. p.150 Photos: Katherine Fogden, National Museum of the American Indian, Smithsonian Institution, 1996. p. 154 Photo: Hattie Cosgrove, courtesy of C. Burton Cosgrove, Jr. p.155 Collection of Michigan State University Museum, Photo: Elbinger Studios, Inc. p.155 Photo: Katherine Fogden, National Museum of the American Indian, Smithsonian Institution, 1996. p.156 Photo by H. R. Voth, courtesy of the Mennonite Library and Archives, Bethel College, North Newton, Kansas. p.158 Photo: Carolyn O'Bagy Davis. p.159 Photo: Carolyn O'Bagy Davis. p.159 Photo: Carolyn O'Bagy Davis. p. 164 Photo courtesy of Buechel Memorial Museum. p.166 Photo by Frank B. Fiske, courtesy State Historical Society of North Dakota. p.167 Photo courtesy of Buechel Memorial Lakota Museum. p.168 Photos courtesy of the Buechel Memorial Lakota Museum Archives, St. Francis, South Dakota. p.170 Photos courtesy of the Buechel Memorial Lakota Museum Archives, St. Francis, South Dakota. p.171 Collection of the artist Photo: Elbinger Studios, Inc. p.171 Photo: Katherine Fogden, National Museum of the American Indian, Smithsonian Institution, 1996. p.172 Photos courtesy of the Buechel Memorial Lakota Museum Archives, St. Francis, South Dakota. p.173 Photos courtesy of the Buechel Memorial Lakota Museum Archives, St. Francis, South Dakota. p.176 Photo: Courtesy of Kaua'i Museum Archives. p.177 Photo: Elbinger Studios, Inc.. p.178 Photo: Janine Jones, National Museum of the American Indian, Smithsonian Institution. p.180 Photo courtesy of Linda Moriarity. p.185 Private collection Photo: Elbinger Studios, Inc. p.185 Photo: Katherine Fogden, National Museum of the American Indian, Smithsonian Institution, 1996. p.186 Collection of Michigan State University Museum, Photo: Elbinger Studios, Inc. p.186 Photo: Katherine Fogden, National Museum of the American Indian, Smithsonian Institution, 1996. p.190 Collection of Michigan State University Museum, Photo: Elbinger Studios, Inc. p.190 Photo: Katherine Fogden, National Museum of the American Indian, Smithsonian Institution, 1996. p.194 Private collection Photo: Carl Hafner. p.194 Photo: Lynn Martin. p.197 Private collection, Photo by Bill McLemore. p.197 Photo: Katherine Fogden, National Museum of the American Indian, Smithsonian Institution, 1996. p.199 Photo by James V. Gleason, courtesy of National Endowment for the Arts. p.199 Photo: Marsha MacDowell, 1993.

Index